Schooling, Democracy, and the Quest for Wisdom

Schooling, Democracy, and the Quest for Wisdom

Partnerships and the Moral Dimensions of Teaching

ROBERT V. BULLOUGH JR. AND JOHN R. ROSENBERG

Rutgers University Press

New Brunswick, Camden, and Newark, New Jersey, and London

Library of Congress Cataloging-in-Publication Data

Names: Bullough, Robert V., 1949– author. | Rosenberg, John R., author.
Title: Schooling, democracy, and the quest for wisdom : partnerships and the
    moral dimensions of teaching / Robert V. Bullough Jr. and John R.
    Rosenberg.
Description: New Brunswick, New Jersey : Rutgers University Press, 2018. |
    Includes bibliographical references and index.
Identifiers: LCCN 2018004605 | ISBN 9780813599922 (cloth) | ISBN 9780813599915
    (pbk.)
Subjects: LCSH: College-school cooperation—United States. |
    Teachers—Training of—United States. | Teachers—In-service
    training—United States. | Mentoring in education—United States. |
    Democracy and education—United States.
Classification: LCC LB2331.53 .B85 2018 | DDC 378.1/03—dc23
LC record available at https://lccn.loc.gov/2018004605

A British Cataloging-in-Publication record for this book is available from the British Library.

∞ The paper used in this publication meets the requirements of the American National
Standard for Information Sciences—Permanence of Paper for Printed Library Materials,
ANSI Z39.48-1992.

www.rutgersuniversitypress.org

Manufactured in the United States of America

In memory of the other Bob and John

Contents

Schooling, Democracy, and the Quest for Wisdom

Introduction

- -

Being Human

> Man by his nature is a social and civic
> animal capable of smiling, born for
> doing good and acting, even to be a
> certain type of mortal god.
> —Giannozzo Manetti, 1438

Democratic manners are the ways of getting along with each other that invigorate a civil society. Young and old might learn those manners, virtues, or dispositions in many settings—indeed, we should strive to do so. However, the central premise of this book is that schools and universities, whatever else they might do (and they do a lot), are uniquely situated to help the young understand, evaluate, and practice democratic manners. We are talking about more than the traditional civics curriculum (classes in history and government)—though we value this strand of our curriculum. We are concerned with something more elemental, because the *manners* of democracy are a priori to the *processes* of government. Finally, we believe that the purposes of schooling, including preparing the young for broad participation in civic institutions, are sustained through robust educational partnerships. This book is about those partnerships, those manners, and those democratic aspirations that bind us together as a people.

Our conversations took place under the shadow of the 2016 presidential election, which for many seemed especially theatrical and unusually significant. A day before one of our meetings, the October 17, 2016, issue of *Time* magazine arrived. Noting the "truth wars" of the 2012 election, which now seem "quaint"

1

(Alter & Scherer, 2016, p. 30), *Time* lamented the accelerating decline of public confidence in public institutions that has historically grounded democratic discourse. Faith in the institutions that once served as arbiters of reality has been overwhelmed by the promiscuity of the information revolution. For much of the population, our mainstream journalism, government reports, and academic research present only feeble truth claims. Busily tracking people on the web, corporate and governmental algorithms direct data mining, crowning as true what is most often said; and decisions that ought to require careful consideration are settled by counting (see Simanowski, 2016). Within some segments of the population, conspiracies thrive and spread like wildfire, jumping over traditional firewalls, unchecked.

Like viewing René Magritte's painting that hangs in Washington's National Gallery—pointedly titled *La condition humaine*—it is increasingly difficult (in Washington and beyond) to distinguish what is "real" from what is fabricated or what is sincerely wished for. Signs of lost trust abound: From 2006 to 2016, Americans became 10 percent less likely to have faith in Congress or the media. In 1958, almost three out of four Americans trusted the government most of the time; now that number is down to one in five. Government, professional journalism, science, public education, and religion (except whichever one I might profess) are losing or have lost their authority. When there is little shared knowledge and even fewer shared assumptions about what is true, factual, and right, there can be no meaningful conversation or compromise let alone the kind of deep change we know as conversion. *Time* concluded, "The nation has lost the common public spaces where we once debated our future" (p. 31). What is left is an extreme individualism, upheld by the assumption that rights are natural and individual, not communal, and a complete breakdown of the "link between the public agenda and private worries" (Bauman, 2012, p. 97). The breakdown becomes personal: "Inequalities and crises of society, such as poverty, social peril, structuralized unemployment, divorce and illness are all 'individualized away' . . . turned into *personal failures* and fiascos, and attributed to the weakness and lack of resources of the individual, and his or her lack of ability to see through and utilize the institutional possibilities that are at all times available" (Sörensen & Christiansen, 2013, p. 50). Moreover, "It is an 'all risk' individualization which forces each individual to bear the weight of the global and collective risks and uncertainties on his or her own shoulders. Life becomes quite a risky affair indeed" (p. 49).

With citizens feeling disconnected, alone, and threatened, subjected to anonymous social and economic forces, political involvement sometimes seems pointless and there arises a disease that sociologist Zygmunt Bauman (2008) describes, somewhat tongue in cheek, as "mixophobia," a "drive towards islands of similarity and sameness amidst the sea of variety and difference" (p. 64). One symptom of "mixophobia" is that people "fail to learn or forget the skills needed to live with difference, they view the prospect of confronting the strangers face-to-face with rising apprehension." Over time, "strangers tend to appear ever more frightening as they become increasingly 'strange–alien,' unfamiliar and incomprehensible—and . . . the mutual communication which could eventually assimilate their 'otherness' to one's own lifeworld loses substance and fades, or never takes off in the first place" (p. 64). The danger is tribalism. Bauman is not the first observer who has fretted over humanity's difficulty with difference. Alexis de Tocqueville (1835/1840/1947), the most lucid observer of our early democracy, worried in the 1830s that natural sociability tended to be local. This encourages "each member of the community to sever himself from the mass of his fellow-creatures, and to draw apart with his family and friends, so that, after he has formed a little circle of his own, he willingly leaves society at large to itself" (pp. 310–311).

Hope: Public Education and the Partnership of Being Human

Responding to employment insecurity and contraction of the middle class, job preparation (mostly) dominates discussions of the purposes of schooling in America. The Great Recession of the early twenty-first century solidified employment as the preeminent school aim. Mysteriously, jobs were thought to be connected to ever-increasing student standardized test scores. Employment is not the only aim of schooling, however, and certainly not the most important one at that.

Public schools and universities are places where young people develop academic skills and are introduced to the disciplines. They also are places where the young learn the importance of good evidence in argumentation and where they develop and refine the languages of affiliation and forms of self-expression. They seek to teach their students how to get along and endeavor to help them overcome their fear of those who are thought to be strangers. And, of most concern to us here, "Public schools are . . . schools of publicness: institutions where we learn what it means to be a public and start down the road toward common national and civic identity. They are the forges of our citizenship and the bedrock of our democracy" (Barber, 1997, p. 22).

Although badly bruised by misguided politicians who support a vigorous marketocracy and by their confidants—ideological fundamentalists (left and right) who confidently profess knowledge of an inevitable future (but are most often wrong; see Gardner, 2011) and live comfortably in "think tanks" on tax-exempt dimes—we find hope in the historical ambition and promise of public education to provide a space, a "moral sphere" (Kane, 2010), within which to think, talk about, and practice democratic citizenship. The importance of the role of schooling in building and maintaining a democratic society is as critical as it is generally underappreciated. We say this even as we recognize the damage caused as the function of democracy and the obligations of national citizenship have been abandoned by capitalism, while globalism has weakened the ability of citizens to unite and press their claims for justice (Streeck, 2016): "Without a solid educational foundation, the democratic state becomes as aimless and vulnerable as a rudderless ship in a storm-tossed sea.... Not only do schools have an essential role to play in the development, health, and well-being of our nation's young, but they are also the only institutions we have for rigorously promoting and sustaining our social and political democracy" (Goodlad, Mantle-Bromley, & Goodlad, 2004, pp. 53–54).

We acknowledge that ours is an aspirational project, an act of reclamation. Most teachers, parents, and policy makers don't talk about or even recognize the democratic purposes of their schools. Meanwhile, schools are asked to do a disproportionate share of the heavy lifting in protecting and preparing the nation's children for the future. Schools can't do everything because they represent only one part of the educational surround (and not the largest part at that); yet schools don't do as much as they can because they too often underestimate their role as mediators of the democratic project. Nevertheless, as flawed as they may be, it is likely that public schools are our "last best hope" for recalling and reclaiming democracy, a topic we pick up in chapter 5.

There is a second source of hope—one deeply rooted in the human experience. Over the centuries writers have offered diverse and often contradictory assessments of the human condition. The *Time* article we described earlier (Alter & Scherer, 2016) is just one of many recent renditions; some are more hopeful. Aristotle, for example, famously claimed that to be human is to be social: "He who is unable to live in society, or who has no need because he is sufficient for himself, must be either a beast or a god: he is no part of a state" (1943, p. 6). Of course, no person can be a god, so the only option left to someone who is above, is beyond, or does not need others is to become beastly—genuinely selfish and self-absorbed. Aristotle's optimistic view is that we are not beastly by nature: we have to learn how to be really, truly selfish.

Another take comes from a story in the Upanishads (Radhakrishnan, 1953) that tells us the first human "had no happiness because he was alone." Eventually he "grew as large as two persons embracing" and subsequently divided himself into two beings, "like two halves of a split pea." From that union "arose husband and wife" (p. 958). Similarly, in Plato's *Symposium* (1953), Aristophanes imagines that our ancestors were completely round, with four arms and legs and two faces—and very proud of their symmetry. Their arrogance annoyed Zeus and he sliced them down the middle "like a sorb-apple which is halved for pickling" (pp. 520–525). These days the halves spend their days seeking reunion: "The reason is that human nature was originally one and we were a whole, and the desire and pursuit of the whole is called love." Lovely tales, both pleasing and problematic, but both remind us that some of our oldest stories teach us that humans are needy and to be human is to be bonded to other humans, to live in relation to others.

Despite discomfort with difference and our desire for stasis, equilibrium, and self-confirmation, we are beings who seek connection, often hesitantly, with others, including with outsiders to our tribe, often because we must; we are deeply and fully interdependent. From his travels across America, journalist James Fallows (2017) reminds us that while a large percentage of Americans are disaffected from a distant federal government, there is also "optimism and determination that are intertwined with desolation and decay in the real 'out there.'" He notes that "a Pew study in 2014 found that only 25 percent of respondents were satisfied with the direction of national policy, but 60 percent were satisfied with events in their own communities. According to a Heartland Monitor report in 2016, two in three Americans said that good ideas for dealing with national social and economic challenges were coming from their towns" (p. 14).

Commenting on his own extensive travels, Fallows concludes, "City by city, and at the level of politics where people's judgments are based on direct observation rather than media-fueled fear, Americans still trust democratic processes and observe long-respected norms." They get along and get things done. What he sees is that most "American communities still manage to compromise, invest and innovate, make long-term plans. They even manage to cope with the ethnic change and racial tension [that is often] so crudely exploited" (pp. 14–15).

Living together, sharing an ecology, a neighborhood, a city, a town, generally brings with it recognition of interdependence, and realization that happiness and misery are shared (think here of the power of GoFundMe when needs cry out). What goes around always comes around, whether, on one side, filthy air, bugs, or blight, while, on the other, a helping hand, the pleasures of farmers' markets, board game cafes, community gardens, high school football games, Fourth of July celebrations, and debates of policies to produce more affordable housing, more after-school programs, healthier births, less aggressive traffic flows, and extended city library hours. We also are restless beings that seek fresh experience and self-transcendence. If for no other reason than feeling bored, to gain relief we venture outside of our immediate tribe and ever so comfortable surround. We take a small risk: perhaps visit for the first time a restaurant that promises a new experience. Or we smile and introduce ourselves to a young stranger who shares our bus and he smiles back and then we chat. Sometimes we risk more: hungry for a new start, perhaps we move to a new city, decide to enroll in a new school, or investigate a new faith. As we do so, we learn, stretch, and grow—and change. However disruptive, learning always requires self-transcendence (Kagan, 1981), the engagement with otherness, something that is "not self."

Some contemporary theorists believe "that the single most potent pressure on human intellectual evolution was the need to cooperate and compete with conspecifics," and that "what makes us humans rather than just apes is the capacity to combine intelligence with articulate empathy" (Bjorklund & Pellegrini, 2010, pp. 65–67, 75). Moreover, we are, as the care theorist Nel Noddings (2010) wrote, predisposed to empathy; we are "prepared to care" (p. 57), especially women (Noddings claimed), and women, of course, comprise the vast majority of teachers, some 84 percent. Empathy arises from the "realm of natural caring" for the young, which speaks to "one of the most powerful motives for being moral—to restore the conditions of natural caring that we regard as good" (p. 56). Perhaps anticipating a tribal transgression, empathy enables and sustains border crossings, for, in the words of the philosopher of ethics Emmanuel Levinas (1969), whenever two people meet, face-to-face, and recognize their shared humanity, a "primordial discourse [opens] whose first word is obligation" (p. 201).

The long history of our species calls us to connection, cooperation, and caring for one another, even as uncertainty and self-interest tug us to return to our tribes—familiar, homogenous, comfortable (but ever so limited). But having once overcome our fears and connected and cooperated with people outside the tribe, we return to it slightly changed, a little different, a bit less parochial, more large-minded, perhaps more curious. Transcendence requires negotiation and compromise; and the greater the risk—"Alas! what differs more than man from man!" (Wordsworth, 1836, p. 322)—the greater the reward.

Here education and partnership enter, and here our interests lie. As Benjamin Barber (1997) argued, schools are sites for building publicness across differences of many kinds. Drawing on this notion, our particular interest is to encourage and extend the publicness of public education by broadening the array of interested parties, including some that may not realize fully the depth and breadth of their investment, in support of public schooling's particular and peculiar historical charge: to strengthen, extend, and enliven the being and belonging that is democratic citizenship.

As a form of community building, partnering is an essential strategy to achieve this aim, a means for softening, perhaps even overcoming and refocusing, some of the experiential, philosophical, and institutional role differences that divide educators: teachers from university faculty, school district administrators from deans and department chairs, teacher educators in schools of education from arts and sciences faculty, school board members from principals, and so on. Partnering involves extending invitations of various kinds to stakeholders to enter a sometimes physical but always shared (and evolving) conceptual and moral space, to join in an exploration of the meaning of democracy and democratic citizenship, for personal, group, and institutional practice. The appeal is not primarily to altruism, but to mutual self-interest, to do something that matters for the self, for others, and for the nation.

Humans are teleological beings whose means most often fall short of longed-for ends, yet somehow we generally keep striving for ever better understanding of our life situations, ever richer meanings and deeper forms of connectedness, and not always for a definite something. Consciousness is intentional; feeling its way along it reaches out into the world, seeking connections and meaning, anticipating actions, and looking for next steps—expanding openness that seeds then fertilizes creativity and increases the capacity to care, perhaps our most *humane* trait. The word gives pause: One might posit that in this final *e* resides the story of this book. To be human is to be constrained; to be humane is to transcend. *Human* can be understood as singular; *humane* is meaningless in the absence of an object of our caring, and that object may be many things including people and cherished ideas, like the BYU–Public School Partnership and those who birthed it and those who have given it life over many years.

What Follows

The American Revolution launched from *commons*—the Boston and New York Commons, the Lexington Green—tracts that colonists set apart for public purposes. We wrote this book because we believe in a few first principles that make it possible to locate common ground from which to prove contraries; we believe that when people of good will identify and protect the commons, difference can be a catalyst for learning; we believe that education is democratic when (and only when) all its constituents are learners, because the openness required of learning is leveling.

We think of this book as offering a framework for considering fundamentals—principles, aspirations, and practices of partnering—an approach to understanding the relationship of the educative whole to its parts, or more precisely, to its *partners*, because however we might define education, learning is partnership: ligature, connection, conversation.

In chapter 1, "The Architecture of Partnership," we explore the evolution of school–university partnerships (sometimes referred to as professional development schools) over the last few decades and try to understand the relationship between their pragmatic impulses—the need to address urgent problems—and the principles and aspirations that inform, inspire, and constrain the practices of partnering. The Brigham Young University–Public School Partnership, in which we both participate, makes the first of many appearances in this chapter, not as an ideal, but as a case to be unpacked and as a story whose dénouement is always being revised. Grounding our discussion in our experience helps us tease out the tension between the abstractions of principles—principles we hold to be noncontingent—and the educational partners (real people) who are rooted in the world of contingencies. Hereafter we will refer to Brigham Young University as "the university" and the BYU–Public School Partnership as "the partnership," our way of expressing the hope that our lessons and our experiences might transcend our particular setting to be relevant to any university and to any partnership. In chapter 2, "Associates and Associating I: Our Story," we take a bit of a risk by presenting an edited transcript of an interview-cum-conversation about the conditions and ideas that brought us together as partners in pursuit of the improvement of teacher education and schooling. In a modern multiversity, intellectual friendships like ours form only when something of considerable gravity pulls them together.

Chapters 3 and 4, "Commons and the Manner of Hospitality" and "From Conversation to Dialogue," describe the virtues of conversation and hospitality that throughout the chapters are coupled with formation of a *commons* and of *planned and shared experience* as essential elements to forging then sustaining partnerships over time. We cast hospitality and conversation as virtues because we believe that they point to ways of being with others that are effectually moral and practically democratic. Hospitality and conversation may have an outer edge that frictions with policy and technique, but their essence is attitudinal and aspirational. Both begin with the question "what are you going through?"—a question that makes it impossible to maintain a view of another as only "Other." Conversation is an expansive idea that can embrace many kinds of relations: pedagogical, organizational, curricular.

Hospitality is concerned with the *border* or *threshold* that marks where the commons begins and works out the conditions of entry. We argue that thresholds are important to partnering. We learn from the etymology of *hospitality*—*hospes*, meaning both guest and host—and emphasize its necessary reciprocity. We claim that conversation is possible only after demonstration of hospitality. Hospitality, a manner, is a condition for conversation, while conversation leads the way to dialogue, a sine qua non for democracy. Hospitality followed by conversation supports formation of a commons, as, in turn, a commons focuses, sustains, and deepens conversation.

Hospitality and conversation call attention to *how* partners will *be together*; the ideal of a commons speaks directly to *where* partners will be together. Moreover, because conversations are necessarily always *about* something and what they are about has importance to their quality, impact, and enjoyment, we also have something to say, albeit comparatively brief, about the place in partnerships of thoughtfully planned activities that invite engagement and reflection—of the *doing* together while *being* together. On becoming the subject matter of conversation, commons, activities, and experiences—memories recalled, stories told, readings revisited, events shared, encounters of various kinds—help hold a partnership and prove its purpose.

Chapter 5, "Talking and Listening: Dialogic Democracy and Education," addresses the first of four Moral Dimensions of Teaching: preparing youth for full participation in a social and political democracy. Proposed by John Goodlad and his colleagues at the Institute for Educational Inquiry in Seattle, the Moral Dimensions represent a guiding "vision" for schooling in a democracy that "encompasses a good and just society" (Goodlad, 1994, p. 4). The dimensions set problems, and recognized and shared problems, as Dewey (1927) argued, are necessary to call into existence a public. Such problems may not be ever fully resolved, but they must be understood, shared, and consistently addressed if, as in this instance, democracy is to be a living educational ideal. The other three dimensions, discussed later, are equitable access to knowledge for all students, nurturing pedagogy, and responsible stewardship of schools.

Chapter 5 revisits the familiar yet central question of the public purposes of schooling. It begins with an exploration of the complexity and confusion surrounding the meaning of democracy as a form of government, comparing and contrasting "full voiced" democracy with more restricted forms, and taking up the notion of democratic manners as a way of speaking about democracy as a shared form of life. The chapter then shifts to criticism of consumer conceptions of citizenship that reduce education to the single purpose of getting a job (and getting ahead), attends to the place of listening as a defining democratic practice, and then invites readers to "dream democracy" as dialogic, thus a foundational partnership ideal and aspiration. Dreaming—imagining the world as it needs to be—is serious business here. Among the evils of our time, perhaps none is more destructive than loss of the ability to imagine alternatives to the givens of social life and to organize dissent in the face of a deepening fatalism (Bauman & Donskis, 2013). Educators are and must always be in the business of hope.

In chapter 6, "Gifts: Access to the Human Conversation through Pedagogical Nurturing," we explore the second and third of the four Moral Dimensions of Teaching: access to knowledge and nurturing pedagogy. The chapter begins with an excerpt from *Children of the Dust Bowl* (Stanley, 1992), a remarkable Great Depression–era story of the Weedpatch School and of the "Okies" of Kern County, California, which serves as a backdrop for posing the question, access to what? Our answer is "the human conversation," a rich metaphor we try to unpack. We present a review of a thin slice of the research related to the effects of the No Child Left Behind legislation (2002) on educational access, including the narrowing of the content of schooling in America. Finally, we turn our attention to the moral weightiness of nurturing pedagogy, a mature expression of the manner of hospitality.

Chapter 7, "Associates and Associating II: A Case Study," represents an attempt to tie the abstractions of the previous chapters to the experience of practicing school and university educators. Each year the BYU–Public School

Partnership sponsors a half dozen Associates programs, study groups composed of teachers, administrators, teacher educators, and arts and sciences faculty to explore and converse about the democratic purposes of education and to nurture allegiances to the moral principles underlying partnership participation. The Associates curriculum explores these principles (introduced in chapter 2). With a focus on participants' understanding of partnership purposes, particularly of the democratic purposes of education, this chapter presents a yearlong participant-observer study of one such group. Associates programs remind us that the partnership is educative as well as educating. Faculty in schools and universities educate, but engagement in the partnership itself should be educating: partners as they partner should learn and grow. While participants report the experience is refreshing and renewing as they encounter new perspectives and ideas while digging critically into old ones, this chapter presents the first attempt to portray the Associates' experience from the inside.

Hospitality. Conversation. Commons. Practicing, doing, partnering. Democracy. Where do these ideas take us? Is the argument simply that partnering is a good and virtuous activity? Dewey's (1938) discussion of how some experiences are educative while others are "miseducative" (p. 25) reminds us that burglars partner and so do mafiosi and street gangs, and that all partnering, for good or ill, generally involves hard work to forge, then maintain a *we*. The question begs a response: why partner? We have already touched on part of the reason: that as humans we are driven toward engagement with others like ourselves for our own fulfillment (though fulfillment might mean successful burgling). Something greater is at stake. Partnering involves a quest and a journey—but for what? Our answer is *wisdom*, a greater measure of wisdom.

Knowing what wisdom is, is not easy, although like Justice Potter Stewart remarked about pornography, we know it when we see it. After a time spent burrowing into the literature on wisdom, hoping to stumble upon a satisfying definition, Stephen Hall (2010) commented, "I found myself silently mouthing [the question] whenever I confronted a problem or dilemma: What would be the wisest thing to do here? . . . Wisdom is more an ideal aspiration than a state of mind or a pattern of behavior that we customarily inhabit. But simply framing a decision in those terms [is] intellectually and emotionally bracing" (p. 10).

We agree. Like the quest for wisdom, itself, partnering involves a journey and an aspiration, an end without an end. The aspiration is to do education more wisely—more humbly, more ethically, more intelligently, more democratically, more of many things that seem wise. Near the end of his journey, like so many others who have trod the same path, Hall concluded that wisdom is "essentially an unattainable ideal." He explained, "It is one of those illusions—like the power of the human mind to imagine a hopeful future or the power of the human heart to surmount a traumatic past—in which even the residue of failure, which may be all we're left with at the end of the day, will leave us better off than if we had not dared to be wise in the first place" (p. 270). With Hall, Robert Kane (2010) argues that it is the search for wisdom, for answers to the question of what is good and true and right to do—not the finding—that matters most. When we act wisely, the world becomes a slightly better place.

We partner because partnering is wise and in order that we may become wiser in meeting the charge of stewardship of children and of public education. Drawing on the fourth of the Moral Dimensions, the conclusion, "Stewardship and Moral Posture," approaches the practice of wisdom as it invites readers to recall the public purposes of public education and to reimagine the roles and responsibilities of educators in relationship to those purposes and to the sacred trust given to educators to care for and educate other people's children—all those who stand at the school's or university's threshold expecting to enter no matter their condition or their promise. Educators are stewards of children and young people, but they also are caretakers of the human conversation and of democracy as that form of civic life that we think best supports *eudaimonia*—the Greeks' word for *human flourishing*.

Pursuing a search for wisdom is not the same as pursuing a degree. We don't test for wisdom; we don't accredit schools and universities based on some quality measure of wisdom attained by graduates. But few institutions that aspire to comprehensive education would renounce the aim that their students increase their "capacity of judging rightly in matters relating to life and conduct" (*Oxford English Dictionary* entry for "wisdom"); their mission statements generally reflect that aspiration, though often with different words. Given that common purpose, we believe that the principles discussed in this book apply equally to universities and schools (though many of our examples relate to school experience). Indeed, our many decades of experience as university employees have taught us that "higher" education has much to learn from the sociologies of schooling, as schools are often more practiced than universities in democratic manners, hospitality, conversation, and the other virtues we describe in these pages. We draw on examples from schools not because we believe universities need not attend to these principles, but because the manners we seek often manifest themselves most clearly and powerfully in the early years of schooling.

We do not expect, or even want, our readers to agree with everything they find in this book. Some may reasonably disagree on terms of interpretation, selection of material, emphasis, political ideology, or moral commitment. We offer our voices as part of a larger conversation, recognizing that our voices were formed and have evolved over time by listening to other voices that we found especially compelling. And we are not finished listening.

1

The Architecture
of Partnership

. . . .

If you weren't an optimist, it would be
impossible to be an architect.
—Norman Foster

Unlike Athena (goddess of wisdom), who popped out of the forehead of her
father Zeus fully developed and wearing a full set of armor, the wisdom of
university–school partnerships has emerged over time. Over many years the language used to talk about partnerships has tended toward construction metaphors: partnerships are built, programs designed, schools restructured, and
standards set, only later to be razed in anticipation of a new building (see Levine,
1992; Petrie, 1995). Considered in architectural terms, partnering might be said
to involve the art, science, and practice of purposefully designing space to create an ambience or environment that represents and supports certain values,
while discouraging others, and enables or inhibits certain actions (e.g., churches
and prisons) while achieving a set of desired purposes or functions.

As with buildings, the shape of programs says a lot about designer intentions
and values. Houses built without porches but with large attached garages, for
example, illustrate how we value (or don't value) neighborliness and privacy.
Once a home or building is constructed, people move in and start living or
working within, and as they gain experience the flaws in design or construction
become apparent. Donald Schön (1987) applies this to the problem of developing reflective practitioners: "Almost always, designers' moves have consequences

other than those intended" (p. 42). Something isn't right; imagination and reality do not quite square. Perhaps the hallways are a bit too narrow, the closets too few, the kitchen inconvenient, and the basement too dark. If the problems are serious enough, remodeling or rebuilding might begin. When the problems cannot be fixed or if the cost of doing so is too high, what was once a model home will be abandoned for a new location and design.

Imagine a blueprint for a hospital that looks like a plan for a big-box store. What would physicians do in such a space? Would new forms of practice emerge? What would patients' experience be like in a hospital designed like Walmart? Or imagine a plan for a preschool or kindergarten classroom set up like a high school science lab. What would the design do to the teaching and learning of young children? What could teachers and students do and not do in such an environment?

Architecture speaks to ontology—to the ways we imagine ourselves as individuals and as a people. It involves a range of decisions that reflect preferences supporting ways of doing, ways of being, and ways of being with others. Athens had its Agora; Rome its Forum. We have churches and social clubs, many now supplanted by malls and big boxes where we might bump into a neighbor or friend accidently, and even online shopping where we do not bump at all. Each supports and in turn shapes its city's and the citizens' way of life. To create successful designs, architects must think carefully about what people will be doing in the designated environment and how they will feel when engaged in the doing. Good design develops from imagination, knowledge, and skill. Equally important are clarity about function and purpose, as well as insight into how processes—what people are to do and how they do it—support purposes.

In this chapter we examine a cross section of the history of the ideas and forms of educational partnerships (sometimes characterized as professional development schools [PDSs]), beginning in the late 1980s and leading up to the rather sedate present. The two terms suggest slightly different aspirations; we prefer *partnership*: a group of people bound together in various ways for various lengths of time in a venture with aspiration that involves identifying, pursuing, and realizing shared aims, values, and social practices. In contrast, the focus on professional development in PDSs suggests greater consideration for the work of those who hold jobs or aspire to find employment in schools—thereby diminishing the contributions that may be offered by university faculty, including arts and sciences professors as well as teacher educators, parents, school board members, and citizens concerned for the well-being of children and the nation. Moreover, partnership, in contrast to professional development, suggests ownership and responsibility for learning—one's own and that of one's partners (see the conclusion).

We begin with the architectural problem of clarifying function and purpose, drawing especially on the three editions of the *Handbook of Research on Teacher*

Education that have addressed the efforts to settle on aims, along with the views of partnership that have evolved over time. In addition, we call attention to a few of the persistently perplexing issues that have intruded when building partnerships, especially related to the challenge of researching partnerships to establish their value and improve their design. By way of illustration and background, we share some of the story of the partnership in which we have worked for many years.

Partnership and Purpose: Two Waves of School Reform

In the first *Handbook of Research on Teacher Education* (Houston, 1990), Jane Stallings and Theodore Kowalski (1990) reviewed briefly the history of PDSs. They placed the origins of PDSs in the famous Dewey School (DePencier, 1967; Mayhew & Edwards, 1936), founded in 1894 associated with the University of Chicago; traced the demise of laboratory schools in the United States; and offered a cluster of reasons for most of these schools being closed by the late 1960s, including (a) high costs of implementation, (b) loss of focus on experimentation, (c) need to broaden purposes and increase influence, and (d) limited commitment to and involvement of faculty in research. Following the much-publicized "plummeting test scores of students in the 1970s" (Stallings & Kowalski, 1990, p. 255), partnerships breathed new life into many of the ideas that initially inspired the founding of laboratory schools.

Framed by the monumentally influential national report *A Nation at Risk* (National Commission on Excellence in Education, 1983), a so-called first wave of school reform began. The response to the report caught President Reagan by surprise (Bell, 1988) as suddenly school reform leaped to the front of federal policy discussions. "Our nation is at risk," the report began: "Our once unchallenged preeminence in commerce, industry, science, and technological innovation is being overtaken by competitors throughout the world" (p. 5). The cause? "The educational foundations [an architectural term] of our society are presently being eroded by a rising tide of mediocrity that threatens our very future as a Nation and a people.... If an unfriendly foreign power had attempted to impose on America the mediocre educational performance that exists today, we might well have viewed it as an act of war" (p. 5). Despite author claims to the contrary, the report castigated teachers and teacher educators. Readers were told that standards were too low, school and college curricula were in disarray, textbooks were lousy, too little time was spent on academic studies, and teachers were poorly prepared to teach. The authors recommended that "schools, colleges, and universities adopt more rigorous and measurable standards, and higher expectations, for academic performance and student conduct" (p. 27). A flurry of activity followed. High school and college graduation requirements were raised and, feeling the pressure, teacher educators began in earnest to rethink the architecture of teacher education.

This was certainly not the first national effort to improve either the effectiveness of public schooling or the quality of education provided by colleges and universities. What distinguished it from other efforts was the presumption of a direct and desired link between schooling and national economic competition, a focus that would fundamentally change expectations of public education (but hopefully not forever!). In an ironic display of simplemindedness, the report's authors conveniently ignored the inevitable lag time separating economic developments from the generational realities of education. Not surprising, as for a century American policy makers and pundits had made (as they continue to make) virtually every social problem imaginable (from teen pregnancies to poverty) first and foremost a problem of schooling, thus excusing other and more powerful social institutions from sharing active responsibility (Bauman, 2011, p. 22; Bode, 1937; Bullough, 1988).

The economy was changing, and the first signs of globalism were evident, signaling the beginning of what became a deluge of strategic disengagements by large corporations from their historical places of business (Bauman, 2011). As corporations were broken apart and the pieces sold off, and as jobs were outsourced, policy makers, desperate to place blame on something other than themselves and their policies, proclaimed education and educators to be at fault. Schools were judged to be in a sorry state, and uninformed promises claimed that getting tough with educators and shaping up schools and colleges would turn the economy around (Standing, 2011). Educators needed to *do* more and *demand* more of students while at the same time public education was beginning to be remade in the image of one-stop shopping.

A second wave of reform followed immediately on the first. Stallings and Kowalski (1990) described this wave: "[It involved] a more in-depth analysis [than the first, that] identified goals for schools that were much broader than gains on achievement test scores. . . . [The conclusion followed:] To develop the type of citizenry required for the twenty-first century, schools must be different, teachers must be different, and colleges of education must be different" (p. 255). Seemingly, everything was to change, and change quickly. Yet the assumption about the power of schools and colleges to alter the wider society remained unquestioned. Business dodged its share of the blame. Fortunately educators were portrayed more favorably than in *A Nation at Risk*. Two documents, *A Nation Prepared: Teachers for the 21st Century* (Carnegie Forum on Education and the Economy, 1986) and *Tomorrow's Teachers* (Holmes Group, 1986), primarily shaped the second wave, driving "the reconceptualization of teacher education toward a model of professional-school partnerships linking colleges of education and schools" (Stallings & Kowalski, 1990, p. 255).

Drawing on idealized outsider images of teaching hospitals, both documents called for rethinking teacher education roles and responsibilities and forging partnerships. Partnerships among university faculty and public schoolteachers and administrators would be based on reciprocity between research and practice and on willingness to experiment with new practices and structures, participate in systematic inquiry, and recognize student diversity (Stallings & Kowalski, 1990, p. 256).

Three of the four principles identified by Stallings and Kowalski involved research: something done to, about, and for teachers. Yet they concluded their review by noting that no credible research had been published on PDSs, although they found an increasing number of descriptive studies that indicated increased interest in and commitment to forming partnerships. Their call was decidedly one-sided. Teachers were expected to need change, to become more research-friendly than they were believed to be. But it was also directed toward university faculty, particularly to teacher educators, suggesting the need for greater involvement in school-based research. As both teacher educators and teachers faced harsh and increasing criticism, colleges of education and public schools clearly needed a shared architecture to move forward.

An Evolving Concept and Set of Relationships

Six years after the first edition of *Handbook of Research on Teacher Education*, Casandra Book (1996) returned to the topic of PDSs and partnerships in the second edition. Much had changed in the intervening years, and the only connection to Stallings and Kowalski's first edition chapter is a minor one. In the six years separating the two handbooks, thought leaders in education had invested a tremendous amount of energy to create school–university partnerships and the idea had spread internationally. A rapidly increasing but primarily anecdotal, descriptive, and celebratory literature emerged, characterized by bold and often unsubstantiated claims. Considering this literature and those claims, John Goodlad (1994) warned of the danger of "rhapsodic twiddle that confuses paradise envisioned with paradise gained" (p. 116). Similarly, representing the deans of the roughly one hundred research universities that comprised the Holmes Group, *Tomorrow's Schools of Education* cautioned against "cheap copies" of genuine partnerships (Holmes Group, 1995, p. 79). Definitional problems over just what was meant by the terms *partnership* and *professional development school* became increasingly insistent.

Book (1996) identified an array of emergent problems accompanying partnership development:

- *Definitional*: "Just what is a partnership?"
- *Conceptual and philosophical*: "What are the underlying assumptions and purposes of partnerships?"
- *Methodological*: "How are partnerships being studied, and what are the best approaches for studying them?"

- *Attitudinal and professional*: "How do teachers and university faculty feel about and respond to involvement in PDSs?"
- *Sociological and psychological*: "What is involved in the transformation of school and university cultures through collaboration? And how are changing roles affecting teachers and university faculty and their professional identities?"
- *Results*: "How does involvement in a PDS affect teachers' (beginning and experienced) learning and development?"

Book's review and especially the writings of Goodlad (1994) helped illuminate just how difficult, costly, and emotionally and intellectually demanding the development of school–university partnerships can be. Partnering requires rearranging and even challenging foundational and familiar architectural features (e.g., professional habits and values) with uncertain payoffs. Moreover, questions of scale loomed: Should an English department in a high school where a few students from a nearby university had been placed for practice teaching count as a school–university partnership? Or would something else and something more be required? Increasingly the literature began to document "obstacles to school/university collaboration": "Schools and universities now occupy different cultures with different views of teaching and learning, organizational structures, role definitions, and reward structures" (Winitzky, Stoddart, & O'Keefe, 1992, p. 6). Questions about the impact of PDSs on student learning would soon begin nagging for attention.

Partnership and Critical Inquiry

After reviewing the available literature, Book (1996) offered yet another warning: "Unless a systematic research program in which many people are invested is developed and the outcomes of the research valued, educators may never know the possible benefits of a PDS. In essence, PDSs could be in jeopardy given the many factors that impinge on their probable success" (p. 206). By 1996 educators began to realize that *building* a PDS was relatively easy; the real heavy lifting would come when trying to move in, live in, and thrive in a PDS over time. Book's warning proved prescient: initial enthusiasm waned as the personal costs of partnering were too much of a strain, particularly for some university or college teacher education faculty, and institutional costs proved too high for some institutions and their partnerships to sustain, especially those dependent on uncertain external funding.

Publication of the third edition of the *Handbook of Research on Teacher Education* (Cochran-Smith, Feiman-Nemser, McIntyre, & Demers, 2008) supported the conclusion that research on partnerships and interest in professional development or partner schools had diminished. Unlike the first two handbooks, this one did not include a chapter on PDSs or partnerships; in fact, *partner schools* and *partnership* were not even listed in the index, although references to PDSs surfaced here and there in the massive volume. Castle, Fox, and Souder (2006) suggested one possible but undoubtedly partial explanation for the situation: "Those involved in PDSs attest to their value; yet because of their complexity, connections between PDS activities and their impact on teaching have been hard to make" (pp. 65–66). Even with relatively clear definitions of what constitutes a partnership or a PDS, outside of qualitative, often descriptive, studies relying on self-report data, causal connections have been very difficult to make across program elements, as have been links to changes in teacher behavior or understanding (Castle & Reilly, 2011; Nolan, Grove, Leftwich, Kelly, & Peters, 2011). Isolating meaningful variables runs headlong into the complexity and uniqueness of individual partnerships, the people who support them, and the contexts within which they operate. Ethical matters complicate the difficulty: in good conscience, how can studies utilizing control groups within a partnership be formed when to do so means withholding from some students the practices that represent teachers' best thinking?

When comparisons among variables are made, they tend to be rather loose. For instance, in the Castle et al. (2006) study noted above, comparisons between PDS and non-PDS teacher education students demonstrated differences of various kinds favoring the PDS participants: PDS students were found to be much further along in their professional development. The actual comparison, however, involved data related to one partnership component, internships, to data from student teaching. The PDS students participated in an intensive, well-supported, yearlong internship in PDS schools selected for their willingness to work closely with the university, while the comparison group was composed of part-time working students enrolled in an "evening course" (p. 67), who participated at the conclusion of the program in two student teaching experiences each lasting seven weeks, one in an upper and another in a lower elementary school grade. It is not surprising that differences were found between the two groups, nor that internships of the sort described were found to offer a more powerful form of professional learning than a part-time program designed to accommodate working adults.

Studies demonstrating positive effects of PDSs on teacher attrition have faced similar difficulties, even when conceived and executed well (see Latham & Vogt, 2007). Clearly, conducting then publishing partnership research that aims at generalization is extraordinarily challenging, conceptually and practically (see Breault & Breault, 2012). Yet this is only part of the story, which may actually lead to a hasty and unfortunate conclusion about the value of partnerships. Within partnerships, two questions must be asked: (a) "What counts as research?" (b) "Research for what purpose and for whom?"

From the beginning of discussions about university–public school partnerships, research has been thought to be an important component, however conceived. In her 1996 review, Book noted, for example,

> The best way to engage teachers, who on the surface may agree with the overall objectives of the PDS efforts, is to collaborate with the teacher rather than trying to direct their thinking. The engagement of teachers in problem-solving issues of teaching and learning that they perceive to be salient holds the best promise of engaging their work on the problems of practice, as well as conducting research about their attempts. It appears that teachers do not value, at least on the first consideration, research being conducted in their schools, but over time they come to support the Holmes Group goals that include inquiry about practice. (p. 199)

No doubt a considerable amount of teacher- and administrator-led research is examining practice in partnership schools in particular and, perhaps, in most schools generally, just not often published and perhaps not even widely shared with colleagues (Bullough & Smith, 2016; McLaughlin & Black-Hawkins, 2004. Such research is of local concern, and no effort is typically made to generalize from the findings, even if the problems addressed may be of far-reaching consequence.

The most ambitious and arguably the most difficult goal to realize within partnerships is to create within them cultures of inquiry that support the simultaneous renewal of schooling and of the education of teachers. While some partnerships have been successful meeting this challenge (Snow-Gerono, 2005), tensions often emerge between differing research ambitions: local studies resonate with teachers and building administrators and with some teacher educators, while university faculty who work within models of research dominated by psychology and sociology generally seek to influence wider audiences through publication (Bullough, 2012). McLaughlin and Black-Hawkins (2004) came to a similar conclusion in their study of a "schools–university research partnership" involving eight schools and the University of Cambridge. Teachers and university faculty, they concluded, often hold different conceptions of research. They argued that "if the creation and dissemination of knowledge beyond the individual teacher is to be an aim and is to happen, then shifts and changes in the structures, roles and relationships of both universities and schools are demanded" (p. 282).

While we agree such changes may be desirable, based on the experience of our partnership, we also believe the two ambitions do not necessarily clash. They may, in fact, coexist symbiotically. The challenge, as Goodlad noted early in the formation of our partnership, is to locate "overlapping self-interests," and this represents a high priority—it does not just happen. Furthermore, while local studies designed to address shared concerns almost always speak to wider audiences and may support publication, reporting is not the primary aim: primacy goes to simultaneous renewal. Still, publication in support of renewal is much to be desired.

University-based researchers sometimes complain that gaining access to schools is difficult and that school bureaucracies are unnavigable. Teachers, they say, can be reluctant to participate in research. Yet ironically, wherever they work most educators who think of themselves as professionals actively seek to improve their practice; this is what professionals do. Often such activity takes the form of research: schoolteachers and university faculty read student papers, and among the reasons they do so is to locate problems of various kinds in the writing, and this involves, as Dewey (1933) argued, research, albeit somewhat informal—questions are posed, data gathered, ideas and explanations tested, and additional questions posed in a pattern of thinking and problem solving very familiar to action researchers. Certainly university-based researchers need and want data and need teachers' help to get it. On their part, teachers sometimes complain that researcher requests represent just another of the numerous and constant external impositions thrown at them that they must manage, seeing them as diversions from the real work of teaching—interacting with students. Yet over the past few years teachers and principals have become heavily involved in data gathering, even if they sometimes do not value the data that are collected, and in data analysis and reporting of results. Moreover, measures of student learning of various kinds are finding their way into teacher and school accountability systems, although most often in forms that cause more consternation than delight among teachers and that may produce tension in partnerships over aims (Bartholomew & Sandholtz, 2009). This situation of university-based researchers needing data and teachers spending increasing amounts of time and energy collecting and analyzing data as they informally but actively study their own practice suggests the possible emergence of a large, increasing, and shared space of potential common interest.

Problems of Definition: Functions and Purposes of Partnerships

In 1991 the Modes of Teacher Education study sponsored by the Economic and Social Research Council was initiated in the United Kingdom. Its general aim was to study change in teacher education in England and Wales over a five-year period and to assess the impact of those changes on teacher professionalism. The study had a lot to say about the architecture of partnerships; nothing of such scope had been done in the United States. Researchers surveyed all the teacher education programs in the United Kingdom and authored case studies on a stratified random sample of forty-four institutions, drawing on interviews with program administrators, instructors, teachers, and students. In a second phase of the study, the authors wrote comparative cases of many of the original sites, and in the autumn of 1995 they distributed a second national survey. Benefiting from this extensive data set and driven by government expectations that "partner schools and HEIs (Higher Education Institutions) will exercise a joint responsibility for the planning and management of courses and the selection, training and assessment of [teacher education] students," the research team attempted to map the "emerging models of partnership" in the United Kingdom (Furlong et al., 1996, pp. 41, 42). To no one's surprise, although models varied dramatically, all claimed the honorific title of *partnership*. Three ideal types formed a continuum: university-led, collaborative, and autonomous partnerships. The collaborative type was described as involving "commitment to develop a training programme where students are exposed to different forms of educational knowledge, some of which come from school, some of which come from [the university] or elsewhere. Teachers are seen as having an equally legitimate but perhaps different body of professional knowledge from those in higher education. Students are expected and encouraged to use what they learn in school to critique what they learn within the [university] and visa versa [*sic*]. It is through this dialectic that they are expected to build up their own body of professional knowledge" (p. 44).

In contrast, reflecting long-established institutional traditions, university-led partnerships used "schools as a resource in setting up learning opportunities for students. Course leaders have a set of aims which they want to achieve and this demands that schools act in similar ways and make available comparable opportunities for all students" (p. 45). Generally this model involved the inclusion of teachers and administrators in consulting roles, and as the researchers found, they could be either "pragmatic" or "principled" (driven by ideals). The authors described the situation represented by the autonomous model: "School and [higher education] are seen as having separate and complementary responsibilities but . . . [with] no systematic attempt to bring these two dimensions into dialogue. In other words, there is partnership but not necessarily integration in the course; integration is something that the students themselves have to achieve" (p. 47). Only a "minority" of courses were classified as autonomous or collaborative. Of the collaborative model, the research team concluded that "few course leaders will be able to adopt or perhaps even maintain the collaborative model in the coming years" (p. 53). The authors concluded that too often partnerships privileged the preparation of teachers over the demands of schooling, that there was no consistent understanding of what constituted a partnership, and that partnerships tended to focus more on process (governance) than on grounding. We consider it worth noting that the writers made no mention of research or inquiry into practice.

As the UK study was under way, Goodlad and his colleagues were busy on the other side of the Atlantic. Based on an extensive study of schooling and of teacher education in the United States, a vision of collaboration developed from Goodlad's (1993) insistence that "the bumping together of university and school cultures would have a positive effect on both institutions" (p. 25). "What comes first, good schools or good teacher education programs? The answer is that both must come together. There are not now the thousands of good schools needed for the internships of tens of thousands of future teachers. The long-term solution—*unfortunately, there is no quick one*—is to renew the two together. There must be a continuous process of educational renewal in which colleges and universities, the traditional producers of teachers, join schools, the recipients of the products, as *equal* in the *simultaneous renewal* of schooling and the education of educators" (Goodlad, 1994, pp. 1–2; emphasis added). Goodlad's response to the discovery that some partnerships were "principled" and others "pragmatic" (driven by matters of convenience such as the ease with which student teachers could be placed in classrooms) was to assert that all genuine partnerships must be principled: committed to collaboration and to a clear, public, and well-articulated and -argued mission. Further, principled partnerships require constant checkups. Partners do more than just get along: they are invested in one another's learning and development and in something bigger than themselves. That vision, Goodlad concluded, must necessarily be grounded in the broader purposes of schooling in a democratic society, a "vision that encompasses a good and just society" (p. 4). Embodied in what came to be known as the Moral Dimensions of Teaching, discussed in the next chapter, the mission, according to Goodlad, should center on four foundational ideals that developed from the historical aspirations of education in America: enculturating the young in a social and political democracy, providing access to knowledge for children and youths, practicing pedagogical nurturing, and ensuring responsible stewardship of schools (p. 5). These principles set an agenda for institutions seeking membership in the National Network for Educational Renewal (NNER)—founded and in its early stages nurtured by Goodlad and his colleagues.

From his and his colleagues' earlier studies of schooling and teacher education, most notably *Teachers for Our Nation's Schools* (Goodlad, 1990), Goodlad developed a set of postulates (see the appendix) defining the agenda's necessary conditions, which "ranged from institutional commitment, to financial resources, to the nature of the student body and faculty, to laboratory or 'teaching schools,' to curriculum designs, to supportive state policies" (Goodlad, 1994, p. 6). Like everything else associated with achieving simultaneous renewal, the postulates have evolved over time, but they remain vital as guidelines for what successful partnerships require of their host institutions (see Goodlad, Mantle-Bromley, & Goodlad, 2004, pp. 183–186).

Early on, Goodlad described partnership in this way:

> A school–university partnership represents a formal agreement between a college or university . . . and one or more school district to collaborate on programs and projects in which both have a common interest. This agreement includes designation of a governing body, commitment of resources . . . an executive officer, a secretariat . . . and an approved budget. The agenda in robust partnerships is made up of activities that require for their vigorous pursuit joint planning and action. Partnerships serve little or no purpose if one partner could carry on the activities just as well without the inevitable demands of collaboration. (Goodlad, 1994, pp. 113–114)

A decade later Goodlad and his colleagues (2004) further elaborated their partnership ideal: "Within partner schools, college and university education faculty members can study the realities of schooling and see how new ideas can affect practice. It is in partner schools that teachers can learn to inquire into their own work and to improve the development of those who are preparing to teach. And it is in partner schools that preservice teachers can learn to question the gaps between theory and practice, and to create opportunities for effective professional dialogue" (p. 118). Goodlad's vision of the centrality of professional dialogue to successful partnering came to hold a central place in our partnership, a topic we discuss in chapter 4.

By the late 1990s, so many teacher education institutions claimed involvement in partnerships or PDSs that the National Council for Accreditation of Teacher Education (NCATE), then the largest of such organizations in the United States, wrote standards for accreditation that would allow for assessing the many partnership claims. Informed by a "process of inquiry, reflection, and discussion . . . supported by research and analysis of data assembled through a national survey, focus groups, and interviews, and by a comprehensive review of the literature" (NCATE, 2001, pp. 2–3), including the work of Goodlad and three years of field testing, NCATE released the standards in 2001. Besides proving useful for accrediting teacher education programs, the standards were intended to support the development of quality PDSs. Underscoring the Holmes Group's early warning about "cheap copies," the authors concluded that the "proliferation of school/university partnerships [was both] heartening and disquieting. It is heartening because so many educators have recognized the potential of these innovative partnerships; it is disquieting because many PDS partnerships are such 'in name only'" (p. 2). In addition, NCATE expected that the standards would encourage research on partnerships that presumably had been constrained by the lack of a "common agreed upon set of conditions that could be used to define the setting and relate one study to another" (p. 2).

NCATE developed five standards to determine the level of partnership development: *beginning, developing, at standard,* or *leading.* Each level included a description of expectations. For example, under Standard 3, "Collaboration," leading evidence needed to support the claim that "PDS work is sustaining and generative, leading to: systemic changes in policy and practice in the partner institutions [and] impact on policy at the district, state, and national levels" (p. 23). NCATE intended that the standards would end the debate over definitions, but they did not: this probably would have been impossible given the policy context and the sharpening and increasingly contentious politics surrounding teacher education. Moreover, setting "best practice" as the standard introduced a destructive expectation: the call for best practice reduces assessment to "right" or "wrong," "yes" or "no" judgments, rather than to the context-sensitive and more helpful determination of "better" from "worse" practice (Bullough, 2012).

Beginning in 1997 and continuing until 2013, NCATE gained a competitor for the education accreditation business with the upstart Teacher Education Accreditation Council (TEAC). In contrast to NCATE's accreditation according to standards approach, TEAC offered an "inquiry-driven" accreditation accountancy model that was more flexible and responsive to differences in program design and purpose. The university in our partnership was among the many institutions that found this model more compatible and embraced TEAC. As TEAC grew and gained official recognition from the US Department of Education, pressure built for merger. In 2013 a combined organization, the Council for the Accreditation of Educator Preparation (CAEP, 2013), was formed (see Bullough, 2014). In the process, the emphasis on partnerships shifted. The second of CAEP's five standards, "Clinical Partnerships and Practice," reads, "The provider ensures that effective partnerships and high-quality clinical practice are central to preparation so that candidates develop the knowledge, skills, and professional dispositions necessary to demonstrate positive impact on all P–12 students." The specific charge begins with the words "partners co-construct mutually beneficial P–12 school and community arrangements" and recognizes that these "can follow a range of forms, participants, and functions" (CAEP, 2013). The initial effort of NCATE to establish a shared definition of partnership faded into history.

The merger of TEAC and NCATE, with its new set of accreditation standards, did little to clarify the nature of partnership work. In response to an increasing need among teacher educators interested in and committed to building partnerships, in 2004 the National Association for Professional Development Schools (NAPDS) was founded. In 2008, rapidly developing and gaining influence (see Bullough, 2016) through its conferences and journal, NAPDS established a framework composed of "Nine Essentials" intended to focus and strengthen the association's partnership efforts. The essentials represent aspects of Goodlad's vision, in particular the postulates he and his colleagues had developed to define the institutional conditions required for partnerships to flourish, as well as recognize the earlier efforts of NCATE. Some highlights represent aspects particularly relevant to partnership development. For example, Essential 1 draws attention to the importance of a "comprehensive mission" that advances "equity within schools and, by potential extension, the broader community." Essential 7 insists that an institutional "structure" be formed that "allows all participants a forum for ongoing governance, reflection and collaboration." Essential 8 requires that "college-university faculty and P–12 faculty" work together in "formal roles across institutional settings." And Essential 9 asserts that partnership work be supported by "dedicated and shared resources and formal rewards and recognition structures" (NAPDS, 2008). While the Nine Essentials have proved helpful for furthering the partnership conversation, there is confusion among accreditation-anxious teacher educators about how the essentials and the new CAEP standards mesh (Polly, 2016).

The position of NCATE in 2001 was that neither the higher-education-led nor the separatist model identified by Furlong and his colleagues in the United Kingdom counted as partnerships. Then NCATE embraced, as do we, Goodlad's conception of *simultaneous renewal* as a central aim and prominent concern of partnerships. Conceptualizing collaboration (the second model of partnership identified by Furlong and his colleagues) as simultaneous renewal represents a radically different partnership vision. Too often *reform* has been the term used to describe the intention of change, suggesting external control directing a rearrangement and reshaping of aspects of established practice. In reform, stuff is moved around. In the 1980s two additional metaphors emerged for the intent of change: restructuring and reculturing. Grounded in the assumptions of behavioral psychology, the architectural metaphor *restructuring* emphasizes changing environments, especially administrative arrangements, as the most essential aspect for changing behavior. In contrast, *reculturing* centers on changing expectations, roles, and relationships as essential to improvement.

Simultaneous renewal, originating in Goodlad's understanding of the philosophy of John Dewey, frames educational improvement as a learning problem. Learning is understood as a sociocultural process involving thoughtful problem solving—which certainly may invite restructuring and result in reculturing. This view holds that the most promising approaches to educational change develop from, draw upon, and enhance the talents and abilities of all those who have a stake in a problem and its solution or its better management. (Most genuine educational problems are not so much solved as managed or, as Dewey [1910] suggested, gotten over.) Simultaneous renewal acknowledges and seeks to identify and then build on the strengths found among educators, including their wisdom and practical knowledge, rather than fixating on deficiencies. Goodlad was clear: if schools are to further the cause of democracy, then democratic values and practices will need to be infused into any and all efforts at change, a position that had and has far-reaching implications for the architecture of partnership, including our own.

The University and the National Network for Educational Renewal

Prior to publication of *A Nation Prepared* and *Tomorrow's Teachers*, college of education leadership and faculty at our institution had been rethinking virtually every aspect of the teacher education program. We were not yet personally involved in this work, but the events that transpired are well documented and for some faculty readily recalled. College leadership reached out to Goodlad for help and guidance. Then dean of education at UCLA, Goodlad had pioneered the development of the Southern California Partnership. Visiting our campus in 1983, meeting with faculty and school personnel, and sensing a strong desire for institutional change, Goodlad posed a question that apparently galvanized the faculty: "What might you have to gain from a close partnership with the schools?"

Goodlad reported what happened following this encounter, a subsequent meeting with area superintendents, and a presentation to both university and school personnel—all over a three-day period: "With incredible speed and unanimity, the combined groups agreed to form a school–university partnership to address [their] overlapping self-interests, which included such themes as teacher education, the preparation of school principals, curriculum development, and research on critical problem areas" (Goodlad, 1994, p. 107). Goodlad spent much of the next year working to develop our partnership, which has been vital and active for more than three decades. Three years after his visit, the work had developed to the point that the university became a charter member of the NNER, a connection that continued until 2010.

As Goodlad and his colleagues' thinking evolved, the initial formulation of the NNER was recognized as too limited, so in 1991 the network was reconstituted and refocused. Over time the agenda was reworked, becoming the Agenda for Education in a Democracy (see Goodlad, Mantel-Bromley, & Goodlad, 2004, p. 19) and the focus and charge sharpened (pp. 118–119). Early members of the network, like our partnership, needed to review their standing and, if membership was still desired, demonstrate commitment. Within our partnership, an extensive revision of our university's elementary teacher preparation program was undertaken (and continues ongoing), part of a larger college renewal effort. Members agreed on the partnership's architectural functions and purposes, but processes needed revision, which required reconsidering roles and relationships and subsequently attending to relationship building in support of dialogue and learning (renewal). Accordingly, students were organized into cohorts for their classes and fieldwork to improve program coherence and continuity and to strengthen relationships; field work expanded and spread across the program along with opportunities to discuss field experiences; teachers reviewed and revised course content; and methods courses moved into the schools to strengthen links between theory and practice and between university and school faculty. An internship program developed enabling students to teach a year in a public school at half pay with benefits as an alternative to student teaching (Bullough, Young, & Draper, 2004). Two interns in one school freed up a site-based educator to serve as a mentor working with university faculty to support teacher candidates' learning and development.

During this restructuring, new positions evolved including clinical faculty associate (CFA), a "bridging" role, connecting and ensuring transit between the public schools and the school of education. CFAs are distinguished teachers hired from partnership schools to work at the university for two or three years in teacher education, funded from resources normally dedicated to supporting tenure-track faculty. They assume responsibility for site coordination and a large portion of fieldwork, and they work with university-based teacher educators to teach or coteach methods courses. Appointed liaisons, initially from among the tenure-line faculty, coordinate programs with the five participating partnership districts and their schools. The aim across all the new roles has been to increase conversation and strengthen support for learning while studying and implementing Goodlad's agenda.

With the strong support and financial backing of university administrators, in 1995 the university established a center of pedagogy—the Center for the Improvement of Teacher Education and Schooling (CITES). Participating with CITES, university arts and sciences faculty who had responsibility for subject area content learning became more active participants in the ongoing conversation about teacher education and public schooling and in the work of simultaneous renewal. Supported by CITES, a tripartite community was formed: a "center of pedagogy is a place where the three primary groups of teacher educators (arts and sciences faculty, P–12 educators, and teacher education faculty) collaborate in the work of building curriculum, field experiences, and the structures that produce good teachers" (Goodlad et al., 2004, p. 116).

The work of renewal is educative. It involves partners in critical inquiry about foundational ideas so that their commitment to those ideals is informed, articulate, and enduring. Consequently, CITES was (and still is) responsible for supporting multiple Associates programs (see chapter 7), study groups of teachers and administrators from the partnership districts along with professors and administrators from the university's school of education and the arts and sciences departments that prepare secondary teachers who meet in a series of retreats. Taking various forms, the retreats support reading and discussion of defining documents and resources related to partnering and simultaneous renewal.

Modeled after a program initially developed by Goodlad and his colleagues, Associates programs were instituted at our university to answer a specific need, as then-Dean Robert S. Patterson expressed:

> The reasons for commencing an associates program were simple. Primary was the need to expand the number of well-informed, committed supporters who would be both able and inclined to assist in advancing the agenda of [simultaneous] renewal that our partnership had pursued since its inception. . . . Although we had been functioning for over a decade, relatively few people within our partnership could articulate the central ideas and purposes undergirding our activities. . . . Using a metaphor from the history of our semiarid land, we perceived that the life-giving water—that is, the vision of the partnership—was not flowing through our irrigation channels to the parched plants at the ends of the rows. (Patterson & Hughes, 1999, pp. 271–272)

Associates programs offer a kind of general education in partnership and function as instruments for forging and strengthening social trust across the diverse role definitions and job responsibilities of partners (see Fisler & Firestone, 2006).

In addition to the Associates groups, early in its development CITES began sponsoring a range of professional development activities that included a pair of two-day retreats held each year for pivotal leaders from the school districts (superintendents, principals, and sometimes school board members) and from the university (central administrators, college deans and school of education leaders). During this time the partnership continued, as it had from the beginning, being governed by a board composed of the five partnership district superintendents and the dean of the college (later school) of education. Meeting monthly, the Governing Board authorizes and oversees projects that strengthen teacher education and schooling, including literacy and arts initiatives, school leader/administrator preparation, a state-approved reading endorsement, language immersion teacher preparation, and many more.

Although many features of the partnership developed from proposals generated by Goodlad and his colleagues, Goodlad was clear that he did not expect any partnership to be quite like another, a position with which we strongly agree. He warned, in fact, that particularly in the "early stages redesigning settings or creating new ones, it is not wise to go forth seeking models elsewhere" (Goodlad, 1994, p. 100). While principles could and should be shared, like the Moral Dimensions and others we discuss in the chapters that follow, each setting was understood to be a site of experimentation from which other educators might learn. There was no expectation of replication. Also, annual NNER conferences were designed to maximize interaction among participants, including discussion and dissemination of promising ideas and practices. No blueprint was offered; none was expected. As Goodlad (1994) wrote, "There is little point in going to the literature or on the road to search for models. To my knowledge, none exists" (p. 129). The institutions associated with the NNER charged into new territory, our university among them.

Partnerships in the Twenty-First Century

As we understand the practice of partnership when driven by the aim of simultaneous renewal of institutions and of people and as we embrace it in our collaboration, our architectural compass draws us to questions about form and space and therefore to human relationships and the quality of those relationships. Any and all aspects of the work of partnering—whether seeking to create rich and interesting practicums for teacher education students, engaging in conversations with partners concerning a vexing problem, or trying to establish and then maintain a research alliance—the kind and quality of the relationships determine the outcome. Partnerships are relationships; thus, the quality of relationships depends on the architecture of partnerships that invite and support engagement in meaningful activity. Encounters across difference within conditions that support acknowledgment of those differences and increase understanding offer participants opportunities to reimagine themselves personally and professionally as citizens and as educators. And maybe even as humans. Overall, rather little attention has focused on the power and influence of relationships to successful partnerships, although relationships are occasionally mentioned as sources of failure. Most often relationships are simply taken for granted even as they require constant tending.

Our intention in *Schooling, Democracy, and the Quest for Wisdom* is to offer and then explore a set of ideas, concepts, and principles that we believe support America's historic democratic aspirations and are central to framing and then productively responding to the tasks of renewing relationships and partnerships. Our hope is that the arguments made in the chapters that follow, the language used, and the concepts presented will enrich and help reinvigorate what is now the rather tired conversation about partnership in education. Partnering needs to regain its place as a central topic of interest and concern, especially among teacher educators across college campuses and within schools.

The chapter that follows is about relationships and relationship building: in this instance, how we (the two authors) came to be involved in the work of partnership at our institution. We do not claim that our experiences are typical, but we think they are illustrative. Ideas, administrative structures, and formally negotiated roles and responsibilities are certainly important to the function of university–school partnerships, but it is building and preserving relationships that give partnerships life, nourishing and sustaining them over time through change and through crisis. Formal structures are ephemeral substitutes for friendship, just as confidence in institutional procedures cannot quell the fundamental human need for trust (see Seligman, 1997) that comes with partnering.

2

Associates and
Associating I

. . . .

Our Story

> A genuine conversation is never the one
> that we wanted to conduct.
> —Hans-Georg Gadamer

Conversations about our common commitment to the public purposes of education brought us together; those conversations led to an intellectual and social partnership out of which this book evolved. Our experience as associates and with associating—conversation to partnership to action—replicates on a scale of two the dynamics of institutional partnerships, studied systematically in chapter 7. Indeed, institutional partnerships endure only as well as the individual relationships that constitute them.

Our institutional partnership depends on ongoing robust conversations involving a variety of educational voices, including school practitioners, school of education faculty, and arts and sciences faculty. We have found it sometimes challenging to engage university arts and sciences faculty in conversations around the public purposes of schooling, especially as many impediments have emerged. For all those reasons, we thought our story might be worth telling. There are other stories that might be told; we recognize that ours is not unique, but it is ours.

We (John and Bob) come from different academic traditions. John is the Washington Irving Professor of Spanish and American Relations at the university. Until 2015 he served as dean of the College of Humanities, before then as an associate dean, and earlier as an associate chair then chair of the Department of Spanish and Portuguese—a history of service of nearly thirty years. He is recognized as a distinguished teacher of Spanish literature and as an innovative and provocative writer and scholar. For many years he directed a National Endowment for the Humanities Summer Seminar for Schoolteachers in Madrid, Spain. Currently he is associate director of the university's Faculty Center where, among many responsibilities, he works with leaders across campus to improve teaching and student learning. He is also a senior fellow in the Center for the Improvement of Teacher Education and Schooling (CITES).

Bob began his academic career at the University of Utah, where he taught social and historical foundations of education and worked with schools and teacher education for many years and was involved with the Holmes Group. Before completing his graduate studies, he taught in an interdisciplinary alternative program for high school students, which stirred an interest in the study of teachers and teaching. History was Bob's first academic love. In 1999, at the invitation of Robert Patterson, who was at that time dean of education at the university where both Bob and John are now, Bob transferred to this university, where he was shortly appointed associate director of CITES. During much of his time here he has taught graduate courses in the history of education and in research and has conducted a faculty research seminar. He is continually studying and publishing on a variety of educational topics: teacher development and well-being, mentoring, models of student teaching, teacher emotion, the Eight-Year Study, and early childhood education policy, among others. We come from two very different worlds. The partnership brought us together.

While refining his ideas about partnership, John Goodlad (1993) thought "the non-parasitic interpretation of the word" *symbiosis* offered a metaphor useful for reimagining how universities and schools could work together: "two dissimilar organisms in a mutually beneficial relationship" (p. 29). Both institutions, he thought, needed renewing: "Good schools require good teachers and good teacher preparation programs require good schools" (Goodlad et al., 2004, p. 22). "Symbiosis," he wrote, "implies satisfaction of the needs of both partners" (p. 30). He imagined something then rare in education, a "three-way faculty collaboration [involving] three sets of actors" (Goodlad, 1993, p. 37)—school and district administrators, teachers, arts and sciences and school of education faculty—"joining in all aspects of designing and renewing the teacher education enterprise" (p. 38). Each partner, he believed, could find meaning and satisfaction in a shared work.

When making his initial case for partnership to the university faculty and representatives of future partnership districts, Goodlad argued that "partnership provides opportunities for people to come together to do things that each organization could not do for itself" (Ray Wittenberg, personal communication to Paul Wangemann, November 5, 2004). Those "things," Goodlad argued, would be found through "the bumping together of university and school cultures" (Goodlad, 1993, p. 25). He knew "bumping together" does not just happen; ever the teacher, Goodlad thought architecturally, exploring the need to create institutional conditions and shared experiences that would enable and nourish relationship building and support sustained conversation.

The body of this chapter is an edited transcript of an unscripted conversation recorded on a summer afternoon in John's office. Bob posed questions to John, and together we tried to unpack a piece of the partnership story we have lived and shared. One of the challenges we have faced—challenges that all who partner educationally must face—has been to learn to speak and to write across our differences, a topic important to the conversation that follows. While we stand in different academic traditions and see from diverse reference points—books, people, places—we have been fortunate to have bumped into one another long enough and frequently enough that we share ownership of a "great thing," that, as Parker Palmer (1998) described, "holds both me and thee accountable to something beyond ourselves" (p. 117). For us, that "great thing" is *our partnership*: the partnership as we live and share it, for partnering is a form of relating that has many and diverse manifestations even as it has a common center and concern.

That center and concern for Goodlad was the charge of moral stewardship for schooling, the focus of the last chapter, but it is more: it is an opportunity filled with the pleasures that come from being engaged in a good work with good people and from doing something that morally matters. With partnership participation has come a language that we share (of which we will have much to say), jargon, parlance, or idiom. Jargon ought not be thought of as pejorative. Different social practices support different languages: the languages commonly used by teacher educators, teachers, school administrators, and school board members are related but different. Taken together, the jargon of education is quite different from the jargon of the various arts and sciences and the jargon of many and various levels of university frontline administration.

The language of partnership supports bridging of differences; but the aspiration of partnership is ultimately greater: to form a sustainable culture that supports a distinctive practice, a work, a way of working, and a cluster of valued identities different from those formed during our everyday work lives. To remain lively, conversation must continuously broaden and deepen, and this necessitates engagement not *across* but *with* difference—understood as a condition for learning and growth. Such engagement may lead to friendship, as it has for us.

Gifts and Invitations

BOB How did your involvement in the partnership come about?

JOHN It began in 1993. I had just been named the chair of the Department of Spanish and Portuguese, and had fielded concerns from the Spanish education faculty about the professional education classes required of students who were preparing to teach Spanish in schools. I reached out to Bob Patterson, then in his second year as dean of the McKay School of Education, and said that I would like to visit with him about what I was hearing. Within a few days Bob came to our conference room, and thus began what turned out to be a decades-long conversation with him about education.

At that time my only experiences with public education had been as a student growing up in California and as the son of a high school teacher. Many in my family have been teachers, but I had no professional background for the preparation of teachers. I knew nothing of our university–school partnership or of the ideas behind it. I suspect Bob sensed that he had an opportunity to make an arts and sciences convert for the partnership. Subsequently, he invited me to attend the partnership's leaders' meetings and made it clear that he was inviting me not because I would get something out of it, but because he believed I had something to contribute. I've thought about that a lot over the years, about how we tend to get that particular part of the conversation backwards—that in trying to engage people in our work we appeal to their self-interest instead of to a spirit of common sacrifice and gift giving.

BOB Why did you respond positively?

JOHN One of the themes of Bob's leadership was giving gifts. All work, but especially educational work, builds on relationships, and those relationships become inherently educational when they are generous—thus Bob's focus on asking us to contemplate the gifts we were prepared to share. And so I began to attend these meetings twice a year, and then a couple of years later Bob told me about a program in Seattle organized by John Goodlad and convinced me that I had a gift to give to that gathering.

BOB Still no pitch to your personal interests: instead an invitation to stretch a little bit, to give something not yet determined and to connect with some people. Who were these people you were invited to give gifts to, and what happened as you got to know them?

JOHN The Seattle meetings involved four or five sessions, each lasting four or five days spread out over a year. So it was a pretty significant commitment with a lot of reading in preparation for each session. Those who formed my particular cohort—there were seventeen or eighteen of us—almost all of them were from schools of education. There were a couple of district board members, superintendents, and one other arts and sciences person.

BOB From all over the country?

JOHN From all over the country. I immediately felt intrigued, stimulated, and completely out of my element because this was a foreign culture I was joining. It was a culture that had its own language, a lexicon largely composed of abbreviations.

BOB [laughing] A bit like walking into a gathering of army officers.

JOHN So I would find myself asking, "What does that mean?" "What was that title about?" "What was that piece of legislation?" There was a tremendous amount of information others took for granted, information that marked the boundaries of their community and designated me as an immigrant.

BOB And when you posed those questions, how were they received?

JOHN Generously, though this background information was only *pretext* for what they really wanted to talk about. In retrospect, I know this was an important moment for me as an adult learner because the insecurity I felt as a holder of alien expertise kept me from taking root in the conversations. I couldn't apply what I knew because the ground was foreign. That's been a helpful reminder when I'm trying to bring people together who have different experiences and expertise. The good will you start with—the necessary and nurturing generosity—is a wonderful blessing and necessary condition, but you have to be able to help everybody take root in a common soil. And that's not always evident and rarely easy.

BOB So why did you not just fold your arms, sit back, and endure the year, instead of continuing to try to find place? The easy thing to do is disengage.

JOHN Well, I did and I didn't. In that particular group I was the quietest. I listened a lot. Many years earlier a friend had complimented my quietness by quoting some unknown source: "Those who talk know what they know; those who listen know what they know plus what the other guy knows." Following that folk wisdom, I was content to be the best-informed person of the group! Of course the flaw in that way of relating is that it is fundamentally ungenerous because it is not reciprocal. The first Seattle experience was a two-act play. In act 1 I listened and reflected. In act 2 I returned to the university and tested my reflections on colleagues to see whether or not they had any resonance.

BOB Do you recall how your colleagues responded?

JOHN Yes. These colleagues were the Spanish education faculty—

BOB Who had met with Bob Patterson?

JOHN Right. And they were simply astonished that a literary critic like me could be interested in questions that would relate to the preparation of teachers because that is not the way departments of foreign language typically work.

BOB So you had multiple divisions to cross, in this instance an internal one between you as a literary critic and these friends as teaching methods folks, who, I'd guess, didn't have all that much in common with you. You had some shared language, but it wasn't about pedagogy.

JOHN That's right.

BOB There are tiers to these divisions, divisions within divisions. It is easy to assume that humanities faculty are humanists, and everyone—people in Spanish and foreign languages, philosophy—everyone, gets along. But you're describing something more complex, an incalculable number of divisions among arts and sciences faculty presenting parallel sets of communication problems.

JOHN Precisely. And as typically happens in departments where the preparation of secondary teachers is decentralized from the school of education, those teacher educators often struggle for a place in their academic departments where they are considered, perhaps, as less expert in the discipline of the department, and there's a hint of marginalization. And so on one hand I was feeling invited and included by our school of education to participate in Seattle with a group from which I felt culturally marginalized, then using that same unfamiliar information to build bridges with a group that was traditionally marginalized in my department. That was a remarkable experience to try and take the intellectual discomfort I had experienced and use it as an impetus for inclusion of others.

BOB It's often a criticism that when school of ed people go to a public school with an idea to do something, maybe even with a grant, everything's impositional. There is a hierarchy operating. Part of what you're describing is the challenge involved in creating a new community, a new culture, where hierarchies are flattened. That's difficult; we're invested in our hierarchies.

JOHN In my case it was a flattening of hierarchies made possible by varying degrees of boundary crossing. Of discomfiting immigration. Willingness to be in an uncomfortable place. Then being able to take something away that enabled conversations that would not have happened in other ways, because I didn't know the right questions, I didn't have the vocabulary to engage in a thoughtful way with my own departmental colleagues on the education side. So even though I came away from Seattle as a novice, at least I was a novice. At least there was a basic grammar that I was beginning to apprehend that could then create some degree of credibility and sympathy with colleagues who had not felt validated before.

BOB At what point did you decide that you'd become multilingual?

JOHN It was probably not until I had done the Seattle experience for the third time. The year I completed the first of these programs it felt like I was doing another master's degree; it was that rigorous and that transformative for me. But the following year I repeated the Seattle experience with two colleagues from our partnership, one from the school of education and one from the superintendent's office in the Alpine School District. The three of us did a variation on the earlier Seattle program, working through a problem in our partnership's secondary education program.

BOB Those who are reading this need a few more details on what that problem was.

JOHN Right. There was a sense, held by disciplinary specialists in the colleges that train teachers beyond the school of education, of two different spheres that were not intersecting. The McKay School of Education was doing its professional education thing; history, English, and biology were all doing their things; and there was very little connecting over common aims.

BOB So you and a school of ed person and a school district administrator went to Seattle together and brought with you a problem to work on. This was your second Associates group experience.

JOHN Yes. We were in another cohort with people from all over the country. But instead of being alone I had two other people from our setting. And we read things that were new to us and discussed them. This time the discussions were all built around the Moral Dimensions of the process of preparing teachers and educating children. For me that was the beginning of some fluency with the ideas, and because of the relationships established with my two local colleagues, I was much more engaged in the conversation than I had been the first time.

And then the third immersion experience came a couple of years later, when the Seattle people invited me to be a facilitator for an Associates group that was to look at the theme of the well-educated teacher, considering ways general education ought to be conceived for preservice teachers. That put me in a leadership role, and at that point when, at least in comparison to the people in our partnership and with regard to the grounding ideas of the partnership, I started to feel like a native in the agenda, comfortable with Goodlad's Moral Dimensions of Teaching. It was apparent to me that the details of the daily experiences of teachers in the public schools or the teachers of teachers in the McKay School were still largely unexplored territory for me. Regarding the principles that brought us together, however, I began to feel that after these three very intensive Seattle experiences I had a grasp of those that was starting to feel somewhat unique.

BOB That just didn't happen; that was planned, wasn't it? This work that you did with the issue here was an opportunity to practice the language and then take some action on the theories embedded in the language. Practicing a language and then testing the theories embedded in that language through a shared project deepens understanding but probably also allows corrections as it enables connections. Then moving into that leadership position, as you described it—that required using language in a different way. But focusing on general education meant your expertise was being tapped: What is it to be a humanist? What is it to be generally educated? And so the education language you were learning was stretched and enriched by the traditions and language of the humanities, your home.

The Seattle Associates group I participated in also required of us some sort of product, a study of some kind. The idea of coming to such meetings with colleagues to work on a problem is a good idea, one supported in the research on effective professional development reaching all the way back at least to the 1930s.

JOHN What strikes me now about the third Seattle experience was the connection between Goodlad's ideas on education generally and general education (GE; also often called *liberal education*). When Goodlad, drawing from Dewey about the necessary connections between vocational and liberal education, between knowing and doing, when he saw education as the breath of civic life, he was making an argument for horizontal learning that demands that we make connections. That is general education. When he talked about securing access for all students to all the subjects that comprise the human conversation, he was talking about general education. And stewardship in any public endeavor—educational, political, civic—starts with stewardship of the mind—that is, with a personal commitment to one's own general education. There is a theory of general education in Goodlad. Is it too much to say that for him all education is liberal education—everything else is training?

BOB That's an important distinction, one that educators often miss. Education is messy business; outcomes are unpredictable. Not so with training, for which aims are known in advance—predictable.

Let's return for a moment to Dean Robert Patterson's initial invitation. Bob invited you to give. Now you're describing some getting. Something changed. You received a language, or you internalized or embraced a language that opened you up, so what were you getting?

JOHN That's the beauty of Bob's invitation, and perhaps of all invitations of that kind: One is inducted through an illusion of one's own gifts to a new society, a new culture, a new group of people, only to discover how much there is to know, how much there is to appreciate, how much of others' experience has been hidden by a veil. And then to have that veil pulled back through reading and conversation and interactions with people who were doing things that I had never done—all this resulted in unanticipated personal growth (intellectually, pedagogically, civically). Only then, ironically, was I prepared to make the gift that Bob had originally imagined.

BOB I want to get you to take another step. You haven't mentioned John Goodlad as a person or described a relationship with him. So there's Bob

Patterson, who influenced both of us in profound ways. Let's add another relationship to the mix: Goodlad. After all, it's relationships that keep the partnership going.

JOHN I hear an echo here. This conversation between us (Bob and John—Bullough and Rosenberg) is possible because of conversations convened by another Bob and John (Patterson and Goodlad). There is a hopeful genealogy at work. My first interaction with John Goodlad was in the first session of that first Seattle program, in which he led a discussion around something that he had just read a couple of years before.

We were sixteen, seventeen, eighteen strangers in the room, unsure of each other and maybe of ourselves, and during the course of the hour and a half that we spent together John learned everyone's name, and each contributed to the conversation in a way that was comfortable for that person. So there wasn't any on the spot putting: "Well, we haven't heard from Bill; Bill what do you think?" I don't quite know how he did it—waiting for the right moment, and then there was just kind of a glance—as in, this is something that you have to offer, this is the place where you can jump in. And without an exchange of anything other than that look, an individual was encouraged to join the conversation.

We were reading about the art of conversation, and so it was this magical moment when form and content became indistinguishable, when we were reading and trying to understand what for many people was a pretty dense piece of writing about the properties, ethical principles, and modalities of conversation, and all along John was demonstrating those very principles without ever drawing attention to the demonstration. John was very active. He was the presenter, he was the convener, he was the facilitator.

In other sessions John was an observer. But he was an observer who would then find opportunities to indirectly reinforce what he was observing. And so he noticed that first year that I was quiet. But both directly to me and indirectly back to Bob Patterson, he made comments like "John is quiet, but when he says something, it's worth attending to." Well I don't know if that was true or not, but what I do know is that receiving that feedback from him gave me more confidence at a time when I was feeling very much like a stranger in a strange land. He had a gift to perceive another's potential and then to craft a circumstance so that potential had an outlet.

BOB Goodlad often used the word *ecology*. There is an ecology of conversation: conditions that open people up. Any time that two people meet and because of the joy of their meeting want to converse or because of some pressing task set things up (or at least try to set things up) for leading, guiding, and being led and guided. As a teacher Goodlad thought structurally, he thought in ways that teachers do, about creating conditions—including a safe yet simultaneously charged space—that supports interaction and engagement.

JOHN This was a part of the thesis of the article that we were discussing that first meeting: Josiah Auspitz's obituary for Michael Oakeshott.

BOB A terrific piece.

JOHN Oakeshott saw conversation as an engaging improvisation, in part because it's enjoyable. But in essays like "The Voice of Poetry in the Conversation of Mankind," he insisted that people who are engaged in conversations (as he understood them) must have something serious to say. That seriousness points to intellectual responsibility (that is, stewardship), and one of the other things I observed in John was a quiet impatience for people who would come unprepared for conversation. It was never unkind, it was never openly critical, but there was evident disappointment when one would come to the table without, for example, thoughtfully considering the reading that was to serve as the catalyst for the day's conversation.

It was easy to see what John and his colleagues meant by *nurturing pedagogy*, as he promoted seriousness and responsibility as necessary conditions for conversation. Pedagogy is nurturing when it cultivates in company with high expectations and undisguised disappointment when a contract of learning is not attended to. But John's was always an interim disappointment; it was always an invitation to come back tomorrow having read more carefully.

BOB It strikes me that what was behind that feeling was Goodlad's respect for other people and for the ideas that captured him. How can a relationship be built that has any kind of depth or power if we don't come prepared? Preparation shows we value that person and that moment. It's an act of love, and it is nurturing.

JOHN And an act of gift giving. Because the gift's value is directly proportionate to the preparation that makes that gift possible.

The Moral Foundation

BOB Back to the story. You're now invested, and the form of that investment, if I understand correctly, is a set of relationships and a flock of ideas. Without the ideas you see no reason to come; without the relationships you find no reason to stay. You've got both of those: relationships and ideas. What big idea had taken hold of you at that time? Conversation was one, but were there others?

JOHN Absolutely. Conversation, I was discovering, is the medium, in the way air and soil are media, but the seeds that were going to be planted—the other big ideas—were the Moral Dimensions of Teaching. I began to discover their context in the first Goodlad book I read, *Teachers for Our Nation's Schools* (which I did not find a particularly engaging read).

BOB That's because you're not a school of ed native.

JOHN But what I did find was important—and this is another core principle— that the theses of the book were not speculative policy: The theses derived from systematic, longitudinal inquiry about the social and economic contexts of schooling. The book demonstrated that having something serious to say during grounding conversations depends on inquiry, on research, on disciplined thought. That was really important because so much of what we do, in practice and in governance at schools and universities, is driven by impression and anecdote, prejudice and self-interest, and by the limitations of experience. The systematic discipline we bring to our scholarly life *infrequently* finds its way to the policy and practices of our institutions of learning.

Critical inquiry brings discipline to the stewardship of partnership. That premise is most obvious when we remember that out of the inquiry of Goodlad's 1984 book (*A Place Called School*) flowed a set of principles that could be called *moral* because they were not contingent. And that is really powerful. If these principles weren't contingent, it meant that no matter how far apart I might be from another person on a whole series of issues, these Moral Dimensions could be a starting point. And because these inquiry-derived Moral Dimensions were not contingent, they would apply not only to what was happening in the public schools, but to what was happening in the partnership and to what I was trying to do in my academic setting at the university. The four Moral Dimensions, derived from and sustained by inquiry and conversation, are the most informing and useful ideas that I have taken away from more than two decades in the partnership.

BOB If we are going to share this conversation, we ought to share a bit of background about the Moral Dimensions and again state the dimensions themselves. (They are first mentioned in the introduction.) Let me read from *Education for Everyone* (Goodlad et al., 2004, pp. 28–32).

> The Moral Dimensions of Teaching are inescapable. When a teacher begins to teach, a whole array of moral choices and decisions inescapably comes into play. What is omitted from a curriculum can be just as consequential as what is included. How information is presented can have a tremendous effect on how it is received. Teaching cannot help but be informed by values and guided by normative principles.
>
> No matter what we do, the work of education involves values. It is important, then, that we be clear about just what values and principles

guide our work. The first dimension, "enculturating the young in a social and political democracy," is often thought of as an overriding goal. The second, "providing access to knowledge for all children and youths" speaks to one of the more important aspects of our democratic aspiration. The third touches on a central quality of teaching, that our pedagogy should be nurturing and grounded in the "art and science of teaching." The fourth dimension touches on the responsibility of educators to be part of the process of institutional renewal through "ensuring responsible stewardship of the schools." Generally, rather little thought is given to just what schools are for and foundational principles tend to be taken for granted—unexamined. But they need to be made explicit. Goodlad spoke of the four dimensions as being like a four-legged chair, each leg crucial to the chair's standing; if one leg fails, the chair falls. Taken together, the four legs form the core mission of the Agenda for Education in a Democracy. Of course, each of these has been the focus of a much writing and discussion. The implications of each dimension are far-reaching if they are taken seriously—what if, for example, all educators from preschools to graduate schools attended carefully to enculturating the young into a social and political democracy? The language used here, of having an "agenda," is important—this is a call to get organized and take action. Schools have all kinds of mission statements, but an agenda suggests rhetorically that we are serious about doing something.

JOHN I find it insightful to draw our attention to the word *agenda*. As you noted, Goodlad and his group insisted on that word—it was a nonnegotiable contract for collaboration. Like you said, forming an agenda is an attempt to distill order from talk. It is post-conversational: after all is said, here is what is to be done. [opening the *Oxford English Dictionary*] Let's see. I wonder what the *OED* tells us about the word *agenda*: "Things to be done, viewed collectively; matters of practice, as distinguished from belief or theory. Sometimes opposed to *credenda*." Interesting. *Credenda*, the "I believe" of credos—articles of faith. The Goodlad agenda carries with it the force and commitment of articles of faith, *except*—and this is important—that in their case they are articles of *inquiry*—not contingent, therefore moral, but demonstrable.

So back to your question about the actions I took that followed from study of the agenda. Early on they took the form of affecting my own pedagogy. I began to implement in my classes ideas taken from the moral dimensions and from the kinds of interactions I had experienced in Seattle. I introduced students in my classes on the literature and art of Spain to ideas of *conversation* and *stewardship*, and I spent time at the beginning of the semester asking, "What do those powerful words tell us for this particular setting?"

During my four years as department chair, the ideas behind the agenda led me to create a mini-partnership consisting of our five Spanish education faculty, teachers from three local high schools with strong programs and capable mentors for our preservice teachers, and me. Our goal was to determine how the university department could help the schools better serve their students and how the schools could help the department graduate better teachers. Though flawed in too many ways, the work did rely on a common commitment to the Moral Dimensions.

Later these same moral principles found their way into central themes I developed during my ten years as dean. We talked about *stewardship* when we emphasized that the value of an individual's work could be measured only by its contribution to the collective project of the department, college, and university. "Access to knowledge" was one of the ways that we generated conversation around the mandate to *assess* student progress toward specified learning outcomes. If we could agree that our students had a right to access the most salient ideas and artifacts that mark the human condition, then we first had to find a consensus around what those ideas were, and to what degree students should be expected to understand and act on them. Assessment, we said, was nothing more (or less) than the final phase of *nurturing pedagogy*—using critical inquiry to understand the varieties of our students' experiences across the breadth of the curriculum. Since teaching is a moral act, knowing how our teaching affects our students is a moral imperative (not an external mandate that requires the lowest form of obedience—known as compliance).

BOB At the same time you were doing the "mini-partnership," wasn't Alpine School District developing its own Associates program?

JOHN Yes, this would have been in '96 or '97.

BOB So it was just about the time CITES [Center for the Improvement of Teacher Education and Schooling, a center of pedagogy] was created and the time the college and the university decided that it would support Associates at a district level. Were those five of your colleagues also participating in Associates?

JOHN Eventually. At about the time that happened I left my assignment as department chair to become an associate dean, and one of the assignments that I asked to have was over teacher education in the college.

BOB You requested that?

JOHN I requested that. And one of the things that I proposed to the new dean was that as these Associates programs sponsored by the districts began to develop, we would invite humanities faculty to become a part of those groups and we would provide them with time compensation to do it. So the invitation would come from the dean and the associate dean to be a part of this conversation with school of ed people and public school people. We would give them a course reduction and tell them that this was an activity that for us had real value.

Partnership and the Challenge of Contexts

BOB   So this thing now is being institutionalized in a certain way within the humanities (and other) colleges, within the schools, and within the McKay School. During that time the university itself started to make some serious commitments to the partnership—up the ante. Were you part of the conversations that led to that increased commitment by the central administration?

JOHN   I was one of the signs of the changing times rather than a force behind the change. By this time I had read *Educational Renewal* (Goodlad, 1994), and what most impressed me in the book were the postulates (see the appendix), a set of conditions and practices that Goodlad and his associates determined were necessary for the education of educators. The first three postulates—eventually there were around twenty—tell us that the university itself, under the leadership of the central administration, must provide a context and the conditions under which teacher education can flourish. That made sense to me. I saw the education of teachers as a university-wide project—one way to transcend the disciplinary silos that afflict the modern university.

  It was a common project that reached across most of the colleges, certainly the largest colleges on campus. So I found the language in those first three postulates to be powerful, and I would occasionally write a memo to that effect to the central administration, memos that I fear may have been a bit too strident, in which I argued for the university project of educating teachers by collaboration involving the education school, arts and sciences departments, and the public schools, and building on the Moral Dimensions and Goodlad's agenda. I wouldn't claim in any way that the things that I did or said influenced the central administration's embrace of the partnership. It would probably be more accurate to say that I was part of a context that was starting to evolve, thanks to Bob Patterson, where people outside the McKay School were starting to understand the university project of improving teacher education and schooling.

BOB   Bob Patterson worked hard to build shared understanding among the deans. Relationships matter. I've had the experience of going to different professional meetings, describing something about the partnership, and having people look at me aghast when I said that this is supported by central administration. It involves real money, and that money is shared.

JOHN   It cut both ways, as far as I understand it, because not only was the central administration willing to provide support, but the dean of the school of education was willing to use his discretionary funds to encourage activities that were much broader than the immediate interests of his own college.

BOB Including the transfer of lines. Takes a lot of trust.

JOHN Yeah. So that was pretty strong leadership for the dean to say, "Come and be a part of this, and this is so important to us that all of our resources are on the table, and we'll put them wherever they need to be in order to have the biggest impact on this shared project." One of the things that Bob organized was the semiannual leaders' meeting consisting primarily of the deans of arts and sciences colleges that had some responsibility for teacher education, the leadership of the school of education, CITES representatives, and the superintendents of the five partnership districts. Bob was masterful in securing the participation of deans from all over campus, I think, by convincing them, as he had convinced me, that they had something important to offer in this campus-wide conversation around teaching. The vitality of the partnership has gone up and down depending on deans' willingness to promote the conversation.

BOB The partnership is in a rebuilding stage once again; there is always an ebbing and flowing. It's remarkable. Over all these years people have come and gone, at least four, five, presidents? I don't know even how many deans, it's amazing how many changes have taken place across campus and in the districts, and yet the partnership endures. It moves along. Sometimes limps along.

There's a new and interesting twist worth mentioning. A year ago the new dean of education, Mary Anne Prater, decided there ought to be a faculty retreat at the end of each year to review the current version of the Moral Dimensions and think about them in relationship to our practice. The second retreat occurred last month. The expectation has been that everybody in the McKay School of Education would be there; more than a hundred people came. There is no doubt that partnerships need constant tending—and it is a tremendous amount of work. Some of those who attended the retreat grumbled, but they came. Meetings of this sort are needed within the schools and colleges. The work is simply endless.

I want to shift our conversation for a moment. You've been involved in the partnership for a long time. Were there ever times when you worried about its future?

JOHN Each time someone is hired there is concern. One of the things that has been really important to survival is that the core non-contingent principles of the agenda have been a part of hiring decisions, and that has increased the likelihood of continuity.

BOB This was part of your selection as humanities dean. I served on the search committee.

JOHN When finding a new dean of a college, especially a dean of the school of education, an important part of that process is to ascertain the degree of familiarity and sympathy with the Moral Dimensions—the degree to which that person is going to provide continuing leadership for these noncontingencies. That provides a critical safety net, because there is no partnership without an evangelical dean of education.

We talk all the time about the need for a vision. Our aspirational rhetoric always looks up: "toiling upward in the night." But we need to toil downward, too, look at the ground at least as often as we look at the sky. By looking at the ground I mean asking ourselves "What are the foundations? What's the core? What's the soil out of which all of this partner stuff is growing?" The partnership can be driven by these powerful moral ideals, yet one can produce a great initiative and over time completely lose sight of the fact that the project was driven by a commitment to access to knowledge, for example. We must make certain what we do is always grounded in this common soil.

Conclusion

The next chapters include some of the manners and dispositions we hold to be central to democratic ways of relating with others. There is a circularity to this discussion in the sense that partnerships are both the cause and the effect of these virtues and practices. Partnerships (and democratic societies) cannot constitute themselves, for example, in the absence of the principles of hospitality and conversation. At the same time, a central objective of educational partnerships must be a continuing commitment to learning about the art and practice of getting along. Let us turn, then, to some of those principles.

3

Commons and the
Manner of Hospitality

. . . .

> While searching for herbs I suddenly
>   lost my way,
> Surrounded by one thousand peaks
>   and the autumn leaves.
> Then I spied a monk returning from
>   fetching water;
> At the edge of the woods, smoke for
>   boiling tea arises.
> —Yi Yulgok, sixteenth-century
>   Korean poet

This old Korean poem, like this chapter, hovers over the possibility of a conversation, and that possibility depends on the hospitality of the monk. Will he share the hot tea, and will the tea sharing be the occasion for a conversation that helps the traveler find his way? Without direct explanation, the poet calls our attention to *place*. The lost traveler happens on a place, a place with the potential to be a shared place—a common place.

There is a geography of association that builds community. Geography refers to the topographies, the characteristics, of the places we cohabit—their size, accessibility, and fertility. There also is an architecture that points to the dimensions and properties of what we build in those spaces. In this chapter we explore geography and architecture as sources of metaphor for two of what we think are the first principles of partnership. The first, *setting a commons* (an area of joint ownership or use), is essential for partnership grounding—emplacement; the second, *hospitality*, thought of as a democratic manner, sets expectations for how we will greet and treat travelers, who include visiting strangers and potential settlers in our commons. Lacking a commons, there is no partnership; without hospitality, partnerships are superficial or ephemeral or both. We begin our discussion with thresholds, boundaries, and boundary setting.

Thresholds

In *Thank You, Mr. Falker,* Patricia Polacco (1998) describes how she began to read in the fifth grade after years of frustration and embarrassment, with a good deal of teasing. Having thought a lot about "Trisha," one day her teacher, Mr. Falker, asked her to stay after school to help clean the boards: "He put on music and brought out little sandwiches as they worked and talked. All at once he said, 'Let's play a game! I'll shout out letters. You write them on the board with the wet sponge as quickly as you can.'" Quickly it became apparent Trisha didn't know the alphabet or recognize numbers. "She threw the sponge down and tried to run."

> Mr. Falker caught her arm and sank to his knees in front of her.
> "You poor baby," he said. "You think you're dumb, don't you? How awful for you to be so lonely and afraid." She sobbed. "But, little one, don't you understand, you don't see letters or numbers the way other people do. And you've gotten through school all this time, and fooled many, many good teachers!" He smiled at her. "That took cunning, and smartness, and such, such bravery." Then he stood up and finished washing the board. "We're going to change all that, girl. You're going to read–I promise you that."
> Now, almost every day after school, she met with Mr. Falker and Miss Plessy, a reading teacher. They did a lot of things she didn't even understand. At first she made circles in sand, and then big sponge circles on the blackboard, going from left to right, left to right. Another day they flicked letters on a screen, and Trisha shouted them out loud. Still other days she worked with wooden blocks and built words. Letters, letters, letters. Words, words, words. Always sounding them out. And that felt good. But, though she'd read words, she didn't read a whole sentence. And deep down she still felt she was dumb.
> And then one spring day—had it been three months or four months since they had started?—Mr. Falker put a book in front of her. She'd never seen it before. He picked a paragraph in the middle of a page and pointed at it. Almost as if it were magic, or as if light poured into her brain, the words and sentences started to take shape on the page as they never had before. "She . . . marched . . . them . . . off . . . to." Slowly, she read a sentence. Then another, and another.

And finally she'd read a paragraph. And she understood the whole thing. She didn't notice that Mr. Falker and Miss Plessy had tears in their eyes. (n.p.)

With Mr. Falker's and Miss Plessy's guidance and support, Trisha crossed a threshold. A threshold is a boundary. It separates who is inside from who is outside—in this case a child who was unable to read from children who were readers (a child who would grow up to earn a doctorate in art history). Thresholds set boundaries between what is familiar and what is unknown, what is safe and what is threatening, what is self and what is other. Growing up we encounter and cross all sorts of thresholds: infant to toddler, child to youth. Homes have thresholds and so do countries, as tourists and refugees discover. Organizations have thresholds marked by signs and symbols of belonging. Thresholds allow people in or keep them out.

Mr. Falker saw another human being—self-aware, profoundly vulnerable, and full of invisible potential—and he crossed a threshold to extend an invitation, while others (apparently) saw Patricia as an object to be worked around. Patricia had attended school for five or six years before a pedagogy that was truly nurturing gave her access to the knowledge that would transform her life. What does this say about the moral architecture of the school?

Moral Architecture

More than three decades ago school and university educators laid the foundation, marked off the threshold, and opened wide the door leading into the partnership. Those who entered and stayed, including five school districts and various organizational and individual representatives of the university, formally promised one another to build a commons—a community committed to the ideal of simultaneous renewal of schooling and teacher education, where all would have equal ownership and access, with opportunities to converse across their many differences. Passing over the partnership threshold meant entering a purposefully planned and constructed moral realm—a realm that included expectations and commitments as well as fundamental beliefs. There was an agenda to be attended to, nourished, and lived by if one acknowledged the foundation of the Moral Dimensions of Teaching. That conditional *if* stretched across the partnership threshold.

Thresholds may be inviting, but they are inevitably exclusionary—as was the reading boundary for Patricia. Not everyone invited to enter comes in or once inside wants to stay even if warmly welcomed. Yet ironically, without exclusivity there is no partnership. The threshold set by our partnership's founders took the form of a credo (literally, an "I believe") composed of the Moral Dimensions—four moral imperatives: I must ensure all students access to knowledge about every subject that makes up the human conversation; I must guarantee this access via pedagogies that nurture authentic learning; because I am committed to all students (not just those in my classroom), I must accept personal responsibility and accountability (stewardship) for what goes on in my building, in my district, in my community; I must do all this because *credo* (I believe) schools provide the threads out of which healthy civic lives are woven.

The partnership's Vision Statement begins with "we believe" (a credo) and proceeds to five "Commitments to Our Future," revised and expanded versions of the original four Moral Dimensions. Entering requires embracing the credo, though, as noted in the previous chapter, these *credenda* are operationalized through *agenda*.

Geography: A Commons

We enter a commons together as equals. Historically, particularly in New England, a commons was a parcel of land that belonged to no one and yet to everyone: "something that . . . can be used by all but appropriated by none" (Holder & Flessas, 2008, pp. 302–303). Recently, under the press of globalism, the idea has broadened to the usage we give it here (van Laerhoven & Ostrom, 2007). Kamola and Meyerhoff (2009) argued that a commons may exist in many places—"classrooms, departments, research groups, labor unions, and student organizations" (p. 6)—and sometimes in no physical place at all. "The term . . . can potentially include anything from the objective conditions of human existence (such as land, food, water, and housing) to embodied skills, knowledge and affective relationships." These authors continued, "Commons are things under general collective ownership by a group whose value practices regulate their use. . . . Within the framework of commons, actors are given opportunities to use the value practices of the group to grapple with those controversies concerning how best to live together" (pp. 8–9).

A commons has been specified as *generative spacing* that "does not simply defend, but which generates new forms of life" (Jeffrey, McFarlane, & Vasudevan, 2012, p. 1249), which we apply to partnerships between universities and schools, involving teachers, administrators, teacher educators, and arts and science professors. Pointing toward the importance of interacting and building relationships within partnerships, members engage in what might be thought of as "commoning" (Moss, 2014, p. 462). Used thus as a verb, it indicates the social practices of a group of people who recognize that their well-being and their futures are inextricably linked and, recognizing their interdependence, choose to act in concert.

As it becomes a form of commoning, our partnership occupies a moral space supported by the "value practices" of the Moral Dimensions. When we insist that these dimensions are moral, we do not claim they are theological, doctrinal, or confessional. They are moral in that they are instrumental for those who participate in commoning to answer questions about themselves as educators individually and collectively: What must I be? What must I (and we) do? How shall I stand (and we stand) in relation to others? How shall I (and we) abide? Educating is abiding; to educate is to abide with, and to abide with supports learning insofar as it is hospitable.

Hospitality and the Commons

The abiding characteristic of partnership educators may be illustrated by the following anecdote, related to John several years ago by the ambassador from Spain.

> The King of Spain greeted his guests at a state dinner in honor of an Asian dignitary. Because a previous dish had been eaten with fingers, a fingerbowl was brought to each guest before dessert. The head of the Asian delegation picked up the fingerbowl and, believing it to be a lemon-garnished broth provided to prepare the palate for dessert, drank the water. The other guests glanced briefly at each other and then down at their plates, not sure how to react to the unexpected breach of etiquette, and surely wondered how the host would respond. The king picked up his own fingerbowl, and without comment drank the water.

All of the rules of etiquette derive from one undergirding commitment: to welcome one's guests, even when their behavior may not conform to the host's norms. Hospitality, a way of welcoming and of being with others—at a dinner or at school or a college football game—transforms the *space* of the commons into the *relationships* of the commons. "Rules" must give way to "an ethical attunement and sensitivity toward the other" (Choo, 2014, p. 74), and so the king drank the water. Over time and with shared experience and conversational persistence, patterns of interaction may emerge that support learning, honor difference, and open possibilities for friendship. But first comes an aspiration toward hospitality that brings with it the potential for deeper and more generous relationships—the kind of generosity portrayed in the undoubtedly apocryphal story about the Spanish king. (The same story is told about Queen Victoria, Elizabeth II, and Eleanor Roosevelt.)

Hospitality has generated a good deal of recent discussion (see Barnett, 2005; Derrida, 2000), much of it driven by issues of international immigration (Macris, 2012). What are the practical limits to hospitality when one's national thresholds (borders) are crossed, sometimes without invitation, by people not like us (Macris, 2012)? What role do thresholds play in defining nationhood? Part of the debate on hospitality turns on the difference between *pure* hospitality and *conditional* hospitality. Pure or unconditional hospitality involves no expectation of return, no conditions, no implied reciprocity. In contrast, conditional hospitality assumes that an invitation involves something from the guest: obeying the laws, not drinking out of the fingerbowl, attending to the Moral Dimensions.

Hughes-Warrington (2012), drawing on French philosopher Derrida (2000), observed that hospitality is "inconceivable and incomprehensible in an unconditional or absolute sense" (p. 317). There are limits to generosity, among them the death of the host or destruction of the commons (see Wu, 2014). The power of pure hospitality comes from its status as an insistent ethical ideal, an aspiration, first developed in imagination (see Choo, 2014). Conditional hospitality is pragmatic: a matter of self-preservation and perhaps of sovereignty as much as anything else. Without some limits on hospitality, our capacity to be hospitable is first diminished and then destroyed. But conditional hospitality can turn wine to water, transforming the *virtue* of hospitality into the halfhearted *accommodation* of tolerance. Often little more than an expression of "false generosity" (Freire, 1970, p. 40), tolerance is passive and disinterested; learning requires something more, a desire for active engagement.

Aspiring to Pure Hospitality

At the threshold and within the commons of the partnership, the ideal is pure hospitality. Indeed, "unconditioned hospitality is prior to and . . . [the condition for] any conventional, public, official or legal conception of hospitality or of 'hosting' a 'guest'" (Wu, 2014, p. 1445). But this ideal has its moral irony: to be generously open to people and ideas is, as Dewey (1916) argued, in one's own self-interest because hospitality is essential to "retention of the capacity to grow" (p. 206). Making a similar point, Burwell and Huyser (2013) suggest hospitality is an important source of "learning opportunities" that come only from the experience of "otherness" (p. 11).

Within most religious traditions hospitality is an honored ideal. An ancient Sanskrit text reads, "Be one for whom the Mother is God. Be one for whom the Father is God. Be one for whom the teacher is God. Be one for whom the guest is God" (Taittiriya Upanishad, Shikshavalli I.20), placing parents, teachers, and guests as godly recipients of hospitality. Tradition attributes to Muhammad this injunction: "Let the believer in Allah and the Day of Judgment honor his guest." The widow of Sarepta's hospitality saved Elijah, and in turn it saved her (1 Kings 17). According to Genesis, Abraham ran to strangers and brought them to his tent to dine (Genesis 18:2). Why? Because Abraham, like followers of many world religions, believed that by entertaining guests, one may entertain angels (or even a god) unaware (Matthew 25:40). The stranger is himself (or herself), but also something bigger, something immanent. No one expects a gift, but nevertheless gifts are given and received, and no one knows just what they are or what they might bring.

The aspiration toward pure hospitality within the commons represents how members ought to treat one another. In recognition of and respect for differing kinds of knowledge and expertise, role definitions soften: teacher, principal, superintendent, professor, board member. Supporting a kind of civic solidarity, the "rule bound behavior of system confidence" (Seligman, 1997, p. 174) that increasingly keeps organizations running is necessarily replaced by trust born of respect, a shared (if emerging) vision, shared values, and a voluntary association made necessary by individual agency—at any time, someone can withdraw with impunity. Hence, solidarity develops from compelling ideas, values, and invested relationships.

Partnering: What Shall I Do?

Philosopher Simon Critchley recently told a university audience that the heroes from Greek tragedy all ask the same question: "What shall I do?" This question expresses the universality of classical tragedy: We all ask and answer the same question throughout our lives. So it is with hospitality: When we ask "What shall I do?" we are also asking "What shall I do together with you?" In different terms, "What sort of partner will I be?" Four partial answers for that question follow, answers that suggest how hospitality is manifested as a democratic manner.

I Shall Not Treat You as an Alien

First, hospitality begins by dissolving the strangeness of the alien. *Alien* and *alienation* represent more than *stranger*: they suggest *strangeness*, something distasteful that must be kept at arm's distance, sometimes with codes and gates and walls. In the opening lines of one of Terence's plays, Menedemus, a sixty-ish nobleman, works from sunup to sundown on his estate, in spite of having wealth and numerous servants (an act of penance, we later learn). Chremes, his neighbor, worries aloud that the old fellow is working himself to death, and that by working himself rather than supervising his indolent laborers, he is not accomplishing much. Somewhat peeved, Menedemus retorts, "Have you so much leisure, Chremes, from your own affairs, that you can attend to those of others—those which don't concern you?" Chremes responds, "I am a man, and nothing that concerns a man is alien to me" (act 1, scene 1). Chremes may be a busybody, and his methods and motives for being interested may be flawed, but he is on to something. He rejects strangeness and difference (alienation) in search for commonality, a common humanity. An explicit recognition (I am a man, and so are you) makes conversation possible.

Monologue is alienating; the speaker perceives the listener only as a vessel into which he can pour the wealth of his words. Hospitality asks us to accept the alien as listener and speaker—to willingly stop talking to attend to another. Michael Naas (2003) stated it this way: "Hospitality requires that a guest be treated as a Somebody, not as a serialized Nobody" (p. 159).

A few years ago David Brooks of the *New York Times* invited fellow columnists to write a "life report," to give a sense of the meaning of their life to that point. One of those who took up Brooks's challenge was a well-known literary critic, a man whose books were read in nearly every English department. Though he was known as something of a curmudgeon, the account of his life he published in the *Times* was astonishingly reflective and confessional. He wrote about the discomfort he had felt throughout his life at parties and other social gatherings at the amount of energy required to try come up with just the right thing to say, with the charming witticism that would reinforce his standing with (and his distance from) others. But then he confessed, "If you regard each human interaction as an occasion for performance, your concern and attention will be focused on how well or badly you're doing and not on the people you are doing it with." When the critic wrote at the end of his essay about "the fellowship of fragility we all share," he crossed the threshold from monologue to conversation, from alienation to hospitality (see Fish, 2011).

I Shall Be Both Host and Grateful Guest

Second, inside the commons we must be both host and guest. A few years ago while reading a novel in Spanish, John ran across the word *huesped*, used archaically by the author to mean *host*. He found that curious because in modern Spanish *huesped* means *guest*. How could a word's history contain both the current denotation and its opposite? *Huesped* comes from the Latin *hospes*, the root of English words like *host*, *hospital*, and, of course, *hospitality*. For ancient speakers of Latin (and modern speakers of Italian), *hospes* (*ospite*) might mean either host or guest. We need to be both, as Anthony Gittins (1994) explained, "Unless the person who sometimes extends hospitality is also able sometimes to be a gracious recipient, and unless the one who receives the other as stranger is also able to become the stranger received by another, then far from 'relationships,' we are merely creating unidirectional lines of power flow" (p. 399). A good place to witness relationships of reciprocal hospitality is in dual language immersion classrooms. In these settings, it is common to find a native speaker of Spanish, for example, tutoring a native speaker of English as each attempts to learn the other's language. What in some settings might be considered a deficit, in this setting is a resource, a gift given of *knowledge* and *expertise*. Finding ways to ensure that every child is as much a giver as a receiver is characteristic of nurturing pedagogy—a practice that grows from the virtue of hospitality (see chapter 6).

Redeeming hospitality requires reciprocity, not in the sense of conditional hospitality (I expect something in return for my welcome) but in the sense that I am willing to become the alien, to cross your threshold, to receive your gift. That is why conversation, the topic of our next chapter, requires two alternating moves, speaking and listening—giving and getting—in which we play out the reciprocal roles of host and guest.

I Shall Be Welcoming and Respectful of Others within the Commons

Third, learning requires a commons—a time and place within which differences can touch, where cultures can bump into one another, as John Goodlad (1993) suggested, and perhaps even embrace. That meeting space must be hospitable. Christine Pohl (1999) described some of the characteristics of hospitable settings: "They are safe and stable, offering people a setting where 'they can rest for awhile to collect themselves'" (p. 152). Hospitable places are not necessarily hushed, just as rest isn't always passive or always still. But they are safe for stasis. Safe for things to be like they are and for people to be who they are—while they figure out where they want to go and what they want to be.

Pohl wrote about "collecting oneself"—an interesting metaphor. We collect stamps. And coins. How do we collect ourselves? The question reminds us that "difference resides as much within the self and with others around us as within the other in another country" (Hughes-Warrington, 2012, p. 319). And so we also "gather ourselves" and "pull ourselves together," necessary responses to being "beside ourselves" and occasionally "out of our minds." These metaphors that suggest otherness from self (as opposed to alienation from others) are ubiquitous. As the spaces of hospitality welcome all strangers, so may they also welcome the strangeness in ourselves. "In such places life is celebrated, yet the environment also has room for brokenness and deep disappointments" (Pohl, 1999, p. 152). In hospitable places the rhetoric of success does not displace relief of distress.

Pohl (1999) continued, "Hospitable places are alive with particular commitments and practices, however guests are not coerced into sharing them" (p. 153). We recognize these commitments and practices as the Moral Dimensions that ground our partnership. As noted, the threshold to the partnership is marked by a conditional *if*: join us if you are willing to judge all you do as educators in light of our moral architecture. Teachers, schools, and districts are free to come and go on the tides of their commitment. In contrast, public school students have no choice: they must attend class. For this reason, the hospitality extended to them must be, at least at first, as pure and unconditional as possible, and always welcoming. Like Abraham with his guests, sometimes teachers need to chase down their students, as Mr. Falker sought out the vulnerable Patricia. To put it another way, our welcome is steadfast and our attitude of hospitality is unrestrained with the young—and to those we recognize as potential colleagues—even when being hospitable is inconvenient and sometimes costly.

Finally, Pohl (1999) reminded us, hospitable places make "provisions for rest and renewal" (p. 182)—for the host and for the guest.

I Shall Be Engaged

Death by Meeting, Patrick Lencioni's (2004) "leadership fable," describes what many educators experience during the array of meetings that require their attendance. The best one can hope for is a quick death. Though such meetings often feel like a distraction from the central purposes of teaching and learning, when leaders who call them have been thoughtful in preparation, these meetings become the commons (dedicated times and places) for partnering and for personal learning and professional development. But when one speaks of gatherings of any sort, there is a difference between mere *attendance* and *attending*. Authentic hospitality is engaged and engaging: It demands that we attend *to* someone or something. It fosters empathy. Empathy is an affective term for crossing thresholds (emotional, psychic, or cognitive). Consider the following tale retold by Simone Weil (1951):

> In the first legend of the Grail, it is said that the Grail . . . belongs to the first comer who asks the guardian of the vessel, a king three-quarters paralysed by the most painful wound: "what are you going through?" The love of our neighbor in all its fullness simply means being able to say to him, "what are you going through." It is a recognition that the sufferer exists, not only as a unit in a collection, or a specimen from the social category labeled "unfortunate," but as a man, exactly like us, who was one day stamped with a special mark by afflictions. For this reason, it is enough, but is indispensable, to know how to look at him in a certain way. This way of looking is first of all attentive. (pp. 64–65)

Weil spends a good deal of time in her essay explaining how one develops this faculty of attention. "Students . . . should never say, 'For my part I like mathematics'; 'I like French'; 'I like Greek.' They should learn to like all these subjects, because all of them develop [the] faculty of attention" (pp. 57–58). "If we have no aptitude or natural taste for geometry," she continues, "this does not mean that our faculty for attention will not be developed by *wrestling* with a problem or studying a theorem. On the contrary it is almost an advantage" (58; emphasis added). The point is to *wrestle*, to work through a difficult problem, to acquire discipline of thought. Too often we succumb to the entitlement of easiness that suggests that if I am *good* at something, it ought to be *easy* (and if it is hard, I must not be cut out for it). Geometry (or French or history) has inherent and practical value of its own, but for Weil all subjects also are vehicles that lead to something immanent and transcendent: the ability to focus on, to *attend to* something bigger than and beyond ourselves, like partnership.

Such attention is active: active in preparation, active in execution, and active in conclusion (hospitality cannot be passive). Attending to ideas (concepts, texts, theories, methodologies) also prepares us to connect with people. Imagine a professional development event whose leaders expect participants to read before the meeting. One can choose not to read. One can choose to skim the texts without engaging with their ideas or becoming open to the changes those ideas might effect in us. Or one can *attend*. In such settings, by attending to preparation one also attends to people.

Hospitality invokes empathy, requires openness, and is reverent, respectful, and filled with surprise, the sort of feeling that arises when curiosity overcomes fear and differing lifeworlds meet. This is the attitude that allowed Mr. Falker to attend to Patricia then teach her to read. "What are you going through?" This should be the first question asked in morally grounded conversations. "What shall I do (together with you)?" This question, posed by classical tragedy, concludes the conversation.

Hospitality and Learning, Again

As a manner, hospitality is a condition for conversation; in that sense it is pre-conversational. Conversation strengthens and sustains the commons. It is the means by which thresholds to membership are set initially and adjusted over time. Thus conversation is both an aim and a means to partnering; it is a defining practice, often a source of pleasure that anchors the desire to belong, and when it involves generous and informed exchange, it is a critical component of learning and a source of personal and institutional renewal. Because conversation involves both speaking and listening, "attentive listening" (Burwell & Huyser, 2013, p. 13) is a rare virtue and a difficult skill to master. Simply wanting to be open does not lead to openness. When no place is provided for turn taking or when the balance of "mutual vulnerability" (Burwell & Huyser, 2013, p. 10) required of conversation is decidedly one-sided, listening may be impossible. In moments when what is said (recall the introduction) is ugly and boldly self-serving, and when the speaker is inhumane and the invitation to conversation insincere, we discover the limits of hospitality. We may also discover that some ideas are simply not worth hearing. And we disengage because we conclude we must.

Here we are reminded of an anecdote from the *Natural History* of Pliny the Elder (1855), praising Alexander the Great's favorite painter, Apelles of Kos. When Apelles had completed a work, he would exhibit it to passersby in a public place and conceal himself so that he could listen to their criticisms, considering that the judgment of the public was undoubtedly in some ways preferable to his own. Tradition records that once he was censured by a shoemaker for having represented shoes with one shoestring too few. Sometimes listening is all that learning requires, but these situations are rare. Despite his lofty status, Apelles showed hospitality to learning, listened to the shoemaker, and reworked his painting. And that can be a hard thing. Some find it easier to open the door to a stranger than to a strange idea. We can feed and dismiss the stranger, but the strange idea, once admitted to mind, often lingers and begins rearranging our conceptual furniture. This is a good thing, though it does not suggest that we surrender our power of discrimination. Some ideas, like a poorly rendered shoe, can be worthy friends, others not so much. The day following his success in correcting the great painter's depiction of a shoe, the shoemaker began critiquing Apelles's rendering of the leg. Rightly discerning that the shoemaker's expertise ended with the footwear, Apelles rejected that criticism. But he had been open to the shoemaker's particular expertise and grateful for it. So we too should recognize and be grateful for the expertise, in all its rich variety, our partners offer.

We find a curious echo of the Apelles story in the Fang culture of West Africa in a tale about a tortoise and tiger who compete to make a superior drum. The tiger secrets himself in the forest and builds his instrument alone; the tortoise constructs his drum in the middle of the main road leading to town, and, like Apelles, hides himself when travelers approach in order to hear their comments. By applying what he learns, the tortoise builds a superb drum, while the tiger earns only scorn for his unwillingness to be open to change.

E. B. DeVito's poem "Graduates" offers a third variation on the initial move of openness that makes us available to surprise.

> Knowledge comes, in a way, unsought,
> as in the Chinese tale
> of the youth who came for daily lessons
> in what there was to learn of jade.
> And each day, for a single hour,
> while he and the master talked together,
> always of unrelated matters,
> jade pieces were slipped into his hand,
> till one day, when a month had passed,
> the young man paused and with a frown,
> said suddenly, "That is not jade."
> As Life is something, we are told,
> that happens while you make other plans,
> learning slips in and comes to stay
> while you are faced the other way.

The "other way" is the one that is unfamiliar, strange, and foreign. Facing the other way, opening to the other way, makes us available to learning and to learners. Facing another way is the posture and manner of hospitality.

In Conclusion: Hospitality and Conversation

Perhaps it is helpful to keep in mind that the Latin word from which we get *hospitality* derives from a Greek idea: *philoxenia*, the love of strangers (the antonym of *xenophobia*). Like democracy itself, hospitality is the product of the triumph of love over fear. It is an invitation and an initiation.

Michael Oakeshott (1959) wrote that education is an initiation into the conversation of mankind. An initiation, by definition, requires crossing thresholds. Clive Barnett (2005) asserted, "Thresholds are the very scenes for the drama of responsiveness, hospitality and responsibility" (p. 13). This drama of responsiveness, hospitality, and responsibility seems a lot like schooling. Schools and colleges have and are thresholds. Often the thresholds offered are not easily crossed, as Mr. Falker knew. Some students, like Patricia, are hesitant, frightened. Some parents are suspicious. Some policy makers are misinformed and distrustful. Some university faculty don't have the time or the interest or the freedom to cross thresholds into places they research and write about. Thus we need a partnership. Through it we collaborate, draw on one another's knowledge and expertise, and with our partners gain courage and strength. By means of it we renew. But mostly, the partnership is the institutional gesture of hospitality.

4

From Conversation
to Dialogue

- - - - - - - - - - - - - - - - - - -

> Every sudden idea has the structure
> of a question.
> —Hans-Georg Gadamer

Hospitality, as we have suggested, is the antecedent to conversation. It sets the place (a commons) and establishes the conditions of openness and welcome that make conversation possible. In this chapter we further explore the conditions and manners that support conversation and set the stage for the emergence of dialogue, understood as a form of inquiry, a defining element of the praxis of democracy.

Hospitality is the mother of conversation. Hans-Georg Gadamer (2011) approached this idea when he wrote, "Use language as a midwife," describing the "maieutic productivity of the Socratic dialogue" (p. 361). *Maieutic*, a word of Greek origin, literally means "obstetric," and the *Oxford English Dictionary* describes a *maieutic* method as one that assists "a person to become fully conscious of ideas previously latent in the mind." The Hebrew tradition joins Socratism in likening speech to birthing, to creating. "And God said, let there be . . ." (Genesis 1:3): speech is power and authority, and *logos* can be both oppressive and liberating.

These ideas of speech as power have their correlation in modern ideas of the gaze. Sartre (1966) described the objectifying gaze (p. 340), the one that apprehends another, controls him, and objectifies him (e.g., iconic image of

Marilyn Monroe on the subway grate in *The Seven Year Itch,* objectified by vary-ing gazes: from the character played by Tom Ewell, from the camera lens, and from the audience in the movie theater). A few decades earlier sociologist Georg Simmel wrote of the "reciprocal glance" of lovers, a gaze that confirms and sustains the other (Weinstein & Weinstein, 1984). Try gazing into a part-ner's eyes for as little as one minute (though it seems like ten). What do you experience? Reciprocity. Fragility. Attentiveness. Vulnerability. Disclosure and self-deliverance. As noted previously, such feelings arise from the "relation with the face" (Levinas, 1985, pp. 85–86) that supports an ethics of obligation.

Deena and Michael Weinstein (1984) claimed that, according to Simmel, "the union or relation constituted by mutual glancing is fragile and is destroyed as soon as one of the participants makes the slightest glance aside" (p. 351). Thus the reciprocal glance is reciprocal by virtue of attentiveness and waitfulness— ideas discussed at the end of this chapter. Further, as included in the section on dialogue, reciprocal glancing works by means of mutual vulnerability: "By the glance which reveals the other, one discloses himself. By the same act in which the observer seeks to know the observed, he surrenders himself to be understood by the observed" (Simmel, quoted in Weinstein & Weinstein, 1984, p. 351). Weinstein and Weinstein conclude that the "social knowledge" made available by the glance "is only possible through self-deliverance and active tran-scendence of the self into the other's vision. Such participating knowledge cannot be attained through observation, but only by offering oneself as a gift to the other" (p. 351). Conversation, as we understand it, is to speech what the reciprocal glance is to seeing.

Gadamer (2011) described the openness necessary for both reciprocal gaz-ing and conversation: "Conversation is a process of coming to an understand-ing. Thus it belongs to every true conversation that each person opens himself to the other, truly accepts his point of view as valid and transposes himself into the other to such an extent that he understands not the particular individual but what he says. What is to be grasped is the substantive rightness of his opin-ion, so that we can be at one with each other on the subject" (p. 385).

Persuasion and Conversation

Anton Chekhov's (1920/1972) story "Home" introduces a father, Yevgenii Petrovitch Buikovsky, procuror of the District Court, who has problems at home with his son who, age seven, has started to smoke. He does not appear to be much engaged in the life of the boy, needing to ask the governess how old the boy is. The father is, however, determined to change the boy's behavior. So he confronts him with formal arguments against his vice. The boy doesn't lis-ten. Bewildered, failing as a teacher, the father wonders what he should do. "What else shall I say to him?" "How can I make him understand? . . . Not in this way." After making an especially clever point, he concludes, "I am a nice teacher." He continues talking but realizes he is not getting through to the boy. Self-doubts increase: "No, I am a bad teacher!"

The clock strikes ten. Time for bed. "Tell me a story," the son pleads. In response the father improvises a tale. It is not a good story; in fact, it's horrid. "The old tsar had an only son, the heir to his throne," the father says, "a little boy about your size. He was a good boy." Then, setting his trap, the father says: "But he had one fault—he smoked." The smoking son in the father's tale gets TB, dies at the age of twenty, and leaves his father comfortless and defenseless against enemies who overrun his palace and cut down his cherry trees. Listening, the child responds in a weak voice, "I will not smoke anymore."

Although pleased his message got through, the father finds his own actions troubling, the dishonesty of "mixtures, always sugared and gilded like a pill. This is not normal. . . . It is falsification, deception . . . a trick." While his son sleeps peacefully, the procuror passes the night pacing the floor, concluding that "there are in nature many useful and expedient deceits and illusions." The end justified the means; the story was a threat, not an occasion to connect with his son, to show love and concern for his health and well-being, not an invitation to talk or an offer to listen. The teacher's task was to persuade, to obtain compliance.

No doubt, persuasion has a place in teaching. Smoking is, after all, dangerous, and seven-year-olds badly need guidance. Debate structures persuasion, but a good debate—a debate that clarifies and elevates understanding and thereby sets the stage for taking a more informed stand on an issue—requires debaters to be reasonably well matched in ability and understanding, else what follows is a setup. But teaching is more than telling and learning is more than complying or conforming. Usually, but not always, when persuasion dominates interaction, unfortunate effects follow: "Persuasion aims to muster thought and feelings in closed ranks; it bends the *will* of other people, making tactical use of their needs and dispositions. . . . Persuasion goes for results in matters of belief and action. To get people ready to act in certain ways, alternatives must be excluded. By its inherent purposes, persuasion eliminates the open-mindedness that justifies confidence [and supports education]" (Buchmann, 1986, 13). As an expression that exercises power over others, real or imagined, persuasion constrains learning; the hearer becomes a passive receptor of the speaker's truth or simply turns off. The goal of persuasion, as illustrated by the Chekhov story, is acknowledgment of a speaker's (teacher's) wisdom and rightness followed by concession. Wealthy (in wisdom), the speaker's truth is superior to whatever the needy (in understanding) hearer might hold to be true. Of course, sometimes the speaker's truth is wise and sometimes the hearer is needy.

The seeds of democracy are planted when the relationship between the speaker and hearer is reciprocal, transactional, jointly invested, and fluid. We then transition from persuasion to conversation, from monologue toward dialogue. Bakhtin's (1984) understanding of the medieval tradition of carnival offers a rich metaphor for thinking about just what conversation entails.

> Carnival is a pageant without footlights and without a division into performers and spectators. In carnival everyone is an active participant, everyone communes in the carnival act.... The laws, prohibitions and restrictions that determine the structure and order of ordinary ... life are suspended during carnival. What is suspended first of all is hierarchical structure.... All distance between people is suspended, and a special carnival category goes into effect: *free and familiar contact among people*.... Carnival is the place for working out in a concretely sensuous, half-real and half-play acted form, a *new mode of interrelationship between individuals*.... Carnival brings together, unifies, weds, and combines. (pp. 122–123)

Conversation and carnival are not the same, but both are modes of relating that appear to "force [people] to renew themselves" (p. 127), and it is partially out of the study of carnival that Bakhtin came to understand what he called "the dialogic imagination."

Because we are interested in and concerned about education and about education in support of democratic social aspirations, and about educational renewal, conversation—not persuasion—is a central departure point for the discussion that follows. Our understanding of conversation has been shaped by many influences, including, as described in chapter 2, our having actively participated over many years in the work of university–public school partnership with many remarkable people. Conversations with John Goodlad and Bob Patterson, among several others, have stirred our thinking. Several additional theorists have captured and stretched our imaginations, as will become apparent, and have added to our understanding.

We begin in the sections that follow an exploration of conversation as both an aim and a means of partnering, as an essential condition for the emergence of dialogue, a form of human interaction that like conversation supports learning but also involves inquiry—the presentation and careful consideration of evidence required by democratic citizenship. The argument is straightforward: Lacking the conditions necessary for sustained conversation, there is no possibility of dialogue nor, finally, of partnership (nor of democracy). Conversation is a particular and peculiar form of human relatedness essential to preparing the ground for dialogue. Conversation opens a space for sharing life experience; dialogue arises when differences and tensions in the understanding of those experiences emerge and insist on clarification and perhaps resolution.

Conversation Defined

In the first century B.C.E., Marcus Tullius Cicero tells us of a visit to a villa where he joined his friends Gaius Cotta, Gaius Velleius, and Quintus Lucilius Balbus in conversation. He reported the conclusion of their talking: "Here the conversation ended, and we parted, Velleius thinking Cotta's discourse to be the truer, while I felt that that of Balbus approximated more nearly to a semblance of the truth." Of this encounter, Stephen Greenblatt (2011) wrote,

> The inconclusiveness is not intellectual modesty—Cicero was not a modest man—but a strategy of civilized openness among friends. The exchange itself, not its final conclusions, carries much of the meaning. The discussion itself is what most matters, the fact that we can reason together easily with a blend of wit and seriousness, never descending into gossip or slander and always allowing room for alternative views. "The one who engages in conversation," Cicero wrote, "should not debar others from participating in it, as if he were entering upon a private monopoly; but, as in other things, so in a general conversation he should think it not unfair for each to have his turn." (p. 70)

Cicero's understanding of the virtue of conversational openness and indeterminacy has appeared in the writings of a number of modern philosophers, including those of Michael Oakeshott.

In part because of his interest in education, Oakeshott, a British political and social philosopher, is among those theorists who have influenced our thinking. Oakeshott's most important writings about conversation can be found in several essays, "Political Discourse," "The Study of Politics in a University," and especially "The Voice of Poetry in the Conversation of Mankind." Oakeshott sees in conversation, through the "humility of honest human self-recognition," hope for overcoming the "rough, coercive, often violent character of political life" (Fuller, 1991, pp. xxi, xix), a life form that has overwhelmed and reshaped what at one time was the relatively placid and more or less convivial agora of education.

In contrast to persuasion, which he characterized as the voice of "argumentative discourse," Oakeshott (1991) offered his alternative:

- In a conversation participants are not engaged in an inquiry or a debate.
- There is no truth to be discovered, no proposition to be proved, no conclusion to be sought.
- [Speakers] are not concerned to inform, to persuade, or to refute one another.
- [Speakers] may differ without disagreeing.

- Certainties are shown to be combustible.
- There is no . . . doorkeeper to examine credentials.
- Voices which speak in conversation do not compose a hierarchy.
- [Conversation] springs from tension between seriousness and playfulness.
- It is an unrehearsed intellectual adventure. (pp. 491–493)

Oakeshott's vision of conversation is appealing but is vulnerable to at least two objections important for our later discussion of dialogue. First, since he affirmed there is no hierarchy, it appears that for Oakeshott all voices were equal, which leaves little room for authorized convictions, for demonstrated authority, based on knowledge or experience. Second, and seemingly more consequential, his ideal of praxis for conversation seems to be nonteleological, lacking an end or goal. If there "is no truth to be discovered" and certainties "are shown to be combustible," what is conversation *for*? Oakeshott's view of conversation might be socially appealing, but it doesn't appear to be especially useful.

Speaking with Authority

To Oakeshott, conversations disallow hierarchy; no gatekeepers check credentials. What we fear is that if no one is in charge, conversation will be displaced by safe chatter, sometimes noise, not even attempts at persuasion, followed by disengagement into snuggly places where all one hears is pleasantly self-confirming. When no one is not supposed to know more than others, or is forbidden or dares not to reveal special understanding or insight, conversation (and teaching) may fail to support learning.

No surprise—internet surfers commonly seek sameness and avoid persons, blogs, or works that might prove disagreeable (Bauman & Raud, 2015). College students avoid encounters with persons and materials that represent contrary and uncomfortable opinions, which may demand a critical encounter with oneself (see Lukianoff & Haidt, 2015). Supporting the "right" to avoidance, some instructors give "trigger warnings" to make certain students won't have to discuss or read anything they would rather avoid. The intent is to root out so-called *microaggressions*—subtle but unintended affronts to someone's feelings. No one should ever feel uncomfortable. Evidence? Not important. In such situations, good feelings and feeling good are the centripetal forces that keep conversation going, even if only in a circle. Under such conditions, to speak with authority is to speak improperly, out of turn. Conversation, then, falters as its area of concern becomes smaller and smaller. Yet conversation may involve a reality check, a sounding, "Am I off base?"

While this represents a reasonable reading of Oakeshott's position, it is certainly not what he had in mind when writing about conversation. He recognized that differences in knowledge and wisdom will always be apparent among participants. He admitted, for example, that "from time to time one voice [in a conversation] may speak louder than others." What he denied is that anyone "has natural superiority, let alone primacy" (1959, p. 55). Oakeshott's point was that "primacy" and assumed "natural superiority," which may take many forms, prevent conversations from getting off the ground. Oakeshott's final distinguishing quality of conversation, noted above, gives space to the particularly wise or seasoned speaker who carries legitimate authority. But that authority finds expression only as it is invited into the conversation, sought as a gift by willing listeners; intrusion suggests persuasion, and persuasion, as illustrated by Chekhov's story, leads to silence—mentally going to bed. If conversation is to be "an unrehearsed intellectual adventure," then all of the talent and understanding of the participants is needed to realize that potential, even as no claim to special position can or should be honored. Such claims set up monologic expectations, and the generosity of conversation embedded in its give-and-take deteriorates into giving without wanting or taking. In contrast, conversation requires full and generous engagement, a manner and a sign of interest and proof of respect.

The Ends of Conversation

Our second objection to Oakeshott's list invites two responses calling attention to the conversational ethos. Conversation requires that each speaker bring something that needs to be said and shared. It continues when my something is allowed to interact freely with the somethings that others bring as their gifts. If I am the only one with something to say, conversation dies stillborn; if I think that what I have to say is what truly matters, at the expense of others' offerings, the conversation devolves into unreciprocated monologues. But when gifts are exchanged, the conversation moves and does so "by the delight of utterance" (Oakeshott, 1959, p. 61); hence conversation has its playful element, a pleasure found in talking and being together that Sax (2016) described in *The Revenge of Analog* as a hopeful force drawing people away from the digital world and into a world that is "more tactile and human-centric" (p. xviii). Humans enjoy and need to converse face-to-face and to touch, both expressions of the drive to make sense of life, to enrich experience, and to satisfy the need to soften feelings of being alone. As mentioned in the introduction, "Man is by nature a social animal," and so we are; we need other people.

As social creatures living on a small planet, our stake in conversation generally involves the life of the species. The kind of discourse Oakeshott (1991) promoted is serious, even as it was sometimes playful, "because without this seriousness the conversation would lack impetus" (p. 493). As opposed to chatter, conversation works only when something serious needs to be expressed and shared, something that matters to us and that we think ought to matter to others—as a subject not for persuasion, but for concern and perhaps communion, pointing toward a shared problem or interest that holds promise of opening space for emergence of a public. This something is the oxygen for conversation, which helps it get going and keeps it moving along. Ultimately, what makes conversation serious is found in its ethos, but also in its form and content.

A fuller response to the question of what conversation is for requires shifting the level of analysis from ordinary everyday conversation to conversation writ large, what Oakeshott characterized as the conversation of mankind or the human conversation (also discussed in chapter 6). In "The Study of Politics in a University," Oakeshott (1991) described how he understood this wider conversation, both actual and metaphorical.

> Civilization (and particularly ours) may be regarded as a conversation being carried on between a variety of human activities, each speaking with a voice, or in a language of its own; the activities (for example) represented in moral and practical endeavor, religious faith, philosophic reflection, artistic contemplation and historical or scientific inquiry and explanation. And all the manifold which these different manners of thinking and speaking compose, a conversation, because the relations between them are not those of assertions and denial but the conversational relationships of acknowledgment and accommodation. (p. 187)

What Oakeshott suggested is that forms of living, "human activities," roughly akin to what Wenger (1998) described as "practices," interact in all sorts of ways and involve all sorts of meetings and adjustments. Lacking speech and often awareness, this conversation swirls around us, happens outside of us, is carried on by others as its results are moving through us, touching, shaping, molding the world we inhabit and the lives living that world for good and ill. Education opens access to the many voices of this conversation—dance, poetry, sport, history, music, science, and theology—but does so at a price but with a promise. The price is active engagement and a measure of openness; the promise is learning, the refining and enlarging of our social and moral sensibilities, and perhaps, for some, membership within the community that sustains a practice.

Conditions for Conversation

When local conversations bump up against the human conversation, or the parts of that conversation that have found place in the language and beliefs of those conversing, a moral position will emerge. From this position life possibilities may be weighed and tested, and reinterpretations of past events become possible. At such moments, the genuinely open and attentive may recognize another's otherness, expressed in various ways, perhaps sharing and validating our sources of sorrow and joy. Recall the moral quality of empathy, the ability to cross a threshold and feel as another feels, yet another human capacity democracy demands. Such moments promise learning and development, which always involve confrontation with limitation, even as our first desire when conversing often is recognition and confirmation of who we take ourselves to be (Harre & Langenhove, 1999). The openness of conversation has a teleology and, like a good book, takes us somewhere; it takes us out of ourselves for a time, so we get to be *other than ourselves* and our world becomes *not as it is*. In conversation we may actually discover we are no longer who we once were: that through conversation we have become renewed, changed. With openness must come attentive *waitfulness*, the pause needed to support reflection and reconsideration (Dewey, 1933). Otherwise, there is no consolidation, no learning.

When conversation participants have no hint of interests or concerns they may share, considerable time and effort may be required for meaningful connections to emerge, if they can be made at all. Such situations commonly occur when worldviews sharply conflict or few life practices are obviously shared. Those who aspire to strengthen democracy and forge effective partnerships need to seek opportunities to share activities and experiences that bridge such gaps among them.

Two people may stand next to each other in line at a credit union. He is in his sixties, with gray hair, wearing tweeds. He is on the university faculty; his life is studying and teaching economics. She is a third grade teacher, dressed casually and recently graduated from college; her mind is on upcoming school test scores. The two might exchange a few words, but they are unlikely to engage in conversation: A credit union queue is hardly a supportive setting, and they might not think they have much to converse about. Generations, lifestyles, and probably worldviews and values separate them.

Perhaps later these same two individuals find themselves sitting next to one another in a school board meeting (or maybe an Associates meeting!). Being in the board room might be a clue that they share some as yet unknown concerns or interests and that each may find something to say that the other will find worth hearing. Perhaps in some ways their differences are less important than their commonalities, now awaiting discovery. Effort would be required to uncover the shared interests inherent in the context. As both speak English, they begin to speak. They may discover that although they share a mother tongue they are not able to speak meaningfully to one another about the issues on the board's agenda. He's thinking about school finances and property taxes. She is thinking about impending cuts to her school's arts program.

But the board meeting may be delayed so both can be *attentively waitful* and *tentatively* open and wanting to talk. So they chat, and they probe one another's language, beliefs, and understanding of the world, ideally seeking points that draw them together. They are curious about one another, and a bit of time has become available. Conversation may occur.

Jürgen Habermas's (1984) description of what he calls the "conditions for the validity of an utterance" (p. 38), the "validity claims" of communication, is helpful for thinking through what is required when conversing. Primarily he focused his attention on three claims. On occasion he addressed a fourth, which is of special interest to us, though often taken for granted: comprehensibility or intelligibility: "The claim to intelligibility is the claim that an utterance is formed out of a language in a specific way so that it can serve some communicative use" (Zinkin, 1998, p. 462). Habermas's other three claims are to *truth*, *truthfulness*, and *rightness*.

When conversation begins there are intersubjective assumptions (a) that those speaking are telling the truth (although, in fact, they may be lying or acting strategically to gain our approval or compliance), (b) that conversants are sincere or truthful, and (c) that "the things said are normatively appropriate considering the relationships among the people and between them and the situation they are in" (Young, 1990, p. 76). Each claim points toward a set of issues. For example, if a person is thought to be untruthful, prone to serious distortions, someone who consistently offers "alternative facts," others are likely to avoid conversation and seek to keep unavoidable interaction as light and as chatty as possible. Lacking intelligibility, conversation is always stillborn, and the promise of democracy is weakened. George Bernard Shaw's witticism that England and America are "two countries separated by the same language" underscores the challenges of conversing even when a language is shared. Sharing words does not necessarily mean sharing meaning, a point of real concern in building sustainable partnerships. For example, jargon can derail partnerships that aspire to engage arts and sciences faculty and school professionals on a common problem. What, after all, are rubrics, SLOs (school learning objectives), ELLs (English language learners)? Or what is AYP (adequate yearly progress)? Jargon is more than specialized vocabulary: it is the power to exclude others as a means of establishing one's presumed authority.

Moving toward Dialogue and Renewal

Often conversation and dialogue are concepts that are used interchangeably. They have important similarities. Both make claims of validity and speak to the human desire for social interaction. Both may be enjoyable, although dialogue might not prove to be as much "fun" as conversation pretends to be. The spirit of conversation resides in dialogue, involving, as Oakeshott states, "tension between seriousness and playfulness." Both seek to represent human experience, and both require participants to identify points of agreement and disagreement. Like conversation, dialogue provides space for discussion of differences in experience and understanding. Both stand in opposition to *persuasion*, the "argumentative discourse" that Oakeshott wished to discourage. True, dialogue may encourage an interlocutor to change a point of view, but its aim is not persuasion, nor is its intent to engage in debate or refutation. Furthermore, consistent with Oakeshott's view of conversation, by operating in what Hamilton and Pinnegar (2015) described as a "zone of inconclusivity" (p. 146), dialogue does not seek to prove propositions or even discover truth, at least not when truth is thought to be a settled and certain conclusion. In both, participants "may differ without disagreeing" (Oakeshott, 1991, pp. 489–490). Finally, like conversation, dialogue involves an "unrehearsed intellectual adventure."

Subtle differences important to our thinking about democracy become apparent as dialogue grows out of conversation. Dialogue and conversation separate over Oakeshott's first proposition, that "conversation participants are not engaged in an inquiry" (p. 489). In contrast, inquiry is the centerpiece of dialogue: "Conversation [becomes] dialogue when it contains inquiry, critique, evidence, reflection, and response" (Hamilton & Pinnegar, 2015, p. 145). Dialogue directly addresses the human conversation and how one participates in that conversation and with others: "The understandings that emerge from dialogue appear in actions taken on the always-public stage of practice. Dialogue is a process of coming-to-know through which meaning is made and on the strength of which we develop assertions for action or understanding" (Hamilton & Pinnegar, 2015, p. 146).

The aim of dialogue, in contrast to conversation, is to influence action in the world, to alter and presumably to improve social practices. In addition, because it involves evidence and reflection in a social setting, dialogue, much more so than conversation, opens a "space of vulnerability" (Hamilton & Pinnegar, 2015, p. 147) that participants must be willing to enter; dialogue requires courage. When the social practices that compose life and support identity are at stake, dialogue may prove deeply unsettling. Recognizing the potential vulnerability of participants whose own practices are under review places responsibilities beyond those typical of the validity claims of conversation. An additional rule applies: "that participants in dialogue listen to one another . . . listening becomes an *obligation* rather than an optional extra" without which "power relations between the interlocutors are more likely to be reproduced rather than challenged" (Dobson, 2014, p. 107; emphasis added). Demonstrating interest and respect, listening softens the tendency to see disagreement as "dissing" and opens an opportunity for learning (see Ruitenberg, 2009). The disposition to listen, then, represents yet another manner essential to democratic citizenship and, more generally, to human learning.

Conversation, Dialogue, and Teacher Learning

Many years ago John Goodlad (1994) argued that the metaphors of reform and restructuring, whether in public schools or in higher education, misconstrue what is involved in educational improvement (see chapter 1). *Renewal*, he asserted, is the more apt and powerful metaphor: improving the education offered until it becomes new again. Democracy is all about creating and supporting citizen learning, and so it is that learning, in one way or another, is the central purpose of partnership—learning and renewing. Within education in recent years a good deal of research, including studies of teacher professional development, has been generated that supports Goodlad's insight. We find it no surprise that much of this work directly or indirectly points toward the centrality of conversation and dialogue to learning. Strong support came with the rise of constructivism and recognition of the influence of teacher beliefs in learning and, importantly, in how people often resist conceptual change.

Three research studies are especially relevant here. Not only do they underscore the central role of talk to learning, they also point toward the institutional conditions that support effective talk. Each study will be presented in sufficient detail to enable the making of comparisons with the sorts of professional development activities commonly experienced by educators within schools and universities where monologue and attempts at persuasion too often dominate.

Drawing on a national probability sample of over a thousand mathematics and science teachers, Garet, Porter, Desimone, Birman, and Yoon (2001) sought to answer the question, "What makes professional development effective?" The resulting study, one of the most important conducted on teacher professional development, focused on structure and what the authors called "core features" that support learning. Structural features included the types of activities teachers engaged in, the length of in-service, and the forms of participation involved. Core features included the content of professional development: focusing on teaching skills, practices, and knowledge; engaging in active learning (observing and being observed, opportunities to connect what was taught in the sessions with teachers' job situations); reviewing student work; giving presentations; leading discussions; and writing. Additional core features concerned "the extent to which professional development activities are perceived by teachers as part of a coherent program of teacher learning" (p. 927). These included the connections between professional development and teacher goals for learning; alignment with various national, state, and local policies, standards, and assessments; and, finally, *"the ways in which professional development activities encourage professional communication among teachers who are engaged in efforts to reform their teaching"* (p. 928; emphasis added).

In contrast to more traditional short-term forms of professional development, such as attending workshops and conferences, the authors' analysis led to the unsurprising conclusion that "professional development is likely to be of higher quality if it is . . . sustained over time and involves a substantial number of hours" (Garet et al., 2001, p. 933). More time enabled more opportunity to engage in active learning: observing teaching and being observed while teaching, along with more involvement communicating with other teachers. Collective participation (educators working together and in the same sites) increased active learning. Program coherence and content focus improved, and the researchers concluded that "activities that give greater emphasis to content and that are better connected to teachers' other professional development experiences and other reform efforts are more likely to produce enhanced knowledge and skills" (p. 933). Finally, these authors found that "enhanced knowledge and skills have a substantial positive influence on change in teaching practice" (p. 934).

As we review the results of this study, virtually every positive finding appears to flow from conversation and dialogue and points toward the importance of forging a commons. Certainly the power of observing and being observed during teaching for a professor as well as for a teacher comes from giving and receiving feedback, from discussing what was observed in relation to what is known about teaching and learning. Greater coherence was connected to collective participation, which suggests that the teachers who knew one another and worked together in the same schools talked about their common activities, and as they talked they apparently found greater meaning and made more connections of the activities to their own professional practices. Enhanced knowledge and skills were strongly connected to change in practice: collective participation, increased contact hours, and extended program duration supported teachers' active learning, which supported enhanced knowledge, which strongly influenced positive changes in teaching practice.

The second study we considered (Penuel, Fishman, Yamaguchi, & Gallagher, 2007) built upon and extended the first, identifying professional development practices that support curriculum implementation. This study involved a sample of 454 teachers who participated in a science inquiry project, examining the impact of various characteristics of several different professional development programs on these teachers' knowledge and program implementation. Generally this study gave slightly more attention than the Garet et al. study to teachers working with other teachers, perhaps indicating a shift in research concerns over the years separating the two studies. Underscoring the power of partnering, in their literature review these authors noted an abundance of research that "suggests that those [schools] that make extensive use of teacher collaboration are particularly successful in promoting [curricular] implementation, in part because reforms have more authority when they are embraced by peers" (p. 929). They also mentioned research supporting the likelihood that "relational trust in a school building" (p. 929) supports implementation and sustains teacher commitment. They reported that some researchers "argue that *interaction among teachers* [is] a resource to teachers in support of their implementation of reforms, which can be considered a [valuable] form of social capital" (p. 930; emphasis added). Finally, based on their review, they concluded that "professional development that incorporates time for instructional planning, *discussion, and consideration of underlying principles of curriculum* may be more effective in supporting implementation of innovations" (p. 931; emphasis added).

Although driven by a slightly different interest, curriculum implementation, the Penuel et al. (2007) study broadly supported the conclusions of the work by Garet et al. (2001), including the importance for educators of having time within professional development programs to converse and work together in support of learning. Several additional findings emerged, including one of particular interest here, that "university-based partners" (p. 950) were valuable in supporting successful implementation.

While there is wide and general recognition of the value of teacher "talk" to teacher learning across many studies (Bullough & Smith, 2016), few have studied the nature and quality of that talk or how it best supports learning. An important exception is the third study we considered, Horn and Little's (2010) analysis of "how conversational routines in two teacher work groups enhanced or limited opportunities for the in-depth examination of problems of practice and hence shaped opportunities for teacher learning" (p. 183). Significant differences were found between two groups that "oriented teachers' collective attention toward or away from a deeper investigation of teaching" (p. 190). The first group developed a routine that enabled them to create "interactional space rich with opportunities to learn about teaching practice" (p. 193) and that included normalizing problems, using questions to clarify problems, and *engaging in inquiry into teaching through discussions* that moved back and forth between specific events and general teaching principles. This group engaged in *conversations* about teaching that evolved into *dialogue*. In contrast, the second group was unable to agree on ways of talking about their work or differences in their perspectives about teaching and struggled to establish a shared understanding of the purposes of their working together. They proved unable to engage in "principled talk about teaching" (p. 208). Both groups were reportedly composed of "energetic, competent, committed, thoughtful teachers who took their professional obligations seriously" (p. 211), but only one group was able to create conditions supportive of dialogue about teaching and their own learning.

Reviewing their data, Horn and Little (2010) did not locate reasons in individual teachers for the two groups being so different. Rather, they concluded the origins of the difference found were in "each group's collective orientation and its contextual resources and constraints" (p. 211). The successful group,

Horn and Little concluded, appeared to develop a "shared language and frame of reference . . . for interpreting problems of practice" and "norms and practices of group leaders" that sustained the focus on "practice" (p. 212). Clearly, not all forms of teacher talk support teacher learning; and dialogue does not just happen.

Chatting fills time. So does conversation, and conversation might be about many things, some or none having to do with work or with those elements of the human conversation that shape educational policies and inform how teaching is talked about and understood. The findings of the Horn and Little (2010) study supported the view that some teachers may need help learning how to talk productively about teaching (Wood, 2007). Others (Bevins & Price, 2014), considering the challenges of partnering, argue that what is required is team and task support. Task support attends to the need, as noted in the Garet et al. (2001) and the Penuel et al. (2007) studies, for educators to have time to meet to inquire into their practice, which may necessitate adjustments to their workloads. Team support points toward the need to develop new skills, including those related to communicating in ways that form norms that support dialogue. Moreover, as we have argued, commitment to building a commons as a space to support inquiry is crucially important.

Classroom teachers are not the only partners who need this help and support. Our experience suggests that some university faculty may bring with them a whisper of hierarchy in their eagerness to speak or more than a little resentment toward suggestions that they too may need to improve their practice. University faculty spend less time than public school partners in leveling conversations about the practice of education (analogous to the "practice" of medicine or law) and more time conversing about the practice of a disciplinary specialty. Those two kinds of conversations have significant differences, as the discourse of research points outward from the university to publication and conference presentations, while the discourse of educational practice points inward to how our students learn and how educator actions and institutional structures facilitate (or impede) learning. We suspect that the conversational cultures in schools *that learn* (as in the research cited above) have yet to evolve fully in many universities.

As suggested earlier in the encounters of the professor of economics and the third grade teacher, building and district administrators, teachers, school board members, teacher educators, and faculty from university colleges of arts and sciences live in very different worlds and, like the British and Americans, share a language only superficially. Attuning to the pitch of another's disciplinary dialect, sensing its resonance, becoming curious about its histories and practices, and seeking connections are conversational strengths needed to make partnership possible. Oakeshott (1991) suggested as much when he wrote, "It seems not improbable that it was the engagement in this conversation . . . that gave us our present appearance, man being descended from a race of apes who sat in talk so long and so late that that they wore out their tails. Education, properly speaking, is an initiation into the skill and partnership of this conversation in which we learn to recognize the voices, to distinguish the proper occasions of utterance, and in which we acquire the intellectual and moral habits appropriate to conversation" (p. 490). Education and educating depend on those "moral habits," and conversation that leads to dialogue becomes both a means and an end of democratic education. Rainer Marie Rilke (1875–1926) composed these verses, used by Gadamer as an epigraph for *Truth and Method*:

> Catch only what you've thrown yourself, all is
> mere skill and little gain;
> but when you're suddenly the catcher of a ball
> thrown by an eternal partner
> with accurate and measured swing
> towards you, to your center, in an arch
> from the great bridge-building of God:
> why catching then becomes a power—
> not yours, a world's.

Rilke wrote of a theodicy, but "catching becomes a power" even when the "partner" is not "eternal." "Catching only what you've thrown yourself" is intellectual juggling that impresses, but it does not renew. The dialogic discipline of the "accurate and measured swing" is what makes bridge building—via educational partnerships—powerful and democracy possible.

5

Talking and Listening

. . . .

Dialogic Democracy
and Education

> It may be an easy thing to make a
> republic; but it is a very laborious thing
> to make republicans; and woe to the
> republic that rests upon no better
> foundations than ignorance, selfishness,
> and passion!
> —Horace Mann

This chapter focuses on the first of the four Moral Dimensions of Teaching: "enculturating the young into a social and political democracy" (Goodlad et al., 2004, p. 29). Our partnership has rephrased and specified it for our purposes: "Civic Preparation and Engagement: The Partnership prepares educators who model and teach the knowledge, skills, and dispositions required for civic virtue and engagement in our society" (see the appendix). Goodlad's language was recast partly because in our setting the conversation has often been impeded by fundamental disagreement over basic terms like *social* and *democratic*. Semantics generate and maintain their own histories, as will be apparent in this chapter.

As a river flows downstream in response to gravity, historical narratives flow toward reductive simplicity in response to natural context. This chapter builds on the principles previously discussed as it recognizes that democracy—in whatever form it might take (and it may take many forms; see Hall & Ames, 1999)—depends on and grows out of the habits of relationship and manners that characterize us as a people and as partners and that grow out of our historical and cultural positions.

This chapter offers a response to the challenge of the philosopher Paul Woodruff (2005) to "keep dreaming democracy" (p. 17) to keep it alive. But what is this democracy, the intent and content of these dreams? We first explore a moment in British political history that opens a window onto some of the complexity and widespread confusion of the semantic challenge. As a concept, democracy is usually taken for granted, assumed, and this is a serious problem, as Roberto Foa and Yascha Mounk (2016) show by their recent analysis of data from the World Values Survey. Questioning the long-held view that once democracy has been "consolidated" it is unlikely to fail, Foa and Mounk's analysis raises the worrisome question that this is simply not true; American democracy, they argue, is in serious trouble.

We begin the chapter with an incident involving Sir Winston Churchill, which works its way into two general questions: What do we mean by democracy? And whose democracy? Like Madison, Jefferson, and Hamilton, Churchill was a complex and sometimes inconsistent thinker—all of these individuals differed even as their thinking evolved over time (Wood, 2006, p. 28). Next we explore democratic manners, then the challenges to democratic citizenship raised by neoliberalism and its reduction of the citizen to the consumer. Finally, we discuss dialogic democracy imagined as a way of life to be lived in schools, balancing the obsession with *voice* (e.g., freedom of speech) when speaking of democracy with the underappreciated obligation of *listening*. We look to public education to provide for the young experience living democratically, the kind of experience that builds memories and provides concepts needed for reimagining what democracy has become in our time and dreaming what it might become in the future.

Democracy as a Form of Government

In the House of Commons on the afternoon of November 11, 1947, Winston Churchill, leader of the opposition to pending legislation, stood to speak. His address included the now famous words often quoted to defend democracy against its detractors: "Many forms of government have been tried, and will be tried in this world of sin and woe. No one pretends that democracy is perfect or all-wise. Indeed it has been said that democracy is the worst form of government except all those other forms that have been tried from time to time." These words echo across the decades and, given the speaker, inspire confidence. Surely Churchill was right.

Considering the context and intent of Churchill's remarks, however, gives one pause. A Conservative member of Parliament, Churchill spoke his now familiar words in the hope of blocking an effort by Prime Minister Clement Attlee and the British Labour government to reduce the period of delay the House of Lords could impose on legislation passed by members of the House of Commons, from two years to one year, intending to clear the way to nationalization of the British steel industry. Scornful of bureaucracies and highly critical of socialism, Churchill was defending the power of the hereditary House of Lords against a "popularly elected government" (Lindert, 2003, p. 316).

Seeking to test the "Churchill challenge"—"Is democracy really the best form of government?"—Peter Lindert (2003), American economist and economic historian, identified three Churchills (just as others have identified multiple James Madisons and Adam Smiths), each indicating a different take on government held at one time or another over a long political career. The first two Churchills were "the great orator endorsing popular democracy as the best we can do, and the conservative defending the last vestiges of hereditary elite power against the excesses of democracy" (p. 316). The third was the "young Liberal rabble-rouser," who supported land taxes intended to produce a "redistribution from landlords to workers and the poor" (p. 316). Lindert wrote, "To ask 'Was Churchill Right?' is . . . to ask 'Which of the three Churchills was right—the populist orator, the elitist Conservative, or the young redistributor?'"

Before offering his own assessment of democracy, Lindert reviewed the available empirical research on the impact of different forms of government, concluding that, on the whole, efforts to address the question "Is democracy best?" fall short. Definitions differ, and many are too narrow to be helpful. "[To] distance their analysis from any hint of circular reasons, some writers have insisted that democracy must be defined only in very narrow procedural terms, as a setting in which there are formal elections for the chief executive and a legislature, and there is at least some opposition. . . . The resulting analysis soundly shows that this narrow definition [what in chapter 7 we will call "thin" democracy] truly has little or no effect on economic growth, within the confines of the chosen models and data sets" (p. 320). The result of such definitions, Lindert asserted, is that many potentially influential variables are excluded from consideration, including differences in who is prohibited from voting, effects of class and income differences, as well as the privileged position given to central governments over local and regional politics in analyses. Moreover, he argued, no notice is given to the unevenness of national development over time, including "long lags" between policy implementation and growth.

Since democracy "has always meant governance by all the people" (p. 320), Lindert turned away from formal democratic rules and toward social measures indicating "channels of influence" that support or limit the extent of "voice": property and political rights, contract enforcement, human capital as investment (including primary and tertiary education). Although representing a narrow conception of democracy, *voice*, for Lindert and many contemporary theorists, is the preeminent concern: it is useful for distinguishing government types and, appealing to historians, changes in type over time. Drawing on history and econometrics, Lindert analyzed the economic development of countries in relation to voice and identified a government typology—more voice equals more democracy: "full voiced democracy" (North America, Switzerland, Australasia) (p. 344), "elite-democracy" (vote-limited democracies; Britain to the 1880s); "firm autocracy" (Thailand), and "benign autocracy"(p. 343).

Based on his analysis and considering the three Churchills, Lindert concluded that Churchill was "right about one thing": "The average democracy has been better for economic growth than the average autocracy, at least in the formative years before World War II" (p. 344). The picture is complicated, however. To develop human capital, firmer autocracies and full voiced democracies invest more heavily in primary education. In fact, "the countries least willing to spend taxes on mass primary education were not the autocracies, but the elite-vote countries"(p. 324), countries like Churchill's England during much of his long life. A conclusion like this gives democrats little to crow about and not much insight into Churchill's views.

Churchill was a transitional figure: at once Victorian, born in 1874 in Blenheim Palace, but also a central player in many of the most significant events of his time, events that reconfigured the social and political world order. In his first book, published in 1898, then a young lieutenant serving in colonial India, Churchill wrote of the "Imperial Democracy" (Churchill, 1898/1989, p. 9) he knew, an unsettling concept. In support of imperial democracy, twice, to his great disappointment, for actions on foreign soil Churchill *almost* won the Victoria Cross, the highest award for conspicuous bravery in the face of an enemy. Later, twice his beloved England warred with Germany, and both times democracy stood as a standard, front and center. He lived long enough to see the British Empire dissolve and the influence of Britain wain, to be displaced by its former imperial colonies that comprise the United States. Of the changes he witnessed, Churchill commented in 1930, "The character of society, the foundations of politics, the methods of war, the outlook of youth, the scale of values, are all changed, and changed to an extent I should not have believed possible in so short a space without any violent domestic revolution" (quoted in Holmes, 2005, p. 6). Given Churchill's experience, James Madison's advice offered in *Federalist* No. 14 seems apt. After referring to the "experiment of an extended republic," Madison wrote, "Is it not the glory of the people of America, that, whilst they have paid a decent regard to the opinions of former times and other nations, they have not suffered a blind veneration for antiquity, for custom, or for names, to overrule the suggestions of their own good sense, the knowledge of their own situation, and the lessons of their own experience" (Madison,

Hamilton, & Jay, 1787/1987, p. 144). Above all else, Churchill respected his own "good sense," and adjusted as situations demanded. An admirer well acquainted with him explained, "Where the ordinary brain is content to add each new experience to the scrap-heap, he insists on fitting it into the structure of the cantilever jutting out from the abyss of ignorance" (quoted in Holmes, 2005, p. 300). Churchill went to war for his beloved England and for English civil traditions, however those traditions might be understood, and for his own glory.

Judged against the largeness of Churchill's life, lived in defense of English (imperial) democracy, Lindert's (2003) attempt to offer an economic proof of Churchill's claim is interesting, but seems almost small minded. So much has been sacrificed by so many under democracy's banner, surely more is at stake than whether or not democracies have more cash value than other forms of government. As political scientist Robert Hoffert (2001) reminded us, "[It] is simply not the case that modern democracy, in the United States or anywhere else in the world, has a singular, coherent, and self-evident structure of meanings and implications. In fact, democracy has simultaneously given coherence to contemporary life and generated many of its greatest conflicts" (2001, p. 39). Digging down into definitions, a kind of conceptual warfare rages beneath the word. To be sure, prosperity is important to a people's well-being, but it is difficult to imagine any nation embracing democracy because of a promise of greater profit, although that argument has been part of "selling" liberalism (Harari, 2017, p. 313). Democracy's appeal lies elsewhere—or ought to.

Republics and Full-Voiced Democracy

Despite widely shared distrust of the people by the founders, the US Constitution necessarily required the approval of the entire citizenry (Ellis, 2016), a voice issue—one that excluded the poor, native Americans, slaves, and women. In making the case for support of the Constitution in *The Federalist Papers*, James Madison distinguished between democracies and republics. His distinction was relatively straightforward: "In a democracy the people meet and exercise the government in person; in a republic they assemble and administer it by their representatives and agents" (Madison et al., 1787/1987, p. 144). These two forms of government were understood to be "two species" of what Madison called "popular government," what might be thought of "in our contemporary terminology as . . . two kinds of democracy: direct and representative" (Tarcov, 1996, p. 26).

As embodied in the Constitution with its checks and balances, the republican form of government was intended to cure what were thought to be the potential dangers—or excesses—of direct democracy. The people could be dangerous and were feared. The introductory paragraph to *Federalist* No. 10

sets the problem: "The instability, injustice, and confusion introduced into the public councils, have, in truth, been the mortal diseases under which popular governments have everywhere perished" (Madison et al., 1787/1987, p. 122). The idea is that a small, wise, and "chosen body of citizens" will filter, regulate, "refine and enlarge the public views" and "best discern the true interest of their country, . . . whose patriotism and love of justice will be least likely to sacrifice it to temporary or partial considerations." In contrast to ordinary citizens, the "public voice" of their representatives "will be more consonant to the public good than if pronounced by the people themselves" (Madison et al., 1787/1987, p. 126). Such a system of government necessarily "presupposes sufficient good sense among the governed for their errors to be only temporary" (Tarcov, 1996, p. 28). In effect, as they vote the public speaks to their representatives, who, in turn, are presumed to speak for (and correct) the public—even *if they have not listened* let alone *understood* the message sent.

On the whole, Americans take popular government for granted, generally assuming the republican form they experience, with its two clumsy political parties and its constitutional checks and balances on power, *is* democratic, *is* democracy. So understood and idealized, American democracy in its republican form is the standard for government against which other countries are judged and often found wanting (see Rose & Mishler, 1996). On this view, for the vast majority of Americans the essential expression of citizenship is a matter of the right to choose, to vote, and rule as a majority, nothing more.

But again the issue is how voice is to be expressed and by whom—the common definition of democracy tends to be procedural, captured by a short checklist of institutional practices deemed democratic. Given this understanding, a dominating concern is that elections be fair; and so voter fraud is a central issue that includes making certain that only those whose voices are authorized are allowed to speak through the ballot box (see Schultz, 2013). No felons, please. At other times no women, no poor white men, no blacks, no native Americans, no immigrants. Subsumed under the category of popular government direct democracy, Lindert's (2003) "full voiced democracy" generally is lost to the imagination or when thought of is dismissed as a bit of nostalgia, highly impractical and of not much importance anyway. Yet in the Western tradition, as philosopher Paul Woodruff (2005) showed in his remarkable study of Athenian democracy, the roots of direct democracy run deep, even if neglected. What is crucial to democracy is how issues and candidates are presented for voting. In ancient Greece, citizens of both Athens and Sparta were permitted to vote in their respective cities, but Sparta was not a democracy, because in Sparta ordinary citizens had no say over what would be put to a vote. In Athens they did. "The *de facto* rule in Sparta . . . is that common people could vote, but not speak, in an assembly. Opponents of democracy applauded such rules, on the grounds that ordinary people are too ignorant to speak about policy. But democracy is guided by the idea that ordinary citizens have the wisdom such matters require" (p. 11). Woodruff wrote of full voiced democracy, "[It] grew along with two explosive ideas—that we all know enough to decide how to govern our public life together, and that no one knows enough to take decisions away from us and do a better job of deciding, reliably and over the long haul" (p. 24). In contrast, the "enemies of democracy . . . fought bitterly for the principle that only the best people should rule [Lindert's elite democracy]. But we have always known that the people who think themselves best—even the people we all think best—can go spectacularly wrong" (p. 25). And so they can and do.

Woodruff (2005) identified seven ideas supporting the Athenian quest for a full *citizen voiced* democratic government: "freedom from tyranny; harmony; the rule of law; natural equality; citizen wisdom; reasoning without knowledge; and general education" (p. 15). Harmony, the rule of law, and freedom were well understood—each belonging "to the ancient art of good government" (p. 30). The remaining ideas hang together and set a standard for citizenship education, one that assumes that democracy represents a particular form of life—not simply a matter of procedure—and a unique social practice. "Athenians believed that good education would make young people better able to use good judgment, to live reverently, and to make decisions with justice" (p. 193).

There was no sense of democracy paying off financially; that idea did not arise bold faced until Athenians built an empire. In fact, citizenship was understood correctly to be costly, a privilege. Family, community life, plays and festivals, and formal instruction taught the children of Athens the virtues associated with the practice of democracy. "To whom . . . should young people look if they wish to become better people? Odd as it sounds, the Athenian answer was 'to everyone,' or, rather, 'to all of us'" (p. 193).

Democracy and Manners

Based on his travels and conversations with a great number of Americans, in *Democracy in America* Tocqueville (1835/1840/1947) identified what he considered to be the "habits, opinions, customs, and convictions" that are "most favorable to [democracy's] maintenance" (p. 212). When writing about America, Tocqueville thought that among Europeans "too much importance is attributed to legislation, [and] too little to manners" (p. 213). Democracy, Tocqueville thought, was something more than just a form of government. "The manners of the Americans of the United States are . . . the real cause which renders that people the only one of the American nations that is able to support a democratic Government; it is the influence of manners which produces different degrees of order and of prosperity that may be distinguished in the several

Anglo-American democracies" (p. 212). By "manners" (a term we introduced in preceding chapters) Tocqueville meant something more than just rules of conduct or customs or even mores, although these were included in his understanding. Manners speak to something deeper, something more fundamental about how we live and make sense of our experience. The literary critic Lionel Trilling's (1950) discussion of manners is helpful for starting to get at what Tocqueville had in mind. Trilling thought that to talk about manners was to address an important but "nearly indefinable subject" (p. 205). For Trilling, the best we can do is to talk around them:

> Somewhere below all the explicit statements that a people makes through its art, religion, legislation, there is a dim mental region of intention of which it is very difficult to become aware. We now and then get a strong sense of its existence when we deal with the past but by reason of its absence [when manners are missing]. As we read the great formulated monuments of the past, we notice that we are reading them without the accompaniment of something that always goes along with the formulated monuments of the present. The voice of multifarious intention and activity is stilled, all the buzz of implication which always surrounds us in the present, coming to us from what never gets fully stated, coming in the *tone* of greetings and the *tone* of quarrels, in slang and humor and popular songs, in the way children play, in the gesture the waiter makes when he puts down the plate, in the nature of the very good we prefer. . . . It is that part of the culture that is made up of half-uttered or unuttered or unutterable expressions of value. (pp. 205–206; emphasis added)

Revealed in small and large actions, in the "arts of dress or decoration" and in the "words that are used with a special frequency or a special meaning," manners "are the things that for good or bad draw people of a culture together and that separate them from the people of another culture" (pp. 206–207). Manners are, then, a deep expression of what makes a people and that people's *way of life* distinctive, a way of being.

Had they been able to read texts of the future, citizens of Athens would have understood what Tocqueville was getting at, as they would similarly have understood John Goodlad and his colleagues' (2004) concern for the development of "democratic character" (p. 41) in the young. Goodlad, like Tocqueville and the Athenians identified by Woodruff, understood that such manners, with their supporting dispositions, do not arise naturally; they must be cultivated and nurtured, then protected. They also understood that manners are learned from all sorts of activities and take all sorts of forms, some of which are hostile to the interests and concerns of democratic citizenship, hence the importance of attending to them in schools.

For better or for worse, manners are taught and learned formally in schools and inevitably learned or more accurately absorbed informally, part of being "socialized" by simply living among other people and encountering and confronting their many various allegiances: being part of a family, spending time with friends, or entering the Agora of Athens to attend to other citizens, exchange goods, share news, and discuss ideas. This process is what Trilling was trying to get at in his description of manners. Today's citizens learn manners by watching television; scanning the internet; being plugged into social media, "liking" and being liked; listening and observing parents, neighbors, teachers, and friends; seeing video clips of the famous and infamous in action; watching people talking, posing, arguing; seeing public figures scowl, point fingers, bark, and bully. Part of a vast informal curriculum of civic life, such actions let the young know how they ought to behave, including when disagreeing, as well as which ideas are to be taken seriously and which dismissed outright. Insular, closed off in some places within some subcultures, young people often learn lessons that are deeply antisocial, antidemocratic: for instance, that disagreements are resolved best with a punch or a bullet—or with less violent forms of intransigence—that strength and independence are matters of being respected, and that anyone outside the recognition of one's own tribe is an enemy not to be trusted. Something quite different follows when an invitation is extended and accepted, say, to be part of a church-sponsored neighborhood park cleanup, or when at the conclusion of a school assembly everyone jumps up in unison and joyously joins in singing the school song.

Enemies and Manners

Both positive and negative identifications—the otherness of the other—are important in self-formation, the tug-of-war that goes into making a self. As we grow and mature we are pulled in many ways, and, sadly, among the least valued and least articulate are those associated with the manners of democracy beginning with hospitality and flowing through those associated with dialogue and inquiry. Moreover, manners are often developed in response to threat rather than as an expression of an inspiring aspiration and desire for engagement. Writing in 1939, reflecting on the rise of Nazism, anticipating war, and worrying about the future of democracy, John Dewey (1939a) called attention to the nature of the internal moral struggle then taking place: "The serious threat to our democracy is not the existence of foreign totalitarian states. It is the existence within our own personal attitudes and within our own institutions of conditions similar to those which have given a victory to external authority, discipline, uniformity and dependence upon The Leader in foreign countries. The battlefield is also accordingly here–within ourselves and our institutions" (p. 49). Sociologist Zygmunt Bauman and his colleague Leonidas Donskis

(2013) expressed a similar concern and made a similar point for us and our time: "To us it seems that evil lives somewhere else. We think it's not in us but lurks in certain places, certain fixed territories in the world that are hostile to us or in which things endangering all humankind take place. . . . But even today we refuse to look for evil within ourselves" (p. 7).

In Dewey's day common enemies were relatively easy to identify and name: Stalin, Hitler, Mussolini, and, some closer to home, perhaps Senator Huey Long and Father Coughlin, for example. As the philosopher and close friend of Dewey, Boyd Bode (1937) commented, "At the present time both communism and Hitlerism use each other as bugaboos [to] justify the fears that are created" (p. 54). Our times seem less simple but the point maintains: there are still enemies that seem to provide easy answers to the complex problems of living. Fear, after all, is contagious. To be sure, enemies prove useful for self-definition, as the sweeping nationalism that followed the 9/11 attacks and their aftermath well illustrate, but manners formed that are reactive and defensive—defined by an enemy—endanger and undermine those required of democratic citizenship. Such identifications justify torture, unbridled citizen surveillance, political correctness, and aggressive policing of free speech. While it may be more difficult now to identify an enemy by name, a person or persons to demonize and assign responsibility for one's grief and grievance, such self-protective strategies live on in conspiracy theories and in the nagging fears encouraged by terrorism and a growing sense that everything is falling apart. With growing fear and deepening cynicism about the future, whole institutions and peoples are excoriated, and most anything having to do with government service and servants.

As in times past when the art of scapegoating was perfected, convenient categories dressed up in sheep's (or wolf's) clothing are offered as explanations for the way things are: every hint of personhood is erased, and what is left are flawed individual people, "illegals," "druggies," "Christian fundamentalists," "radicalized Muslims," or even Democrats or Republicans. *Lacking* (i.e., the absence of personal stories in the construction of social categories) is a positive ideal and identity: something to believe in, something to stand for, something to be. And it is for this reason there is urgency to any and all efforts to reclaim and revitalize democratic citizenship as an educational and social aim and its supporting manners. Dismissiveness of others and blaming are immobilizing and poor substitutes for critical analysis and citizen engagement.

Democracy: Thinking beyond the Manners of Consumerism

America, we are often told, is a consumer society: that the purpose of good government is to promote the life, liberty, and happiness of citizens is now basically a platitude, replaced by a different aim—taking care of business. One result is that the nation-state has become a porous corporate plaything charged above all else with assuring an uninterrupted flow of goods and services, maintaining labor market flexibility to keep costs down, and, to maintain institutional legitimacy, ensuring personal security (almost) no matter what the cost. The citizenship of *homo sapien sapiens* (*wise men*, capable of self-governance) has been shoved aside by *homo economicus,* no longer the rational economic man, but a "preferred customer" or a worried worker who has come to see democracy through a consumer lens—the inalienable "right" of individuals to choose, and to choose everything.

The image of the consumer-citizen is hardly inspiring. The day after Thanksgiving, Black Friday, anguished women and disgruntled men line up very early outside of discount stores, competitors hoping to beat out the competition to "win" some sort of deal. Economic growth necessitates perpetual dissatisfaction, and advertisers seek to answer the call. New needs need to be created, needs that cannot, must not, be fully satisfied: fancy cars that do things no one needs done; exotic trips; designer jeans replaced by other designer jeans; gated McMansions; plastic surgery and plastic surgery again, but for different disappointing body parts. The aim is *more*, more of everything, and to gain more one lives in quick time all the time and in fear of the loss of one's possessions—which is the loss of one's self. Observing such trends, Bauman (2008) concluded, the "consumer is the enemy of the citizen" (p. 190). His point was that "competitive individualism divides people rather than brings them together around common public interests" (Bullough, 2014/2015, p. 16). Consumption fails as social glue.

Ironically, when Adam Smith wrote of the wonders of markets, he assumed a marketplace situated within a moral order composed of people who knew something about and were sensitive to the importance of being a brother's keeper. That order has been lost. Believing that markets would produce a "liberal reward of labour" (Smith, 1759/1937, p. 80), Smith was convinced they would support the well-being of families and the children of the working poor whose hard lives he found deeply troubling. Unable to imagine how extending markets could destroy moral virtue, elevate selfishness, and crush families, Smith envisioned a future of material abundance shared by all—still a distant hope.

The irony is that while free markets have, to a degree, enriched many individuals and nations, simultaneously they have impoverished large portions of those very nations' populations, persons who form massive underclasses and for whom life is precarious (Standing, 2011). As Madrick (2017) argues, increasingly workers are "contingent" and occupy what are "careerless" jobs (Standing, 2011, p. 15). As Harari (2017) warns, "It is dangerous to trust our future to market forces, because these forces do what's good for the market rather than what's good for humankind or for the world" (p. 382). The problem is not markets per se (we are not conjuring a world without markets); what is troubling is what results when markets are thought to be natural forces that generate *the only values that matter*. Such values underpin social policies that support ever-widening inequalities of wealth, justify a revolt of the rich against the poor (see Obermayer & Obermaier, 2016), and accept as inevitable the shrinking of the middle class, the class upon which the health of democracy historically has ultimately depended.

Neoliberalism, a dominating form of economic rationalism, has taken hold, and its manners have displaced democratic manners. Often now taken as common sense, neoliberalism "reduces all human dimensions, social relations, and activities into consumer exchange" (Mullen, Samier, Brindley, English, & Carr, 2013, p. 188). Driven by neoliberalism and realized in globalism, like every nation, every person has come to be in competition with every other person for the sometimes meager goods of life (Bauman, 2011). Under neoliberalism, markets have been extended broadly including into teacher education (Zeichner & Conklin, 2017) and schooling, as private interests advertise and sell the "goods" of education and rush about bold-faced collecting public dollars for their supposedly generous public service (Bullough, 2014/2015; Ravitch, 2013; Schneider, 2016). Moreover, with the maturing of the web and the advent of "big data," algorithms and statistical tools that reduce the social to the numerical and support the ranking and rating of just about everything sweep aside the values associated with human deliberation and reason as they "remove any need for the articulation of opinion and replace it with an act of silent [consumer] voting" (Simanowski, 2016, p. 73). As "technology [of algorithms] has overtaken politics" (Bauman & Donskis, 2013, p. 7), the commons has been subdivided into gated communities.

Man does not live by bread alone, but formal education is now all about earning one's daily bread, even as globalism and internal and external outsourcing in pursuit of ever lower labor costs have made certain there are not nearly enough good jobs to go around, as the "precariat" (Standing, 2011) has learned (the word *precariat* represents a blending of *precarious* with *proletariat*). As Standing argued, "The neo-liberal state has been transforming school systems to make them a consistent part of the market society, pushing education in the direction of 'human capital' formation and job preparation [which is] one of the ugliest aspects of globalization" (p. 68). Mullen et al. (2013) added, "The educational manifestations [of neoliberalism] are far reaching, resulting in a shift of education from primarily a cultural to an economic concern: Managerialism, audit cultures, values of commodification, efficiency, and effectiveness from a wholly alien sector—the industrial economy—reduce education to an export-import trade" (p. 222).

With this view, schools offer a tame citizenship by teaching *about* democracy while ignoring manners: who may do what; how a bill becomes law; how the judicial, executive, and legislative branches of government function, and how voting is the incarnation of the muffled voice of the people. Specific courses, usually in the social studies, are expected to take up the charge and tidy the issues of self-government. What is left of citizenship, as Woodruff (2005) concludes, are democracy's "doubles": voting, majority rule, and elected representatives (pp. 9–15), nothing more. Of this approach to education, Bode (1937) remarked, "Teaching democracy in the abstract is on a par with teaching swimming by correspondence" (p. 75). He was right.

Education and the Democratic Dream

Earlier we mentioned Foa and Mounk's (2016) study, which raises serious questions about the vitality of American democracy. To underscore their concern, we mention a few of their more unsettling findings. They note a disturbing difference in generational responses to the question of whether it is essential to live in a country that is governed democratically. Of those born before World War II, 72 percent marked 10 on a 10-point scale of democratic essentiality; of millennials (born in the 1980s), around 30 percent gave the question a 10. "In 2011, 24 percent of U.S. millennials (then in their late teens or early twenties) considered democracy to be a 'bad' or 'very bad' way of running the country" (p. 8). Similarly discouraging numbers were reported for support of democratic institutions and engagement in democratic processes. Most alarming of all was the increasing support for authoritarian alternatives. For example, in 1995 only one in sixteen respondents felt that for the "army to rule" would be a "good" or "very good thing"; today that number has increased to one in six. While those who hold this view remain in the minority, they can no longer be dismissed as a small fringe, especially since there have been similar increases in the number of those who favor a "strong leader who doesn't have to bother with parliament and elections" (p. 12).

Findings like these make ever more urgent the call of the first Moral Dimension: to prepare the young for participation in a social and political democracy, a preparation that has to be foregrounded and explicit, consistent and grounded in inquiry and engagement if educators are to counter the trends identified by Foa and Mounk. We recognize, as Standing (2011) argued in his call for a "politics of paradise that is mildly utopian and proudly so" (p. 155; see pp. 155–183), that much outside of schools and universities needs to change for democracy to become a living concept. However, our concern is narrower and explicitly dilated on the importance of forging educative cultures in our schools and universities, most especially on establishing the *informal* and *formal* conditions needed to support development of *the manners of democracy* in the young (and in their teachers).

Our position is supported by political scientist Benjamin Barber (1998), who argued that "Thomas Jefferson preferred education to representation as democracy's guarantor" (p. 163). With Barber, we further agree that "the logic of democracy begins with public education, proceeds to informed citizenship, and comes to fruition in the securing of rights and liberties" (p. 220). Moreover, the charge is to develop "civic literacy [that] encompasses the competence to participate in democratic communities, the ability to think critically and act with deliberation in a pluralist world, and the determination to identify sufficiently with others to live with them despite conflicts of interest and differences of character" (p. 221).

John Dewey (1916) provided a helpful reminder as well as a useful point of departure for the remainder of this chapter. First, he reminded us, "We never educate directly, but indirectly by means of the environment" (p. 22). Second, he set the problem of what sort of environment is needed to nurture democracy by calling attention to what is involved in building "neighborly" communities, places within which democracy "must begin" (1927, p. 213)—commons—like schools or universities. Of community, he wrote, "Men live in a community in virtue of the things which they have in common; and communication is the way in which they come to possess things in common. What they must have in common in order to form a community or society are aims, beliefs, aspirations, knowledge—a common understanding—like-mindedness as the sociologists say" (1916, p. 5). By "like-mindedness" Dewey was pointing to democratic manners.

Dewey set a standard useful for thinking about our communities and for determining just how democratic they are. He suggested we ask two questions: "How numerous and varied are the interests which are consciously shared? How full and free is the interplay with other forms of association?" (p. 96). Applying these standards, Dewey concluded, as we have argued, "A democracy is more than a form of government; it is primarily a mode of associated living, a conjoint communicated experience. The extension in space of the number of individuals who participate in an interest so that each has to refer his own action to that of others, and to consider the action of others to give point and direction to his own, is equivalent to the breaking down of those barriers of class, race, and national territory which kept men from perceiving the full import of their activity" (p. 101). Drawing on the manner of hospitality, referencing of actions by way of making one's own behavior more intelligently purposeful establishes the task of conversation and the charge of dialogue. Finally, Dewey (1939a) set the larger problem: "We are learning that everything about the public schools, its official agencies of control, organization and administration, the status of teachers, the subject taught and methods of teaching them, the prevailing modes of discipline, set *problems*; and that the problems have been largely ignored as far as the relation of schools to democratic institutions is concerned" (p. 42). Such an ambition certainly is mildly utopian, perhaps more than mildly, but it is also provocative and helpful for thinking about the responsibilities of educators on all levels for democratic citizenship and, more specifically, for building partnerships.

Listening for Democracy

Goodlad and his colleagues (2004) observed that few of us "really think much about what it means to live in a democracy or what is needed to sustain one" (p. 36). As noted earlier in this chapter, even when recognized, notions of democracy are often confused and confusing. Seldom is it realized that different kinds of social systems call forth different kinds of schooling; thus, unless we are driven by a desire to change America into China or Singapore, it makes very little sense to assess the schools of the United States in comparison to those of other nations. As Bode (1937) argued, "A democratic system of education is ordinarily supposed to mean a system which is made freely accessible to all the members of the group. That it should also be distinctive in quality or content is not taken for granted in the same way" (p. 63). But it should be. It must be.

Since "democracies never *just happen*" (Goodlad et al., 2004, p. 36), let's do some thinking and perhaps correcting. A metaphor generated by philosopher Robert Kane (2010) is helpful for thinking about the relationship between schooling and the manners of democracy. We might think about a school or a college as a "moral sphere" within which a community, a moral commons, is to be formed. Within the sphere, not just any community is desired, but one dedicated to *maximal participation* and *maximal openness* as preconditions to learning as well as to the utility of getting things done. Maximal participation supports *voice*, which, as we have noted, dominates discussions of democracy. Willingness to speak up and with an informed voice certainly is a manner of democracy. But maximal openness requires something different, something more: a robust commitment to *listening and "listening out for" the other* (Dobson, 2014, p. 177). At his ninetieth birthday party, John Dewey remarked that "democracy begins in conversation" (Lamont, 1959, p. 58), and, as we have argued, so it does. While gaining voice is widely thought to be the most essential element of democratic citizenship, as Andrew Dobson (2014) convincingly argued, that voice matters only if someone is listening and listening carefully. Without listeners there is only noise—not conversation, and certainly not dialogue, that form of structured conversation that seeks to deepen understanding across differences.

What is needed, then, is a *dialogic* democracy, one that unites and balances voice with the openness required to hear others' voices. Listening is more than a skill. Like Dobson, we think it is a critically important *virtue*—a manner and an expression of hospitality—that must be learned though it cannot be directly taught. Involving education of the emotions (see Ruitenberg, 2009), as Dobson (2014) suggested, as an educational problem, "to listen involves cultivation rather than teaching" (p. 79). Certainly, some traits associated with good listening (e.g., active listening, motivational interviewing) can be acquired through training. But the training is a polished surface sustained and maintained by an informed attitude about other people's worth, about the value of their voices—something that is possible because of the attentiveness that transforms listening from a technique to a virtue.

Extending our argument in chapter 4, as a precondition for dialogue (Dobson, 2014, p. 77), listening must be grounded in respect for other speakers and perhaps energized by curiosity; it is a source of humility needed to be silent, more concerned with what is being said than with "reloading" for one's anticipated response (p. 52). Speaking of humility, Paulo Freire (1998) warned of what is at stake when status or other differences interfere with listening: "How can I listen to the other, how can I hold a dialogue, if I can only listen to myself, if I can only see myself, if nothing or no one other than myself can touch me or move me ... [The danger is that I will become] entrenched in the circuit of my own truth" (p. 208). Being so self-entrenched promises stupidity and supports foolishness, even among the powerful. Freire continued, "No one knows it all; no one is ignorant of everything. We all know something; we are all ignorant of something" (p. 208). Listening is part of validating voice and a sign of recognizing (potential) community membership. As the other half of dialogue and as an essential condition for refining and deepening compassion, listening supports the formation and maintenance of democratic institutions, including schools and universities. However, given what is at stake when voice dominates, listening may sometimes need to be forced (as when a child takes hold of her mother's face, a hand on each cheek, and eyes lock and the child speaks and a mother listens). Often citizens must insist on being heard, and to this end they do and must organize.

Goodlad's colleague Roger Soder (2001) offered help to educators in thinking about the conditions for developing *democratic manners* or *character* within schools and in support of a dialogic democracy. He made several suggestions— some are actions, some reflect knowledge that needs to be developed, and some represent needed attitudes or inclinations. He began by noting the importance of building trust (which we think logically follows, not precedes, exchange). Next, there needs to be situations requiring some sort of exchange (of ideas, goods, and services) that support interaction, possession, and development of social capital. Respect follows next: respect for equal justice under the law and for civil discourse. Then comes recognition of the need for *e pluribus unum*. The point here, as Soder explained, is that "there must be some sort of glue that holds the whole together." Free and open inquiry precedes knowledge of rights (which we think requires a shift from the focus on natural rights toward an understanding of rights as expressions of community and cultural commitments and duties). Freedom follows ("the power to exercise freedom and the insight to value it"). Freedom requires recognition of tension between freedom or liberty and order, recognition of the difference between a persuaded audience (see chapter 3) and a more thoughtful public, and ecological understanding (pp. 189–193). Finally, Soder suggested that a community must be "responsive to the challenges of pluralism and uncertainty" but, we suggest, also avoid "the dangers of a strong relativism, a [community] that recognizes the limits of tolerance as a social aim while exploiting the educational value of otherness" (Bullough, 2014, p. 252).

As Dewey (1939b/1988) wrote (echoing Bode, 1937), the intent is to make democracy a "personal, an individual, way of life" (p. 226). To achieve this aim requires that careful attention be given to both the informal and formal ways a community molds the young and to the quality and relative abundance of the spaces opened for speaking and for listening. Theodore and Nancy Sizer (1999) wrote of one aspect of the informal modes of teaching, "How we adults live and work together provides a lesson. How a school functions insistently teaches" (p. 116). Perhaps no writer more aptly described the formal citizenship charge to education than Boyd Bode (1937) when he wrote, as the world drew closer to a second world war, "The school is, *par excellence*, the institution to which a democratic society is entitled to look for clarification of the meaning of democracy. In other words, the school is peculiarly the institution in which democracy becomes conscious of itself" (p. 95). On this view, every aspect of schooling—the entire social life of the school, indeed every interaction that takes place in a hallway or on a playground or in a lunch room, in science labs and math classes—provides opportunities to learn about *and* to practice the manners of democracy, manners that "must be woven with everything else" (pp. 94–95).

In support of learning, subjects need to be taught in ways that maximize student voice and support the self-transcendence empathetic listening requires. Students need to be brought into class governance—and this involves the simple recognition that classes are, in fact, always jointly managed by students and teachers. How activities are planned also offers educational opportunities, perhaps as rich as those found when subjects are more formally taught and teacher-led. We are not suggesting that schools become places where anything goes and the authority of teachers is weakened. Nor are we suggesting that educational settings are only about the quality of relationships and not about academic learning. We are suggesting, however, that if dialogic democracy—the language and the practice—is taken seriously as a prominent educational aim, the quality of educational relationships will change and improve. We agree with Bode (1937) that the "essence of freedom [lies], not in the lack of restraint, but in the character or quality of the restraint"

(p. 43). And we are suggesting that students will perform better academically (see chapter 6).

Democratic and dialogic *ends* require democratic *means*. There are no quick fixes: just as beliefs resist change and evolve slowly, we expect development of more democratic manners and formation of more democratically centered cultures within schools to require time and involve a lot of experimentation. Copious amounts of studying and talking are needed to guide us in reconsidering the nature of the work of education that needs to be done.

Like Goodlad and his colleagues (2004, p. 27), we believe there are no standardized "blueprints" for this work—really good schools are not like the indistinguishable units of tract housing. Educational communities are inevitably different, and such differences are important to the culture and character of schooling. But thinking about the work of education through a democratic "frame of reference" (Bode, 1937, p. 79) of the sort we have described, one that takes hold of the moral imperative to return democratic citizenship to its rightful place as a central aim and concern of public education, promises improvements that are sorely needed. These include greater clarity of purpose, a clearer mission, and a more compelling moral vision—a vision that is, unlike consumption, worth living for. As we have said, reducing the purposes of public education to jobs alone has created a crisis of institutional legitimacy.

It is in democratic citizenship that public education finds its unique reason for being. In contrast to the fragmentation and cynicism that flow from neoliberalism into the body politic and throughout our social institutions, educators must stand for hope and for democracy. For the work of university–public school partnerships, the recovery of democracy is, as Bode (1937) described, "an adventure," one that "stands or falls by its faith in the common [person]" (pp. 14, 115) and his or her ability to become fully and wisely self-governing. Democracy can survive on no other moral foundation: "For democracy is always about *public* willing and *public* goods and the *common* weal" (Barber, 1998, p. 268).

6

Gifts

- - - - - - - - - - - - - - - - - - -

Access to the Human Conversation through Pedagogical Nurturing

> What the best and wisest parent wants for his own child, that must the community want for all of its children.
> —John Dewey

Chapter 5 ended with Benjamin Barber's assertion that democracy "is always about" the will to be a caring public. Much political discourse centers on the locus and accountability for caring. Who is responsible? Under what conditions? And at what cost? One can aspire to a just society without being naïve about its obstacles and counterfeits. And occasionally one finds a story, a true story, that justifies our dreaming.

> When Leo Hart was elected superintendent [of schools], hostility in Kern County [California] toward "Okies" was at a fever pitch. Policemen and civilians formed armed patrols called Bum Brigades and guarded the county's borders to keep Okies out. In 1938 a mob headed by the sheriff burned down an Okie migrant camp under the Kern River Bridge. Then irate farmers armed with pitchforks, guns, bricks, and clubs attacked Weedpatch Camp at night and tried to drive the Okies out. Hundreds of Okies went to jail for defending

themselves and their families, but not one local was arrested. In 1939 Kern County banned *The Grapes of Wrath.*

All the while, Leo continued to visit the Okie kids in the field next to Weedpatch. During this period of violence against Okies, Patsy Lamb later recalled, "Mr. Hart was our only friend." First Leo tried to place the Okie children in the outlying rural schools of Kern County, hoping they might blend in with the sons and daughters of farmers and ranchers. But he met stiff opposition. One high-ranking school official in the Vineland School District called the superintendent's office and scolded Leo: "You're not going to spend our money for these sons-of-bitches!" The parents demanded that Leo remove all Okie children from all the public schools. At least two educators called Leo a communist and warned that his job might be in jeopardy, even though he had held it only a few months. . . . When [the children] went to school each day, most of the teachers ignored the migrants, believing that Okie kids were too stupid to learn the alphabet, too dumb to master math, and too "retarded" to learn much of anything. . . .

The opposition to the Okie children angered Leo. Edna Hart recalled that her husband would come home from work so upset that he couldn't eat or sleep. "I could never understand," Leo said, "why these kids should be treated differently. I could never understand why they shouldn't be given the same opportunity as others. Someone had to do something for them because no one cared about them." . . .

In 1940 Leo decided if no one wanted the Okie kids in the public schools, then maybe the Okie children should have their own school. It would be a different school, he thought. It would be more than bricks and buildings, more than lessons and homework in math and writing. It would teach practical skills, such as masonry, mechanics, and agriculture. It would also teach the children to be proud of who they were. It would instill self-confidence in them so they might succeed in life on their own. It would provide the Okie children, Leo said, "with educational experiences in a broader and richer curriculum than were present in most schools." Above all else, Leo insisted, it would be "their school." (Stanley, 1992, pp. 41–42, 38–39, 44)

Thus was born the Weedpatch School, a school for the children of the migrants of the Dust Bowl, some half million of whom headed west as their land parched and the soil blew away. The children, their parents, and teachers built the school themselves. While they built, the children were "also attending classes, doing homework, and taking tests on a regular basis. Besides practical training in aircraft mechanics, sewing, cobbling, and canning fruits and vegetables, they learned the basic subjects taught in elementary and junior high school: English, arithmetic, geography, history" (p. 60). They were supported by an extraordinary and dedicated faculty recruited by Hart. The principal brought a C-46 aircraft to the school for the children to work on. They raised pigs, sheep, chickens, and cows; they learned butchering, planted a large garden, and studied what the kids in other schools studied. It was not long before parents who had not wanted the Okies in their children's schools wanted their own children enrolled in Weedpatch. "One day [the superintendent] started to dig at the east end of the field between the school and the campus. Twelve-year-old Bob Farley asked Leo what he was digging, Leo said, 'swimming pool.' Leo told the children if they did not 'goof off,' and 'if they kept up on their academics,' they could dig [the hole for the pool] in their spare time" (pp. 58–59).

And they did.

Reminiscing with Jerry Stanley, author of the book about Weedpatch School, Hart pointed to a photograph of himself holding a small girl who was wearing his hat; both were smiling. Hart remarked, "Weedpatch school 'had a happy ending.' 'See that girl.' Sometimes when she wasn't ready to go to school, I had to hold her and walk her around outside until she was ready. She liked to wear my hat" (p. 75). The school became a community center for the camp, changing the lives of the Okies and their children, many of whom went on to careers in business, education, and industry.

In this chapter we address issues related to educational access and pedagogical nurturing. Providing access to knowledge for all children and youths and practicing pedagogical nurturing while providing that access represent the second and third of the four Moral Dimensions of Teaching (Goodlad et al., 2004, pp. 30–31), both critically important to achieving the first Moral Dimension, "enculturating the young into a social and political democracy" (see chapter 5). For Leo Hart, determination to provide children access to high-quality knowledge and the ability to deliver it with nurturing pedagogy were two of the qualities he looked for in the teachers he recruited to Weedpatch.

Nurturing pedagogy has much to do with the expression of hospitality, pure hospitality: teacher to student, human being to human being, and more. A school superintendent dared bring hospitality to Weedpatch, nurturing the derided as he carried and comforted their children.

Rereading the conversation shared in chapter 2, we were surprised by the number of times the word *gift* occurs in describing our early partnership experience. The Weedpatch children received the incomparable gifts of respect, education, and hope. We too have been recipients of gifts—often unaware of them as gifts—offered in hope and without expectation of reciprocity. Access and nurturing are among them. The bounty given to us by both Dean Robert Patterson and John Goodlad has included access to that portion of the human conversation that touches on partnering and schooling, which has changed us and our thinking about education. Nurturing pedagogy calls attention to how access is given: the spirit in which the gift is given and the knowledge of teaching that underlies that spirit.

Seeking Access: The Second Moral Dimension

Throughout the history of American public education, access issues have loomed large. In 1909, for example, the Russell Sage Foundation published Leonard P. Ayres's pioneering study of "retardation and elimination in city school systems" (i.e., students who fall behind and drop out). This study was concerned with finding the reasons why large numbers of children did not progress through the grades in a timely fashion. "Since retardation is ascribable to only two conditions, late entrance and slow progress, and since late entrance is found to be only a small factor, slow progress, however caused, is proved to be the great factor in bringing about the existing condition" (1909, p. 4). Children were not learning as they should or as quickly as they should, and the cost of "repeaters" caused concern. "In the country as a whole about one-sixth of all of the children are repeating and we are annually spending about $27,000,000 in this wasteful process of repetition in our cities alone" (p. 5).

Much of our struggle to provide educational access has been impeded by a common assumption: different levels of access and very different kinds of experiences need to be provided to different "kinds" of kids by virtue of family income, race, color, national origins, gender, ability, and even rural/urban residence. At times the national conscience has burned over access issues. Consider, for example, the upheaval following the Supreme Court's ruling in *Brown v. Board of Education* (1954) that overturned the long-standing *Plessy v. Ferguson* (1896) ruling that upheld the doctrine of "separate but equal" education for black and white children. Think of the riots after the court order to desegregate the Boston public schools (1974–1988) by busing children. Passage by Congress and the presidential signing of the No Child Left Behind Act (NCLB, 2002) were hailed as another step in the long drive toward achieving greater educational equality as well as a means for increasing America's economic competitiveness. The title of the act reflected an admirable aspiration and commitment: we won't lose a single child. Fulfilling that moral imperative was more complicated than legislating it.

Although schools remained seriously underfunded, the fanciful belief was that the law would close the achievement gap separating poor and minority students from their more privileged peers. Under NCLB all public schools that received federal funding were required to administer statewide achievement tests in reading and mathematics in third through eighth grade and at least once in high school to demonstrate adequate yearly progress (AYP). A punishing psychology dominated federal policy. Failure to meet AYP across student categories could result in eventual school closure. In a bewildering and stupendous flight of fancy, a goal was set that by the end of the 2013–2014 school year all children would achieve at a proficient level or above. Although definitions of proficiency varied by state, results were to be disaggregated to identify performance levels of various student groups by race, economic status, disabilities, and limited English proficiency; one group's near miss in meeting a standard cast the entire school as failing.

As 2014 drew nearer and the inevitability of failure became apparent, more and more states applied to the US Department of Education for waivers to some provisions of NCLB. By 2013 waivers had been granted to thirty-four states and the District of Columbia. Remarkably, after years of rigorously enforcing NCLB, Arne Duncan, US secretary of education, promised the waivers would "unleash local leaders' energy for change and ensure equity, protect the most vulnerable students, and encourage standards that keep America competitive" (US Department of Education, 2013). Having been unable to reauthorize NCLB, finally, with bipartisan support, on December 10, 2015, President Obama signed into law its replacement, the Every Student Succeeds Act (ESSA). In its original form, ESSA altered some of the requirements of NCLB, including giving a measure of flexibility to the states to meet federal standards and softened some of the more punitive institutional consequences of low student standardized test scores. At the same time, emphasis on teacher and school accountability, student testing in mathematics, reading, and science, and the performance of English language learners and nonwhite and disabled students remained, although more nuanced measures were called for. Greater emphasis also was placed on increasing student access to advanced classes and reducing student suspension rates.

There is no doubt that NCLB was helpful in bringing attention to student groups that were not benefitting as they should from public education. And this was and is terribly important. But this is not all the law has left behind. Deeply embedded in the national consciousness, in state educational policies, and in political rhetoric is a simplistic view of student achievement, misrepresenting the complexity and diversity of social and cultural factors that influence learning, "the strongest of which is parental income" (Rose, 2015, p. 22). Long excluded from policy discussions and blamed and punished for being unable to meet impossible expectations, a battered and demoralized teacher workforce remains, and so does a simplistic "pinched" (p. 27) conception of teaching. Discounting how context-sensitive and remarkably varied really good teaching is, assessing in terms of observable "sequences of (discrete) behaviors and routines" (p. 25) is now considered proof of teacher effectiveness and of teacher education program quality.

Finally, a cluster of assumptions about the purposes of public education so starkly stated in *A Nation at Risk* (National Commission on Excellence in Education, 1983; see chapter 1) also remain and are now deeply embedded in the national consciousness and in state educational policies. The primary function of education is understood to be economic, about jobs and the development of human capital to "keep America competitive," as Secretary Duncan remarked.

Within the tenure of Secretary Duncan and President Obama, like the tenures of President Clinton and President Bush before them, the values of neoliberalism have reigned supreme and are likely to continue to enjoy preeminence long after the Trump presidency. Indeed, with the legislation no longer having bipartisan support, in March 2017 Congress quietly voted to repeal select regulations of ESSA, most particularly those associated with access. The intention appears to be to extend greater freedom to the federal Department of Education to further the marketization of public education, most especially in support of corporate charter schools and vouchers. Discounting the public purposes of public education, purposes that speak to collective citizenship responsibilities, the move is defended by its proponents as essential to extending greater access to educational consumables, a matter of choice and of states' rights.

There is scant evidence of our ability to elude the neoliberal seduction that has infiltrated federal education policy for decades. Responding to the enticement of free markets with their presumed reformative powers, the Department of Education has generously spent public funds in support of a wide range of private money-making school ventures, from easy-access and quick-exit online teacher preparation programs to Teach for America. The flow of public funds is likely to increase in support of teacher preparation programs that are allowed to skirt quality standards—admission and exit—required of programs at universities and colleges. The department also generously funded development of National Board Certification, which is now managed by Pearson Education, a large British corporation headquartered in London, and the edTPA, a widely used portfolio assessment of beginning teachers required as evidence for certification. Aspiring teachers pay to have their portfolios scored by Pearson employees, who, in effect, decide who is qualified to teach in America.

Claiming a strong commitment to access of a consumer kind, the department has encouraged development of voucher programs, including those that support private sectarian schools and for-profit and corporate-managed charter schools that appear to be more interested in collecting management fees and advertising their wares than in educating for citizenship. This trend is increasing despite strong evidence of the strength of American public education, including the fact that public schools (when comparing similar demographics) generally outperform private schools and charters (Berliner & Glass, 2014; Lubienski & Lubienski, 2014; Ravitch, 2013), as well as the failure of every state voucher initiative at the ballot box. More damning still, research fails to support vouchers (see Carey, 2017).

Access Denied: Ingrained Inequity

Given the power and influence of NCLB to reshape how Americans have come to think about public education and what they expect of it, we believe it is important to review a small slice of the research on its legacy. Many policies have unintended consequences, but rarely have the effects of a policy been so diametrically opposite its publicly espoused intent, challenging the truthfulness of those claims (see Berliner & Biddle, 1995). Informed criticism of governmental policy and policy ambitions is an important part of building an effective democratic citizenship. Among the more insightful critics, probably no one is better informed than David Berliner, a distinguished researcher and educator who explored the effects of what he called MCLB (Much Curriculum Left Behind), an access issue. Access claimed has become access denied.

> Survey research by the Center on Education Policy [captured a] frightening trend. The center looked at 350 school districts and learned that about 62 percent of those districts had increased the amount of time spent in elementary schools on English-language arts or math and that 44 percent of the districts cut time on science, social studies, art and music, physical education, lunch, or recess. The group discovered, however, something more frightening: 97 percent of the high-poverty districts (where more than 75 percent of students are eligible for free or reduced-price lunch) had policies that restricted the curriculum offered to their students. (Berliner, 2009, p. 286)

The curriculum—from the Latin *currere*, meaning to run (a race) or to proceed—to which students are given access, Berliner, among many others (Croft, Roberts, & Stenhouse, 2016), argued, has been pruned for some children but not for others. The course some young people are expected to run is not very engaging, mostly direct and dull; the route for others is rich in possibilities: encounters with music, poetry, dance, concerts, pottery, field trips, inquiry projects, and interesting people—some living, some dead. These students are given opportunities to write essays, make arguments, and engage in dialogue about topics that matter. The result is an "apartheid system of schooling" (Berliner, 2011, p. 292), one sort for a ruling class, another sort for those who are to follow, with comparatively little interaction between the two. Poor and minority children are dramatically affected by the narrowing, with its focus on "mastery of rote procedures" (p. 296). School time is time to study mathematics and language arts and to prepare and practice for upcoming tests. For these children, "the arts are rationed" (Berliner, 2011, p. 291) and so are history and science. But the more fortunate students are given abundant and diverse opportunities to develop their talents and to demonstrate they are "good at something" (p. 294). Where, one asks, is the fairness in this?

Berliner has reminded us that, assuming a strong connection between public education and democratic citizenship, the "founding fathers of the United States did not want a narrow curriculum" (2009, p. 289), nor should we. Parents don't want narrowing, nor do most teachers and professors. Teachers comply because they believe they must; they are but responding rationally to an irrational situation (Berliner, 2011).

While there is much current talk about a teacher shortage, rather little attention has been given to a simple explanation: for many teachers, policies like NCLB have dimmed the luster of teaching. As they fear unforgiving and punitive future assessments and recognize they have rather little control over their work, many teachers struggle with a "disjunction between practice and beliefs about practice" (Rooney, 2015, p. 489). They are double-minded. Under such conditions, the intrinsic motivation that drives so many to teach, a reflection for some of feeling "called" to teach (Bullough & Hall-Kenyon, 2011), withers, as access to the relationships, service, and joy they expected has been supplanted by technicist forms of teaching.

As policy makers have turned to testing as a "magic bullet that can be fired by school leaders and teachers to effect a cure for low achievement among the poor, English language learners, and among many minorities" (Berliner, 2011, p. 288), teachers have come under continuous heavy pressure to comply, to do what is necessary to generate acceptable student scores. As a result a "narrowed curriculum has reached into teachers' classrooms and interfered with teachers' abilities to use their skills and judgments as professionals" (Rooney, 2015, p. 493). Their capacity to provide access to education, not just narrow training, has been greatly diminished.

In response, "just as reforms have been growing nationwide, so have national, state, and local resistance efforts by educators, students, and parents/caretakers" (Croft et al., 2016, p. 86). Seeking relief, some parents have pulled their children out of public schools and placed them in charters or private schools where teachers may enjoy greater freedom. Ironically, even if testing could be made meaningful and more supportive of student learning and teacher development, as Berliner (2011) has argued, getting away from (computerized) bubble sheets in a generally underfunded system of public schooling competing for dollars with charters would be prohibitively expensive. Value-added testing is even more expensive and raises numerous and serious conceptual, ethical, and technical difficulties (see Everson, 2017; Papay, 2011; Pivovarova, Amrein-Beardsley, & Broatch, 2016; Smith & Imig, 2016).

Access Required: The Human Conversation

Along with the moral imperative for equal access comes an inevitable question: Access to what? To answer this question, Goodlad and his colleagues, as we noted in chapter 4, drew on insights of philosopher and political theorist Michael Oakeshott (1959), who saw the "conversation of mankind," or the human conversation, as a metaphor for civilization and for the interlacing ways of knowing that constitute a civilization. As Goodlad et al. (2004) explained,

One of the most commonly expressed goals for schooling is to promote the development and use of the intellect through encounters with various bodies of knowledge. Too often, though, what is understood to be "knowledge" amounts to little more than inert bits and pieces that, taken together, amount to little more than the leftovers or refuse of what could be called the "human conversation." Mere exposure to this refuse is not the same as genuine, substantive participation in the conversation itself. . . . Participation in the human conversation and access to all the varied knowledge that goes with it are important because they are what develops a person's intellectual and social skills and abilities and what best prepares that person to interpret the human experience. (pp. 29–30)

Within the human conversation, as Oakeshott (1959) suggested, are different voices representing different forms of social capital (see chapter 5), each a "reflection of a human activity" with its own "specific character and . . . manner of speaking." While there is "no fixed number of the voices which engage in this conversation," two, the voice of science and the voice of poetry, are "most familiar" (p. 12).

The metaphor is rich and suggestive, but requires unpacking. Richard Rorty (1979) offered a helpful point of departure. For Rorty, the human conversation speaks to the "ultimate context within which knowledge is to be understood [as evolving and negotiated] standards of justification, and from there to the actual changes in those standards which make up intellectual history" (pp. 389–390). *Justification* has to do with giving reasons, making arguments, providing evidence to explain or support a belief or the cause of an event or an action. When conversants are united by standards of justification, the rudiments of a discipline emerge.

Thus the origins of the disciplines arise in relationships and, as Stephen Toulmin (2001) argued, friendship: "the phila [love] that unites people whose interest lies not in profiting from one another's situations, but in enjoying together shared good things" (p. 34). With this view, a discipline is a bounded discourse community, part of the whole of the human conversation. A sign of disciplinary membership is knowing "what things to pay attention to and what to set aside, for the purposes of our particular activity or argument" (p. 42). Being part of a discipline means holding a lively interest in a set of problems and standards for inquiry within a community and sharing ways of seeing and doing (methods for noticing and manipulating), and talking about and exploring those problems. But membership also comes with a warning: institutional conventions and habits, what Toulmin called "professional blinders" (p. 114), can result in domestication of the experience and in the understanding of inquiry provided to the young.

Although centrally important to schooling, the formal disciplines do not exhaust the content of the human conversation. Conversation is culturally bounded, and learning also comes from involvement in all sorts of groups and through all sorts of human practices, many of which are valuable to our growth and development as human beings, especially to our social and emotional growth—clubs, churches, and soccer leagues, for example—but not necessarily part of the formal curriculum of schooling. Sometimes such activity is described simply and somewhat oddly as "extracurricular," somehow valuable but tangential to serious learning. But the issue is more complicated still. There is an informal or what is often characterized as a "hidden curriculum" (Apple, 1979). As Dewey (1938) reminded us, people learn not only what they are studying, but much more: "Collateral learning in the way of formation of enduring attitudes, of likes and dislikes, may be and often is much more important than the spelling lesson or lesson in geography or history that is learned" (p. 49). Students learn simply by what they are allowed and encouraged to do (see chapter 5 on "manners").

Some of what is learned in school incidentally is planned though not highly structured, part of how a learning environment is organized; and, for good or otherwise, some learning just happens. Berliner (2009) observed that certain "nonacademic competencies" are of critical importance to academic learning (p. 290) as well as to success in life: "improved work habits, increased sports skills, increased leadership skills, better prosocial behavior, and more responsibilities for success" (p. 290). No doubt Leo Hart and the Weedpatch faculty thought carefully about activities that promised certain kinds of collateral learning for the Okie children, along with their concern about the subjects that were part of the formal curriculum. But still much was learned that was unplanned but perhaps hoped for, a result of children working together to dig the pool or of Leo carrying the little girl wearing his hat as they walked and talked. Similarly, John Goodlad and Bob Patterson planned all sorts of activities for partnership participants, but neither could predict the learning outcomes that would follow, outcomes we as beneficiaries recognize as "gifts."

Access through Experience

"Access" to the human conversation and all it represents—knowledge, skills, manners—proves to be a much broader and more complex issue than simply providing all students with a list of courses to choose from along with a class schedule; they must also experience being together and working together. As discussed in chapter 5, the question touches virtually every nook and cranny of the lifeworld of schooling, revealing just how important it is to get and stay clear about aims. Clarity of aims makes a dramatic difference to how curriculum decisions of this kind are made and to the breadth of their area of concern.

Consider, for example, the implications for the formal, informal, "hidden," and "extracurricular" (sometimes referred to as "cocurricular") elements of schooling when the dominating intent of public education is understood to be thinking about and practicing democratic or some other kind of citizenship. The concept of the individual, particularly of each individual's worth, is perhaps the most distinctive feature of Western civilization—the taproot ideal of democracy. The ideal gives rise to concern about citizen rights, generally thought of as inalienable and inviolable. Yet, from living with those rights and from suffering because of their diverse and sometimes troubling and often contradictory expression, our attention is drawn to citizen responsibilities and the social conditions that define, shape, constrain, and ultimately make that ideal possible. Within such a context, where there is genuine concern for student (and teacher) rights *and* responsibilities, very little of a school's or college's program is not rich in potential learning opportunities. As we have argued, we learn the manners of democracy by living them.

A helpful way of framing the issue, of dividing it up for discussion, comes from Harold Alberty's thoughts about curriculum design (Bullough, 1999). Alberty was especially interested in general education that "part of the program which is required of all students at a given level on the ground [thought to be] essential to the development of the common values, attitudes, understandings, and skills needed by all for common democratic citizenship" (Alberty & Alberty, 1962, p. 203). Alberty illustrated what he had in mind by singling out the importance of respect for differences, "a very precious value," warning that "the protection and enhancement of this value is only possible when it is held in common" (p. 119). The requirement is to forge, then protect spaces—commons—and to plan activities that support engagement across our many differences in lunch rooms, in classrooms, and on playing fields. Alberty contrasted general education to specialized education to indicate "the point where special interests can no longer be effectively dealt with in groups organized primarily in terms of common concerns" (p. 202). Specialized education has as part of its area of concern developing and nurturing individual student talent and ability. In an aspiring democracy, the claims of both kinds of education need to be met and kept in balance: civic responsibility on one side, individual interest and choice on the other. But the call of citizenship necessarily places limits on the right to choose, a point often neglected in arguments over school choice and vouchers.

Alberty's categories help us make what might be thought of as first-level distinctions useful for educators at every level. So are we talking about experience with disciplinary knowledge and planned activities that ought to be part of the school experience of every student (general education), or are we talking about parts of a program that target some students and their specific interests or challenges and not others (specialized education)? Moreover, are we talking about activities that may potentially support learning but really do not belong in the school day or as a formal part of a university program (extra- or cocurricular)? Especially for younger students, general education has priority over specialized education, but general education remains a concern at all levels, in part because the obligations of citizenship remain insistent.

A set of helpful second-level distinctions was offered by education philosopher Harry Broudy from his analysis of what he called the "uses of schooling." Broudy (see 1988) describes four such uses: (a) replicative, (b) applicative, (c) associative, and (d) interpretative.

Broudy and his colleagues described replicative learning in this way: "When we read a newspaper, compute a sum, look up a word in the dictionary, read a map, or recite a poem, we repeat an operation performed many times" (Broudy, Smith, & Burnett, 1964, p. 48). Much of what is taught and practiced in school, particularly elementary grades, aims at automaticity: multiplication tables, spelling, lining up in class, raising hands to speak, using an "inside voice" when speaking, and so on. However, the college curriculum (e.g., legal and medical studies) also requires a good deal of replicative work that comes with apprenticeship and emulating a practice.

Applicative learning tends to lack structure, with varying demands on and opportunities for the learner. Broudy et al. (1964) explained, "Learning— usually in the form of some principle, generalization, or statement of fact—is used to solve a problem or to analyze a situation. . . . Sometimes the situation is so unstructured and open that the bulk of the cues must come from the problem-solver himself" (pp. 50–51). Associative learning involves more spontaneity and recognizes individual difference. It was defined by Broudy et al. (1964) as follows: "Many learnings, while not subliminal or unconscious, have an air of the accidental about them, as when something we have learned comes to mind because it has something in common with what is before us. . . . When we are asked to respond to a question, we resurrect from memory something or other that the cue suggests. The laws of association—resemblance, continuity, and satisfaction purport to tell us what learnings the given cue is most likely to elicit" (p. 46). Finally, the interpretative was presented: "Much of what in ordinary language we call application of knowledge is better regarded as interpretation, a process related to application but far less specific and detailed. . . . The interpretative use of schooling . . . is primarily for orientation and perspective rather than for action and problem-solving. Although interpretation is a necessary preliminary to all the other uses of knowledge, there are many situations in which orientation toward a problem is as far as we can go, that is, in virtually all of the situations in which we cannot function as specialists" (pp. 54–55). The orienting function of the interpretative uses of schooling calls attention to the importance for the young of gaining a "democratic frame of reference," as described in chapter 5.

Moving into and through a discipline, students find themselves engaged in activities that fall into each of the four uses of schooling in varying measures.

From an instructional perspective, recognizing what use is intended and why has crucially important implications for access and for citizenship. Under pressure of standardized testing, as Berliner (2009) noted, greater emphasis is placed on replicative and applicative uses of schooling than on associative and interpretive uses because they are easily taught and tested. As a result, far too few students have "opportunities to question or to explore new ideas" (p. 291) or to consider carefully and critically the consequences of policies, plans, and personal actions on the lives of others, including those far removed in space and time. Both activities are central to democratic citizenship.

Ironically, now recalling former education secretary Duncan's pronouncement on the importance of keeping America economically competitive, the current emphasis on basic literacy and basic numeracy, echoing the failed competency movement of the 1970s, supported by an overarching concern with minimally meeting externally set performance standards, will likely weaken America's economic competitiveness by wasting and misusing an abundance of talent. Moreover, a curriculum of this kind undermines the development of democratic manners and character, which depend on making connections, seeing similarities, and finding and holding common ground across our many differences.

Contrary to the parsimonious curriculum encouraged by the testing fetish that dominates federal and state education policy, democracy requires a generous curriculum. It must be sufficiently broad to support general education and, because we cherish the individual, sufficiently abundant and deep to enable through specialized education the development of talent in its many expressions. A rich general education supports the associative and interpretative work—the thinking—required for understanding and productively responding to the problems of citizenship and of living. Living in a democracy brings about insistent demands from difference and diversity along with the expectation of cooperative and corrective social action. To this end, the content of the human conversation must be culled to locate the disciplines, or parts of disciplines, subject areas, key concepts, ideas, modes of inquiry, forms of discourse, and social activities, that support the development and enactment of democratic citizenship. This includes history, literature, science, and much more, including how to form an argument and marshal evidence in its defense. Because a dialogic democracy relies upon thoughtful and informed inquiry to remain vibrant, attention must also be given to the conversational content that supports immanent critique: the skills and abilities to question the demands of citizenship "whenever they appear to threaten the foundational ideals of democratic sovereignty, such as respect for persons" (Gutmann, 1999, p. 52).

Much of the value of the informal and hidden curriculum comes in supporting the formation of what Thomas Green (1999) called the "conscience of membership"—the idea of being part of a *we*, a democratic aspiring (college or school) community with people united by shared (but often unrecognized) needs, concerns, and aspirations. In addition, the informal and hidden curriculum more or less intentionally supports internalization of community norms and the manners that express those norms. Reminiscent of Woodruff's comment that the entire citizenry of Athens educated the young and our discussion of democratic manners, Green argued, "One does not learn the norms of cooperation and then apply them . . . one simply comes to be cooperative. One comes to be normed" (p. 49), strongly or weakly, so careful thought needs to be given to the norms that are to be learned and lived. Learned one way or another, if ignored or taken for granted, the norms that come to be learned might turn out to be mind numbing, spirit crushing, and undemocratic.

As preferred ways of acting, "oughts," norms (like manners) are interwoven throughout the institutional fabric of schools and universities, a pattern of weaving that should to be carefully considered and purposeful. Some norms have to do with getting along, so we ask, "How ought we live together in this place at this time?" and "How ought we treat one another?" John Gardner (1984) speaks of additional norms important for a free society, ones that also are central to the concern of schooling: "Men and women doing capably whatever job is theirs to do tone up the whole society. And those who do a slovenly job, whether they are janitors or judges, surgeons or technicians, lower the tone of the society" (p. 161). Doing one's best in "every phase of life" is what democratic citizens do; it is part of their contribution to the life of the commons. Gardner continued, suggesting that such societies "need individual excellence in all its forms—in every kind of creative endeavor, in politics, in education, in industry, in our spiritual life—in short, universally" (p. 161). To meet the obligation of access through general and specialized education, schools and colleges must not only support established student interests and skills and celebrate their maturing development but help create new ones. Nurturing pedagogy, to which we now turn, gives students the support needed to develop and extend those interests and skills.

When considering the outline of the general education currently available to students, the temptation for educators is to immediately turn attention to resisters, young people who demonstrate unprincipled noncompliance. The result is that suddenly we are talking about general education not for all, but rather for select students, ones we like and/or find interesting or know are willing to give us, their instructors, the benefit of a doubt without complaint.

We insist once again, for the young, the first teacherly obligation is "pure hospitality" (see chapter 4). When refusal results, Amy Gutmann (1999) offers a general guideline for thinking through the threat: "Inequalities in the distribution of educational goods can be justified if, but only if, they do not deprive any child of the ability to participate effectively in the democratic process. . . . [There is] a moral requirement that democratic institutions allocate sufficient resources to education to provide all children with an ability adequate to participate in the democratic process" (p. 136). For some children, this standard means additional resources must be allocated, resources beyond those an individual teacher may possess. Access sets a standard of justice, not of fairness (see Woodruff, 2005).

Nurturing Access: The Third Moral Dimension

The third of the Moral Dimensions provides us with guidance in how access must be provided: "*practicing pedagogical nurturing* with respect to *the art and science of teaching*" (Goodlad et al., 2004, p. 30). As part of creating a *we*, a sense of community belonging, practicing pedagogical nurturing, representing the first part of this dimension, involves more than simply being nice to students— as important as niceness is to getting along. Schooling is compulsory for young people; many would prefer to be doing something other than sitting in class, and this complicates teachers' efforts to be inclusive and to be perceived as nurturing. The almost inevitable tensions between personal preferences and values and institutionally set role expectations also are complicating. Children are not born students; *studenting* is a role they must learn if they are to succeed in school, and for many young people, including college students, settling in and finding place do not come easily (see Bullough, 2007).

Many beginning teachers have a parallel experience when they first step into the teacher role. Many are facing large groups of students and may find themselves by necessity in the reward and punishment business, which makes the high institutional value of consistency in role enactment a source of personal moral ambiguity, particularly when they first enter a classroom as a teacher. Other ethical issues arise: consistency in meting out punishment or reward may offend justice even when honoring fairness, and crowd control makes loss of the individual student all too easy.

The second part of this dimension—"with respect to the art and science of teaching"—brings with it knowledge, skill, and dispositional demands. Educators have invested time and energy in studying what is known about how students learn, and they are committed to improving their pedagogical practices, not in the belief that they will ever achieve once-and-for-all "best," but in the hope of finding ever better practices for the benefit of students (Bullough, 2012). To this end, nurturing pedagogy requires educators at all levels to become students of teaching and of their own teaching practice. John Dewey (1904) commented on teachers learning and becoming students of teaching: "The teacher who leaves the professional school with power in managing a class of children may appear to superior advantage the first day, the first week, the first month, or even the first year, as compared with some other teacher who has a much more vital command of the psychology, logic, and ethics of development. But later 'progress' may with such consist only in perfecting and refining skill already possessed. Such persons seem to know how to teach, but they are not *students of teaching*" (p. 15; emphasis added).

By calling attention to the nature and quality of teacher-student relationships, the first part of this dimension, the imperative of nurturing, is more complex than the second part. Cognitive scientist Daniel Willingham (2009) set the problem: "The emotional bond between students and teacher—for better or worse—accounts for whether students learn" (p. 65). The kind of human beings we are as educators and the ways we connect to those we teach profoundly affect student access to knowledge; thus the two Moral Dimensions considered in this chapter intertwine.

In his interest in the development of conscience, Green (1999) touched on a particularly motivating aspect of nurturing pedagogy: to think about nurturing pedagogy, the teacher's half of the teacher-student relationship is to consider just what sort of person she or he is. As Green wrote, "It is the reflexive character of judgment that . . . is essential to conscience. Each of us has the capacity to be judge of our own conduct and our own affections. This is judgment that each of us makes in our own case. Conscience is often described . . . as an interior voice of the self speaking to the self, offering advice, counsel, judgment, and reproach" (pp. 23–24). What is done to and for students and how they respond call forth the voice of conscience, suggesting at times a need to awaken to our moral obligations, obligations that force the question "What sort of person am I?" Van Manen (1991) had it right: the humanity of teaching is found in relationships.

All educators work in a charged moral space. But if they stop what they are doing in class to deliberate over what to do in every situation that has moral implications they would morph into Camus's Clamence in *The Fall* (1957) and, freezing, become unable to do anything but sit in a bar sipping a drink alone. In contrast, "most of our ordinary, everyday moral deliberation is . . . barely reflective and . . . only marginally self-conscious" (Johnson, 1993, p. 60). To get their work done, teachers often set aside their moral burdens and rely on established routines of thought and of action that grow out of layers of past experience. Reflecting in action (Schön, 1983), educators make decisions on the fly. They stop to consider a particular situation only rarely, most often in a quiet moment when they may experience the weightiness or wonder of what was done and, based on what they have studied and know, ponder how they acted and how the students reacted. In such moments, teachers may sometimes feel regret, reconsider, adjust their moral compass, and then plan for recovery and restitution. And hopefully they learn and become a bit more wise.

Ultimately the moral weightiness of teaching is embedded in the pedagogical relationship, responsible educator to learner, as van Manen (1994) described it, referring to the student side: "The [pedagogical] relation is a life experience that has significance in and of itself. . . . Our relation to a real teacher—someone in whose presence we experience a heightened sense of self and real growth and personal development—is possibly more profound and more consequential than the experience of relations of friendship [and] love" (p. 143). In such caring relationships, when a teacher or professor and a student have an "experience of contact" (van Manen, 2012, p. 24), when they bond—she is "my teacher" and "I am her student," and we are part of something together—they recognize obligation and responsibility. Recognition brings expectations, and with expectation comes vulnerability (Kelchtermans, 1996), the possibility of disappointing and of being disappointed by the other.

Sometimes nurturing teachers must do hard things and tell difficult truths that can be told only by someone who is recognized as caring—caring deeply about a student's future, beyond merely the individual's current happiness. Part of teaching is to be a voice of warning (see Bullough, Patterson, & Mayes, 2002), in addition to designing a curriculum and living a life that supports imaginative ventures into possible worlds peopled by different selves: different conceptions of what a student is and might become—more capable, competent, interesting. Inevitably teachers model something, consciously or not, but probably too few of us know just what we represent.

Vulnerability is part of teaching, a necessary condition for learning, but it is also a source of pain on both sides of the pedagogical relationship. Rejection by either side is experienced as deeply personal, the teacher (or professor) because teaching (or professing) is not just what she does but teacher (or professor) is who she is. When she is feeling acutely vulnerable, the desire for self-protection may cloud an educator's perception of student vulnerabilities; she may forget for a time that to nurture is also to forgive, forget, and give second chances, sometimes third and fourth chances. Locating limits results in disappointment and failure, both very much a part of learning and an opportunity for growth for both students and their teachers.

Unconditional Hospitality

John Goodlad once remarked that the best evidence for the goodness of a school is that children are happy when there. Among the many criticisms directed toward schooling is that public schools overreach their bounds when they move beyond academics. Economic uncertainty, family instability, poverty, and fear of violence are very much a part of the global world and thus of children's lives. Many children are not faring well despite doing the best they know how at home and in school. Schools are constantly being asked to do more, to help pick up the pieces of children's lives dropped by other institutions, including the family. Nel Noddings (2003) offered a powerful reminder of why the focus on nurturing pedagogy is so very important:

The best homes and schools are happy places. The adults in these happy places recognize that one aim of education (and of life itself) is happiness. They also recognize that happiness serves as both means and end. Happy children, growing in their understanding of what happiness is, will seize their educational opportunities with delight, and they will contribute to the happiness of others. Clearly, if children are to be happy in schools, their teachers should also be happy. Too often we forget this obvious connection. Finally, basically happy people who retain an uneasy social conscience will contribute to a happier world. (p. 261)

That "uneasy social conscience" is what led Leo Hart to see the otherwise invisible Weedpatch children and to be attentive to them. Seeing them, he recognized their humanity and sensed their promise not only as citizens but as young people capable, with some help, of forging happiness from the disruptions of poverty and marginalization. Hart knew that education is an optimistic enterprise, or it is not education at all.

7

Associates and Associating II

. . . .

A Case Study

> Those who go out in search of knowledge
> will be in the path of God until they
> return.
> —Sunan al-Tirmidhi

In chapter 1 we introduced one of the educative mechanisms of our partnership, the Associates program. There are three versions of Associates conducted each year: leadership, district-focused, and school-based. *Leadership associates* involve participants who occupy formal administrative and decision-making positions across the partnership (school board members, district and university level administrators, deans and associate deans, department chairs, and CITES faculty, among others). *District-focused associates* include university faculty in addition to educators and administrators from a single school district. Currently operating in one of the five partnership districts, *school-based associates* include teachers and administrators from a single school. All gatherings share a common aim: to study and attempt to practice the partnership's version of the Moral Dimensions of Teaching.

This chapter presents a participant-observer study (Dewalt & Dewalt, 1998) of a single district-focused associates group that goes beyond participant observation to include case study (Yin, 1989) data gathered through interviews, questionnaires, and a focus group. "Participant observation is a way to collect data in a relatively unstructured manner in naturalistic settings by ethnographers who observe and/or take part in the common and uncommon activities of the people being studied" (Dewalt & Dewalt, 1998, p. 261). The data included observation notes written while participating in shared activities (or shortly thereafter). Observing and participating in shared activities provide informal opportunities for gaining insight into group dynamics and beliefs, including changes in belief that might otherwise be missed or be presented differently when viewed through other research lenses including interviews and questionnaires. We considered participation crucial to presenting a rich picture of the Associates experience, most especially of the place of first principles in partnering, including hospitality, commons, shared activities and experience, relationship building, and conversation (moving to dialogue). We hoped to provide evidence of program effects and value.

The Context

Supporting Structure

Organizing leadership and district-level Associates groups is a responsibility of the Center for the Improvement of Teacher Education and Schooling (CITES). All Associates groups serve as partnership commons: dedicated spaces enabling persons who have responsibility for one or more of the interrelated facets of education and the development of educators but occupy distinct institutional roles to come together to reflect and learn.

Describing how CITES operates as a center of pedagogy, Robert Patterson, the founding dean, wrote,

> CITES does not control or exercise authority in a typical sense; rather it coordinates through persuasion, through inviting and building consensus among participants in various units within the university and in the schools. It does not seek to alter or diminish organizational entities such as colleges, school districts, or schools. Administrators within CITES recognize that collaboration cannot be mandated or legislated; it must be entered by choice, with a conviction that the benefits of the relationship are sufficiently compelling to cause participants to surrender a degree of their own autonomy in the interest of the common good. The establishment of CITES is an attempt to build a community of educators across the university and schools who do not feel threatened or diminished by collaboration, a community sustained by an unwritten social contract to which educators have entered of their own volition to promote shared ideas, beliefs, and commitments. ... CITES was created to build a new cultural perspective centered on collaborative relationships and commitment. (Patterson, Michelli, & Pacheco, 1999, pp. 131–132)

A primary concern of CITES is culture building, which involves formation of multiple commons in support of shared experience and sustained conversation. The intent is to build robust relationships across institutional boundaries centered in a shared moral vision of the work of teaching and teacher education. Given constant turnover in school, district, and university personnel, once such relationships are achieved, they require constant tending and care. New superintendents, principals, teachers, deans, and university faculty as well as school board members and personnel within the state Office of Education need to be brought into the partnership conversation in a way that they find compelling, not because participation is expected but because it makes a positive difference. Because the politics of both public and higher education are complex, often exhausting, and sometimes deeply disturbing, longtime participants as well as new participants need strengthening.

Origins and Development of an Idea

Over the past several years, enhanced teacher collegiality and collaboration have become important aspects of school improvement in many countries. Recognizing the power of distributed leadership and the importance of building and then tapping social capital, instructional teams and professional learning communities or teacher professional communities (Bullough & Smith, 2016; Hargreaves, 2013; Stoll, Bolam, McMahon, Wallace, & Thomas, 2006; Webb, Vulliamy, Sarja, Hamalainen, & Poikonen, 2009) have become commonplace in schools. But the purpose for that collaboration must be considered. Bode (1940) nicely made the point: "Co-operation in itself is scarcely an issue. The totalitarian states of today are all examples of large-scale co-operation. What is important is, first, the end or purpose that is to be achieved, and, secondly, the appropriateness of the means to the end" (p. 270).

Since passage of NCLB, with its aggressive accountability measures and its championing of technical views of teaching, such efforts have often become narrowly strategic, focused mainly on raising standardized test scores. Under such conditions, collegiality may feel "contrived," unnatural, forced, bureaucratic (Hargreaves & Fullan, 1992, p. 229). Too seldom do cooperative activities, focused on test scores, attend to wider issues of concern: the purposes of teaching and schooling, the well-being of children and families, or the challenge of building school cultures that sustain nurturing child-adult relationships and interesting and ethical adult relationships. And rarely do they focus on the education of educators: books that educators ought to read that explore our times, reports that critique public schooling, or beautiful cultural works that lift and fill the human spirit (see the discussion of "stewardship of the mind" in the next chapter). Here we are reminded of a comment by three distinguished teacher educators of an earlier era: "The first requirement for growth of teachers through any means is that they work under conditions which are favorable to their growth as persons, and that to be a good teacher one must be first of all a good human being" (Giles, McCutchen, & Zechiel, 1942, p. 231).

Appealing to the broad human interest in personal development, book groups or book clubs and study groups have long been part of American life. Besides offering social opportunities, such groups give expression to participants' desires to better understand and perform the practices that structure our lives and give life meaning. They also open opportunities to go far afield, to turn inward then outward, to ask questions related to where one's life meets the world one inhabits: Why do I do what I do? What sort of good comes from my doing? What are the sources of my deepest contentment? Do my actions square with my identity, my moral aspirations? Do I have moral integrity? One invitation offered by such groups is to pause, to step out of fast time for a time, and to *think*, to contemplate, to reflect, then engage with others for the sake of enriching experience and broadening perspective and understanding. "Only by wrestling with the conditions of [a] problem at first hand, seeking and finding [a] way out, does [a person] think" (Dewey, 1916, p. 188). And to think is to "find and test meanings" (Bode, 1940, p. 251).

Until recently the Ladies Literary Club of Salt Lake City, founded in 1877, was located near the home of one of the authors. Many teachers have been members of the Literary Club over the years. Just like Literary Club members, many teachers organize themselves for the pleasure of associating and discussing interesting novels or expanding their understanding of a topic or practice by reading and conversing about select professional publications (see Burbank, Kauchak, & Bates, 2010; Riley, 2015). Such persons are, to use a popular phrase, "lifelong learners." They are curious people—models of educated citizens—who not only enjoy talking about ideas with interesting people, but want to make ever better sense of their experience and to live a life that matters morally.

This tradition, within the give-and-take of a seminar, underpins the idea of the Associates program. The word *associate* was carefully chosen. The verb form comes from the Latin term *associare*, to join with, to unite with. It's adjective form, *associatus*, suggests being allied, connected, or paired. Often, it seems, professors, teachers, and school and university administrators fail to appreciate that they ought to be allies, that they share those they teach. As noted, a focus of Associates groups is relationship building, but the larger intent is to build a community of educators united by a moral cause and shared vision.

Linking the word *associates* to the work of building and sustaining university–public school partnerships was an initiative developed by Goodlad and his colleagues in the Institute for Educational Inquiry in Seattle as a form of professional development, a way for planting and nourishing the seeds of ideas then being developed that would deepen and expand into the Agenda for Education in a Democracy. The aim was not to set chairs for group recitation of an educational catechism or even to locate fellow travelers, but a generous offer to join an uncertain "journey with adventurous company" (Kridel & Bullough, 2007, p. 224), a process aimed at nothing less than the simultaneous renewal of public schooling and teacher education. The process involved studying, thinking about, and rethinking the personal, professional, and institutional practices and commitments that bear the work of teacher preparation and schooling.

Expansion in the BYU Partnership

Both authors have participated in Associates groups with Goodlad. John's multiple experiences, including a turn at being a facilitator, are described briefly in chapter 2. Shortly before the founding of CITES, the general structure and intent of the Associates model developed by Goodlad were embraced but initially conceived in the more familiar form of a professional "seminar."

> The first seminar included eighteen participants from across the university, the five school districts, and the State Office of Education. It met four times during the year, in a resort setting not far from BYU, to explore a set of readings and issues similar to those studied by the Seattle Associates group. After CITES was established, it extended this activity considerably. During its first year of operation, CITES conducted two seminars or cohorts, one for personnel from the total BYU-PSP [Public School Partnership] and one primarily for [one of the school districts]. A year later, six groups were organized to meet throughout the year: four in the partnership school districts and two for the BYU-PSP overall. Participating principals and faculty from one or two schools subsequently began to use a modified form of the model to promote professional growth in their individual schools. (Patterson et al., 1999, p. 137)

From this beginning the current iteration of the partnership-wide Leadership Associates has been meeting twice annually in two-day retreats. The most recent retreat involved eighty-three participants, including three school board members, the five partnership school superintendents, eighteen district administrators and staff, fifteen deans and associate deans and numerous department chairs from the university programs involved in teacher education, and five university-level administrators, among others. In addition, year after year for twenty years, five and most recently six district-level Associates groups have been sponsored by the university and the partner school districts, one of which is described in this chapter. These groups meet in two-day sessions five times across an academic year. Substitutes are provided for participating teachers. In total, there have been more than two thousand district-level participants.

For several years principals in the largest of the partner districts (many of whom have participated in past Associates groups) have been encouraged to apply for funding to support building-level study groups. Each year, at district expense, from twenty to twenty-five (of the eighty-six) schools form such groups to meet monthly to discuss selected readings and to explore and make better sense of their experience in public education. The district provides books and some meals to support these voluntary gatherings.

The Study

Facilitators

Under leadership of the CITES director, school district leaders and university staff linked to CITES meet annually to plan district-level Associates sessions and to set responsibilities; at the end of the year they meet again to assess the program and make future plans. Groups are led by three-member teams, each team including a CITES representative.

The team that led the group studied for this chapter was composed of two assistant superintendents, John (Patten) and Kimberly, and a former superintendent, Vern, a CITES staff member. Although very busy, district-level Associates leaders typically volunteer for the assignment, as did both Kimberly and John. Principals and teachers are invited to participate in Associates; whether they choose to do so is voluntary. In a late-year focus group with the three facilitators, John commented on his reasons for being involved: "It is very satisfying to facilitate teachers' development, [their understanding] of the 'why' behind what they do. . . . I love seeing the lights come on when they have a greater sense of the moral purpose to what they're doing. . . . It's very, very invigorating." John and Kimberly had both recently become assistant superintendents to a new district superintendent, also a champion of the partnership. John explained: "When the change was made with the superintendent, . . . I asked if I could keep [Associates]. I knew [the new job would involve] another significant learning curve, and . . . it's been brutal, it's like having the first year of teaching all over again, in terms of the busyness and everything. But I thought that if I take [Associates] off [my] plate now, it'll never come back, I'll never find room. I just enjoy [Associates] so much. I just wanted to keep it, and it's been awesome." Kimberly, whose mother was a teacher who had been a participant in a district-level Associates group, told a similar story. After ten years of teaching, she was invited as a new principal to be part of an Associates group with two of her teachers. "I just fell in love with it, and every year [while] I was a principal, [I] continued to do Associates with [my] own faculty. . . . I was ecstatic [after I came to the district office] at having the opportunity to be a facilitator."

Participants

Schools were invited to participate following suggestions from district-level supervisors, who were well acquainted with the building principals and their schools, having worked closely with them. Their judgments were based on principal and faculty interest and on school need. The intent was that the Associates opportunity would circulate and eventually extend to every school faculty. University faculty and administrators were invited by the director of CITES. The final composition of the group studied was weighted toward teachers, principals, and district personnel, with twenty-three of the twenty-seven participants representing six schools (four elementary, one middle, and one high school). The university contingent was composed of an associate director of an institute with an interest in education, a professor of teaching methods, and an assistant dean of education who worked closely throughout the study with the author of this chapter. We wish more university faculty could have been part of the group studied, but the group was already large and resources were limited. As two of the four university faculty involved were conducting the study and thus could not be sources of data, we decided to emphasize the experience of the public school participants. Of the educators who completed the initial survey, eleven were men and ten were women; ages ranged from thirty-one to fifty-eight, with an average of forty-two years. Of the initial interview respondents, thirteen held master's degrees, seven held bachelor's degrees, and one, a male administrator, had a doctorate. Three district administrators, seven school administrators, including assistant principals, and eleven teachers completed the survey.

Elementary and middle school administrators invited two teachers to join them in Associates; the high school team included four teachers. Three participants came from the district offices.

Organization and Curriculum

The group met five times during the school year in two-day sessions, each held in a resort hotel an hour or so from the university campus, at partnership expense. Participants came to each session having read a set of assigned materials and prepared for conversation about those readings. Each session focused on one of the Five Commitments to Our Future. As noted previously, these commitments (see the appendix) represent a partnership-specific revised version of Goodlad's Moral Dimensions of Teaching. The commitments serve as points of orientation for the partnership and as the school district's published mission statement—formally approved and supported to varying degrees by members of the school board. The dean of education and the director of CITES, with the superintendents of the five partnership school districts, compose the partnership Governing Board. As Associates group participants from this district were reading and thinking about the commitments, they were in effect exploring the values underpinning and sustaining the work of their own school district as well as those of the partnership and the teacher education programs at the university.

The first session of the Associates group in the study focused on Civic Preparation and Engagement; the second treated Nurturing Pedagogy; the third considered issues of Access to Knowledge; the fourth dealt with Stewardship (see the conclusion); and the last drew things together with Simultaneous Renewal, the commitment of teachers, teacher educators, and arts and sciences faculty to improve simultaneously in their respective roles, always for the benefit of students.

After breakfast at the hotel, sessions began with participants entering a large conference room, looking at a wall chart for table assignments, which changed frequently, then sitting at the specified table. To facilitate planned activities, one member was designated temporary leader at each table, with all being a leader at least once. In addition to meeting agendas, in the middle of the table was a laminated triangle tower that on each side stated the commitment that focused the meetings, with a statement of supporting and specific session aims.

The first associate session began with a brief orientation, including introduction to the commitments. "At Associates, we'll get our questions answered and our answers questioned," participants were told. "Buddy time [will be] during meals." Introductions followed. Participants came having read a cluster of articles on the nature of conversation and dialogue. The first topic was "Dialogue: What is it and how does it differ from discussion?" The group generated and agreed to rules for group interaction, which would be reviewed in subsequent sessions: "Listen to each other's ideas with respect," "Participate actively," "Come prepared," "Be okay with disagreement," "Be fully engaged," "Begin on time," and "Have fun and laugh."

"Democracy will be the thing today and tomorrow," Kimberly announced. In its entirety, the first commitment reads: "Civic preparation and engagement: The Partnership prepares educators who model and teach the knowledge, skills, and dispositions required for civic virtue and engagement in our society." (Frankly, we prefer Goodlad's more direct and more memorable statement: "enculturating the young into a social and political democracy.") Kimberly's statement "democracy will be the thing today and tomorrow" indicated to the group that the session would be focused around the place of the school in building democratic thinking, feeling, and behaving citizens, reminiscent of Bode's (1937) concept of democracy as "a way of life" that Dewey also developed (1939b/1988), or a "distinctive way of coming at life" (Hullfish & Smith, 1967, p. 261). Educators, we found, rarely think about democracy; like other citizens they take it for granted and rarely interrogate it as foundational to practice.

To prepare to explore this commitment, participants came having read sections of Paul Woodruff's *First Democracy: The Challenge of an Ancient Idea* (2005) as well as selections from *The Public Purposes of Education and Schooling* (Goodlad & McMannon, 1997). Table discussions began on the first day with this leading question: "Why is the public school essential to perpetuate civic virtue and engagement in a democratic society?"

After table discussions, the entire group was brought together and focused on a question designed to generate discussion: "What do we mean by democracy?" A vice principal responded, "equitable voice." Asked to respond, a teacher remarked, almost apologizing, "Ten days ago [before completing the preparatory reading], I probably would have said, 'to vote.' The concepts [we're discussing], I've never really considered." He was not alone. A task followed: "What I want you to do now is identify the least democratic and most democratic society you've been in. Describe why." Another question followed: "Do you agree that public education is the cornerstone of a civil and prosperous democracy?" A lively discussion commenced, during which a middle school vice principal, who agreed with the statement, soberly said, "Democracy is fragile, next week it could fall apart"—a conclusion he reached without reading Foa and Mounk (2016; see chapter 5).

That evening, like every Thursday evening during Associates meetings, participants gathered at a restaurant for a meal together, more conversation, and some "buddy time."

The second day began with focus on the importance of making democracy visible. After viewing clips from two classic motion pictures, *The Ox-Bow Incident* (1943) and *12 Angry Men* (1957), discussion turned to identifying some of the social and intellectual skills associated with living democratically. From there attention moved to *First Democracy* (Woodruff, 2005), with five groups rotating around the room, reading and then responding in writing to statements taken from the book, which had been posted on the walls. One quotation addressed "doubles" (mentioned in chapter 5): practices that appear to be essential to democratic function, like majority rule, but that distort and narrow how democracy is understood and confuse its social intent. Another posted quotation focused on the "enemies of democracy." "When have people traded freedom for perceived safety because of fear and/or ignorance?" Responding to this issue, one teacher wrote that in the quest for efficiency in education, educators and administrators tend to "focus on systems [but] democracy focuses on people." Democracy, he thought, was an afterthought to keeping "systems" rolling. "Democracy is you," he later said in discussion. Journal writing as self-reflection followed.

After a break, participants analyzed an article on public education by editorial columnist David Sarasohn, identifying statements with which they agreed or disagreed. They shared the quotations they had selected and their reasons for choosing them. A school decision-making simulation followed, leading into discussion of a handout on the "Five Habits of the Heart That Help Make Democracy Possible," taken from Parker Palmer's book *Healing the Heart of Democracy* (2011, pp. 44–46):

1. An understanding that we are all in this together
2. An appreciation of the value of "otherness"
3. An ability to hold tension in life-giving ways
4. A sense of personal voice and agency
5. A capacity to create community

This turn of discussion had a double purpose: to reiterate the norms governing interaction within Associates as well as encouraging consideration of participants' own relationship to democratic values and aspirations, including their behavior in the simulation. The session ended with a return to the obligations and opportunities of dialogue, with discussion focused on "The Indispensable Opposition," a 1939 *Atlantic Monthly* article by social critic and political theorist Walter Lippmann. His concern was educational: the importance of protecting "the right of our opponents to speak because we must hear what they have to say" (p. 186). "Do we listen?"

A roughly similar pattern was followed in each of the subsequent four sessions: Participants (mostly) came prepared, discussed readings, engaged in role plays and simulations, analyzed film clips that addressed issues pertinent to meeting themes, compared and contrasted points of view, and identified life events on which they self-reflected in their journals. In one session we went bowling, but not alone, and reflected together on Robert Putnam's analysis of the erosion of civic bonds in American culture. Subsequent sessions additionally included briefly reviewing previous sessions and revisiting the selected conversational norms.

Readings varied widely, including books, chapters, and articles. For sharing, cooperative learning groups might be formed around different books from which participants could choose. For example, options for session 3, on equitable access, included several books about access challenges children face: *Out of My Mind* (Draper, 2010), *Look Me in the Eye: My Life with Asperger's* (Robison, 2007), *The Minds of Boys* (Gurian & Stevens, 2005), *Uncertain Lives* (Bullough, 2001), and *Odd Girl Out* (Simmons, 2003). Everyone read *Children of the Dust Bowl* (Stanley, 1992), discussed in chapter 6, which tells the story of the Weedpatch School for "Okie" children, built under leadership of Superintendent Leo Hart and the remarkable educators he recruited to his cause. Visionary and committed leadership of the sort demonstrated by Hart was linked to the work of providing all children access to the knowledge and the skills needed for living more meaningful lives and functioning more effectively as citizens.

Data Gathering

With district, participant, and institutional review board approval, data gathering began with an initial anonymous survey and an interview with each participant conducted prior to the first Associates session. In addition to obtaining demographic data of various kinds, the survey was intended to establish a baseline for group members' views, especially their ideas about the aims of schooling, their understanding of democracy, their beliefs concerning the relationship of schooling to democracy and political engagement, and their concerns regarding the first of the five commitments. Following an extensive literature review, which produced very few pertinent studies, the initial survey was created as a significant revision of an instrument developed by the Global Doing Democracy Research Project (GDDRP). The GDDRP involves "some 70 scholars in over 20 countries examining perspectives and perceptions of democracy among pre- and in-service teachers, teacher education academics, and educators, in general" (Zyngier, 2012b, p. 2). We found sufficient overlap in interests with GDDRP that we anticipated that some of the conclusions from their research could prove useful for gaining perspective on and understanding our data set.

The initial surveys were distributed through Qualtrics, and all but two of them were completed. As anticipated, length and depth of survey responses varied widely. Prior to the first Associates group meeting, a preliminary round of telephone interviews was conducted by a very able student research assistant. The following items were among the questions asked, each with probes: What do you think is or ought to be the primary aim of schooling in America? What is the most important job of teachers? As you reflect on your career in education, what big ideas or central values have been most important to your work? Rate on a one to ten scale how optimistic you are about the future of the students you currently work with. How optimistic are you about the future of students in general? Rate on a one to ten scale how optimistic you are about the future for teachers in the United States. Thinking back, why did you enter the field of education?

A brief anonymous survey was distributed at the third session to assess participants' views of the direction of the program and the value of the experience. At the end of the year an assessment instrument was used across all district-level Associates groups, including self-reported gains in respondents' understanding of the Five Commitments, among other critical information. Results of this survey were shared with the authors. A second telephone interview was conducted late that spring, and a brief email survey was sent a month after the beginning of the new school year. As noted, extensive observation notes were written across the sessions and were drawn upon for illustrative comments and analyzed thematically in relationship to first principles.

Results

A Question of Purposes: Initial Anonymous Survey and Interview

Of the questions asked in the initial interview, two addressed participants' beliefs about the purpose of their work: (a) "What do you think is or ought to be the primary aim of schooling in America?" (b) "What do you think is the most important job of teachers?" Overall, twenty-one interviews were conducted (excluding interviews of the university participants). Of the findings, most noteworthy was that only four respondents—two teachers, an elementary school principal, and a district administrator—spoke of citizenship aims generally as primary purposes of schooling. A teacher wrote, "[Students] should be taught how to go about researching the candidates that best serve their interests and protect the things that matter to them." Well familiar with the Five Commitments, the elementary principal remarked, "I mean it's really the [district's] mission to educate each and every child to ensure the democracy of tomorrow, and I fully believe that." Among elementary school teachers, preparing students for movement to the next higher grade was often mentioned as a driving purpose, along with gaining "basic skills"—social and academic. When speaking of older children, participants noted preparation for the responsibilities of "adulthood," especially for "careers" and for the "job market." Loving children, promoting a "love of learning," and "building their confidence" were most often mentioned as the most important job of teachers.

Of the twenty-one survey respondents, ten stated all five of the commitments; eleven did not state any. Responses indicated wide variation in expectations of what would be gained from participation in the Associates program. "Not sure. I am always looking for ways to be more effective as a teacher." "Collaboration amongst peers. New insights on relevant topics. A type of rejuvenation." A building principal wrote, "I hope to find more information that will help me be a support for my students and teachers." Most teachers expected their teaching would improve as a result of Associates group participation, but were uncertain just how. Only one respondent, a female district administrator, noted a connection with the partnership: "I expect to gain a greater understanding of the partnership, principles, and the role of the university in public education. I hear from other participants that the conversations and experiences are career changing. I look forward to learning with and from others in the program."

Respondents were asked to define democracy. Again views varied. Similar to the teacher who in interview mentioned the importance of learning how to "research candidates," the dominant view expressed in the survey, one that cut across roles, was that the essence of democracy is to vote, a means for exercising "voice" and for choosing leaders. Of the eighteen district educators who responded to the item, thirteen expressed this view: "People choosing leaders by voting" (male building administrator); "Democracy is a system of government in which the majority of people decide on the rules for everyone" (female teacher); and "Demos = People, Kraten = Rule; the people rule, majority rules" (female teacher). Offered by four respondents, the second most common response centered on the phrase *government by the people and for the people.* A building administrator offered a singular variation: "A system in which differing views/backgrounds/beliefs work together for the common good of the people." Eight respondents elaborated on their views, indicating feelings of concern, especially that the dominance of moneyed special interest groups has moved government ever further away from the people and their lives.

Respondents reported very little personal participation in political activity. All but one respondent stated that he or she often or "all of the time" voted. But not a single respondent reported being "very actively engaged in democracy." Of the twenty-one respondents, fourteen said they belonged to a political party, but not one respondent said party membership was very important to him or her. Some were party members only because membership was a requirement to vote in primary elections. Consistent with the shared view of the meaning of democracy, for most of them active political participation was defined as making an effort to "be current and informed and to vote." One specified, "I stay in touch with the news, locally, nationally, and worldwide. I try to keep myself up to date with what is happening." Not one respondent mentioned participating in party caucuses. Two noted placing candidate signs on their property as evidence for being "more actively engaged" in politics.

A series of questions were asked about participants' views of the health of American democracy. Three indicated that they *disagree* or *strongly disagree* while nine said they *agree* or *strongly agree* with the statement that "racial or ethnic minorities are fully part of the US democracy." When given the statement that there "exists equality of opportunity for persons in the US," fourteen agreed or strongly agreed, while only three disagreed or strongly disagreed. All respondents believed that *sometimes* ($n = 4$), *most of the time* ($n = 11$), or *always* ($n = 6$), "teachers should strive to promote understanding of democratic citizenship in students."

Views of social justice varied dramatically. There was basic agreement on importance: Of eighteen respondents, fourteen believed that "issues of social justice" are *very* or *extremely* important to democracy. However, one respondent thought they were *very unimportant.* Drawing on the metaphor of "life as a race," a female district administrator commented, "We look out for those who begin the race with a disadvantage in hopes that they can complete the race. Fair? Not everyone thinks so. But it's an attempt to improve [things] for everyone." A male teacher wrote simply, though perhaps a little cynically, that social justice is "getting what you deserve." A female teacher was critical of the concept, even as she noted its importance: "Socialist term meaning equality for everyone, basically. I don't agree with it." A school administrator offered, "Everyone gets the same shot." Beneath the diversity of statements was a widely shared view of the importance of equal opportunity, although long-standing inequalities were generally ignored.

Discussions: Thin and Thick Democracy, Fairness and Justice

Findings from research by the GDDRP proved helpful for thinking about the associates' early views of democratic citizenship and education. "Through the notion of *thin* versus *thick* democracy, the GDDRP conceptualizes the visible tension between the superficial features often associated with teaching *about* democracy . . . and the fundamental scaffolding which permits people to appropriate the deeper meaning of teaching *for* democracy across the curriculum" (Zyngier, 2013, pp. 8–9). The distinction, as Zyngier drew it, represents three different "core assumptions" about democratic citizenship and its responsibilities, a continuum: "[The] *personally responsible citizen* solves social problems and improves society, by having a good character; they must be honest, responsible, and law-abiding members of the community. The *participatory citizen* solves social problems and improves society through active participation and leadership within established systems and community structures. Finally, the *justice oriented citizen* solves social problems and improves society by questioning, challenging and changing established systems and structures when they reproduce patterns of injustice over time" (p. 9). Calling for a more "engaged" citizenship (p. 17), thick democracy "goes beyond the championing of electoral and legislative processes, rule of law, and basic civil rights" mentioned most often by survey respondents. "It acknowledges the legitimacy of collective citizen and civil action as external to government and business. . . . It is a commitment to individual and collective agency that ensures inclusiveness" (Zyngier, 2012a, p. 81). Further, the aim is to provide students with experience in democratic living and knowledge that will "shape a more democratically literate, engaged, and inclusive society—rather than [merely] teaching *about* democracy" (Zyngier, Traverso, & Murriello, 2015, p. 4).

As has been evident, participants in the Associates group began the year with a rather "thin" conception of democracy. When they thought of democracy at all, their conception, drawing on Woodruff's (2005) argument, confused the "doubles" (e.g., voting, majority rule, and elected representation [pp. 10–15]) with the concept itself. Something more is required, as our analysis has indicated.

Just as democracy is often understood by educators *thinly*, as essentially passive, as Zyngier and his colleagues concluded (2015, p. 8), social justice is similarly often misunderstood. In exploring the relationship between fairness and justice, Woodruff (2011) offered helpful perspective on what was said: "Fairness and justice are truly at war with one another. Fairness is not wise. Fairness is following principles wherever they may lead. . . . Fairness is a trap in which justice and compassion die. . . . Yet fairness has often been thought to be the heart of justice. This cannot be correct. The heart of justice is wisdom" (pp. 62–63). Fairness imposes rules—outcomes must be equal, procedures the same. Justice requires a higher standard, one that speaks to compassion, as Woodruff explains:

> Justice is a kind of human wisdom that is shared by members of a community. When justice is present, the community has the capacity to settle disputes in such a way that anger goes away, or at least that anger falls back far enough that the members of the community can work together. That succeeds only when the individuals involved have justice in their souls. . . . In a soul where the wisdom of justice is present, compassion and respect are there too; they are a moderating influence on the springs of anger, on the love of honor, and on the fear of shame. . . . [It] is justice [we hope for in] our everyday lives. (pp. 63–64)

Using the three categories of democratic "thickness," we call for movement toward more participatory, dialogic, and eventually justice-oriented conceptions of democracy and forms of citizenship. Such movement, as Zyngier (2013) argued, is difficult in part because educators "own school biographies" (p. 15) and experience proves limiting. Yet such movement is essential to doing the work of democratic education, as ultimately it is for the health of the nation.

End-of-Year Survey and Interview: Changes in Views

An anonymous survey to be analyzed statistically was sent electronically to each participant in the Associates group after the last session. Respondents used a five-point scale from *strongly disagree* (1) to *strongly agree* (5). Items probed individuals' experiences: "I understand the purposes of the [partnership]" ($M = 4.64$). Subsequent questions included the following: "I feel our institutional participation in the partnership is worthwhile" ($M = 4.72$); "My commitment to the role of public education in our nation has increased" ($M = 4.64$); "I have changed or altered some behavior in my employment responsibility" ($M = 4.42$). Questions also were asked about the effectiveness or value of various aspects of the sessions; the same scale was used. These items and results were typical: discussions about readings ($M = 4.84$); group discussions/conversations ($M = 4.92$); small-group interaction ($M = 4.72$). The outcomes were indeed very positive.

Twenty-two participants (excluding the university group) were interviewed by the research assistant who had conducted the interviews at the beginning of the study. Some of the questions were chosen to get at understanding participants' feelings about the commitments. Questions were different from but complementary to those on the final survey:

- "What are two big ideas, important concepts, or strong conclusions you have taken away from your participation in Associates?"
- "What is the purpose of public schooling in America?"
- "What was the best thing about your participation in Associates this year?"
- "Would you want to participate again?"
- "Do you plan to do anything different next year because of your participation in Associates?"
- "If you could change anything about your experience in the Associates program, what would it be?"

Analysis of the interview responses revealed very strong themes with little variation, similar to the survey results. "Big ideas" identified by the participants frequently connected to one of the Five Commitments (which were used to organize the sessions): citizenship; equitable access to knowledge; nurturing pedagogy; stewardship of public education; and personal, partnership, and institutional renewal.

The respondents were asked to identify an activity or "source" for the concepts they mentioned. Specific readings were often mentioned as influential. Speaking about the moral responsibility and the importance of their personal stewardship for public education, two respondents, for example, said they were strongly influenced by having read *Lest Innocent Blood Be Shed* (1994), by Philip Hallie, a story of how the inhabitants of a small protestant French village came together during World War II to protect the lives of refugees seeking safety in Switzerland. Three respondents pointed to *Education for Everyone* (Goodlad et al., 2004) as strongly influencing their thinking about renewal and the social aims of public schooling. A teacher remarked about equitable access, "I read *Out of My Mind* [Draper, 2010]. . . . That really . . . opened my eyes to the challenges [my kids that have IEPs] are facing."

Some respondents mentioned specific activities that influenced their thinking. For example, a teacher said a clip from the movie *Radio* underscored for her the power of nurturing pedagogy to change lives; the film portrays a true story about Coach Harold Jones, who befriended "Radio," a mentally disabled African American student, showing the effects that a simple act of decency had on an entire community.

Most responses were more general, however. Every interview respondent mentioned being strongly influenced by the "conversation," "dialogue," "talk," "small group interaction," sharing of "different perspectives on something great," and simply "being with [other associates]." Talk about the importance of building relationships pervaded the interviews. When asked what they considered the "best thing" about participating in Associates, respondents consistently mentioned "getting to know other educators," forming friendships, reading and conversing about important ideas, and getting to "chew on stuff and come back and talk about it." A teacher remarked, "I feel a lot more connected in a broader circle [of educators] than just [with those at] my school. I feel like I have connection points; that was really cool." Another teacher said, "[I feel] I'm not out there alone."

Some mentioned feeling renewed, energized, and strengthened in their commitment to teaching; one teacher said he felt he had been given a "refresher about why I became a teacher in the first place." Similarly, a secondary teacher commented, "It renewed my sense of commitment to education . . . it kind of confirmed to me that I was doing something meaningful, and that was the reason I had chosen this career path in the first place: [to] do something that [is] worthwhile." All said they would gladly participate in Associates again if the opportunity presented itself: "Yeah, absolutely!"

In contrast to the results from the initial survey and interview, at the end of the Associates sessions twenty of twenty-two educators interviewed spoke, many of them eloquently, about the importance of teaching *for* democracy. Strong evidence of their understanding of democracy becoming "thicker" was found. One teacher seemed surprised at the thinness she discovered in her friends and colleagues: "One of the big ideas I took away from Associates was just how important it is for there to be a public dialogue or conversation about the purposes of education . . . [I've] started asking parents, moms in my neighborhood, 'What is it exactly you're hoping for from your kid's education?' It's funny, they always give me these vague answers. . . . [No one] mentioned . . . preparing people to be citizens in a democracy." Others agreed with this teacher's emphasis on the role of schools in preparing students for democratic citizenship. When asked to state the purpose of public education, an assistant principal turned to page 35 of *Education for Everyone* (Goodlad et al., 2004) and began reading a quotation from political scientist Benjamin Barber: "Public schools are not merely schools for the public . . . but schools of publicness: institutions where we learn what it means to be a public and start down the road toward common national and civic identity. They are the forges of our citizenship and the bedrock of our democracy." A male school teacher remarked, "Public education's purpose is to inform students of what democracy looks like, feels like, acts like."

Follow-Up Survey: New Year, New Responsibilities, New Perspectives

A month into the following school year, five months after this group of Associates was finished, we emailed a brief survey to the school and district participants. After we had sent three reminders, we received twenty responses. The survey items requested that respondents (a) define/describe democracy, (b) briefly discuss whether participation in Associates had affected their thinking or practice, and (c) indicate (*yes* or *no*) whether their school sponsored a school-based Associates, and if so whether they were participating.

Responses to the first item were consistent with a "thickening" and deepening of participants' understanding of democracy and its educational importance. Many respondents focused on aspects of communication and/or civility. Concluding her definition, for example, one teacher wrote, "It is the idea of coming together to benefit the common good of the community, not necessarily through political means [like voting], but through social circles and other forms of important communication." Another teacher stated, "Democracy encourages dialogue. Differences should be discussed and all sides of an argument should be considered with an open mind."

Some focused on how we ought to treat one another. A principal concluded that democracy demands that "[we] take care of everyone"; a vice principal commented on the requirement for greater "equity." Another teacher focused on the importance of respecting differences in opinion: "[Democracy] involves involvement. It allows for everyone's voice to be heard, for the 'common good.' [It] requires respect, because in order for a democracy to work people need to work together for a common goal. It [requires] suspending judgment and allowing disagreement to happen. It [encourages] dialogue." With a handful of exceptions, procedural views of democratic citizenship were replaced by more complex understanding, often touching on what we have described as democratic manners. The nature of the contributions shows the depth of participants' thinking. They noted the importance of participating more fully in decision making, respecting differences and "appreciating others' perspectives," caring for and listening to others' *voices*, recognizing the centrality of dialogue, solving problems together in the community to achieve common interests, and, in the words of one teacher, being "willing to make personal sacrifices for the good of [the] community."

Three themes emerged from reading the responses to the second item, whether there had been any lingering effects of the Associates experience on their thinking or practice. Several respondents noted gains in *understanding the bigger picture* of the purposes of public education, including those represented in the Five Commitments, and of the challenges involved in achieving "equal access to knowledge." As one teacher wrote, she better understood "the barriers [to learning] my students may be facing and ways to break down [those] barriers."

Another theme cutting across the responses was *greater awareness*, which included the importance of strengthening relationships with parents and increasing community engagement in schooling. In addition, several teachers said their *confidence* in themselves as educators and their *commitment* to teaching were given "a boost." While these generalities are consequential outcomes, of the twenty respondents only four teachers and a principal mentioned specific activities that had been inspired by their Associates participation. These findings suggest a taming of participants' ambitions for change once the new school year with all its busyness was under way.

Those who *were* making changes in their practice shared some of their efforts. Concern for reaching out personally to students was attributed by two teachers to increased awareness developed in Associates. One teacher explained that she had adjusted her planning for instruction to be more attentive to access issues, particularly for children who were struggling. Another wrote that she had been focusing on being more "engaging" as a teacher and making the classroom more "nurturing."

Two additional teachers reported increased awareness of the need for more specific efforts to expand community involvement. One of these teachers wrote, "I am trying to find ways to reach beyond the school sphere and into the [wider] community." To that end, she volunteered to "help lead" an after-school program that "has been great for our school and community." The second teacher said she had increased her efforts to communicate better with the community, to show she was "willing to LISTEN to their concerns and questions." The elementary principal explained how he was changing his school culture by "incorporating the Associates teaching model (with its emphasis on reading and conversation) into the professional development activities."

Responses to the third question, whether or not a teacher's or building administrator's school was sponsoring an Associates program, were complicated by four respondents having been reassigned to different schools. Of the original six schools represented in the Associates group, two—one an elementary and the other a middle school—had Associates programs. Three elementary schools and the high school did not, but that was about to change. One of the Associates participants from the high school said he approached the principal to ask about whether such a program would be made available. He was assigned to start one. Of participants who were moved to a new school, a teacher who is now a new vice principal in a middle school reported that the school has such a program, as does the school of a transferred elementary school teacher. A participating principal whose school had not sponsored a study group suggested he might begin one. We will return to the place of the school-level Associates meetings shortly.

Analysis of the Observation Notes: Participant Observation Themes

Analysis of the observation notes, which included a large number of verbatim quotations, involved making comparisons across the five Associates meetings, noting not only what was said, but the language used and the nature or quality of the interactions. Three themes emerged: strengthening intimacy, leveling established hierarchies and practicing hospitality, and developing a common language.

Intimacy

The first session began with considerable uncertainty. As noted previously, participants were quite confused about what the purpose of Associates was and why each person had been invited to participate. As the description of the first gathering suggests, conversation and dialogue were emphasized from the beginning. Trusting relationships quickly formed.

By the second session, evidence of trusting and being trusted was abundant. "I want you to think back to your experiences with school: When you first started school, what were the barriers you brought with you to school?" The discussion that followed was poignant and powerful, and the comments made were honest and heartfelt. An elementary teacher spoke openly about how her "alcoholic father" had hurt the family and how she had developed strategies for protecting herself. Another teacher spoke of being terribly shy and of struggling to figure out "how things [in school] worked." A principal described the challenge of growing up as a military child, including his difficulty in moving from school to school and making friends. A district administrator described his academic struggles, and one of the facilitators told of the frustration he had felt in trying to learn to read. A charge was then given: "Self-reflect: How did I overcome one of [my] barriers?"

The personal examples helped participants connect emotionally with other group members, as well to the topics to be discussed. Transition followed, and the group generalized to discussing the barriers children face in school and the importance of maximizing access to knowledge. District statistics on poverty rates and academic achievement underscored the challenges of achieving greater equity. Conversation was open, lively, and appropriately intimate.

In the third session during a table discussion, an elementary teacher spoke tearfully of having just attended the funeral of a first grade child in her school. Shaken, she needed to speak, and everyone at the table listened empathetically.

Hierarchy and Hospitality

The three facilitators were or had been high-level district administrators. In addition, the group included two university faculty members, an assistant dean, and an academic institute administrator. There were eleven teachers, seven school building administrators, and additional district administrators. Such perceived status differences often underpin assumed differences in the right to speak, as Oakeshott (1991) warned.

While role differences were evident in how issues were conceived and discussed, the conversational norms set in the first meeting and reinforced across all sessions were maintained: most notably, "Listen to each other's ideas with respect." Attention to differences in background and experience faded as conversation focused on a third thing, as discussed in the introduction and chapter 2: a "great thing" that "holds both me and thee accountable to something beyond ourselves" (Palmer, 1998, p. 117). For those in this group, that third thing was the readings and, more broadly, the project of partnership and renewal.

A third "thing" and a written norm to be respectful of others and listen to others, however, do not guarantee openness in conversation. Something more is required, as we discussed in chapters 3 and 4. That something more is hospitality, an active reaching out to embrace the other and the other's worldview. As Freire (1998) observed, "No one knows it all; no one is ignorant of everything. We all know something; we are all ignorant of something" (p. 208). Being blinded results in stupidity; the flattening of hierarchies opens the possibility of learning. A telling moment came during the fourth Associates meeting when a university professor made a comment and without hesitating a teacher piped up, "I beg to differ," and gave reasons for his disagreement with what the professor had said. He had a point. The two disagreed, but both listened.

Common Language

From the first to the last interview, from the first to the last survey, the language of the participants changed. Over time, as was readily apparent in the observation notes, the shared vocabulary of partnering swelled and appeared to deepen: *democracy, access, nurturing pedagogy, stewardship, simultaneous renewal*. Each concept cut across differences in experience, as reflected in the many and diverse assigned readings, and touched down for most participants in personally profound ways, as acknowledged in self-report. Opportunities provided for self-reflecting were intended to help make the connections which vivify the first of the "habits of heart" (Palmer, 2011) noted above, "an understanding that we are all in this together" (p. 44). Conversation, as we have discussed, requires a shared language, and common speech is best built by sharing a commons, a place in time and over time for sharing experiences. An elementary teacher touched on the power of the Associates' commons when she wrote, "I loved the group that we were with. . . . I loved going away and staying in nice places. It gave me a chance to put my worries and cares aside and focus [on something important]."

Forging a shared language fashions another sort of commons—a commons that is conceptual. A conceptual commons sets terms of community membership and provides passageways for forming and transforming identity. It mediates relationships and, as participants said on the last day of the final session, Associates is all about relationship building: "The biggest thing I'll take away is the [importance] of relationships!" Thus the changes in awareness and understanding, supported by changes in language, are important participation outcomes: indications of changes in consciousness, in personal theories of good educational practice, and in imagination.

Problems, Processes, and First Principles

In the year-end interview we asked participants, "If you could change anything about your experience in Associates, what would it be?" Everyone was very positive, each pleased to have been invited to participate: "I don't think they should change a thing. It was great. All of the locations were great. All of the readings were great, and the presenters . . . fabulous."

However, eleven respondents offered suggestions for improvements of various kinds. A high school teacher said she would have appreciated spending more time with her colleagues in the school, which has a very large faculty. A principal echoed this desire: "There were a lot of times that we weren't able to discuss how [a particular concept] was going to apply within our everyday work at our building." A few remarked that "some of the readings got a little long" and, as another teacher observed, some were dated. But as a teacher who had commented on the dates of some readings said, "Other[s], like Goodlad for example, [are] seminal. Not going to change, true now just as they were [when written]." The later remark strikes us as compelling. But we wonder what makes a reading seminal.

A teacher and a university faculty member commented on having inadequate time to discuss each reading or process some of the movie clips. "I don't want to sound critical, but over and over again it felt like we had to move on when we were really still in the midst of [talking about] important things." After saying that, she commented that she "love[d] all the people involved, I know them all and I love them, they're good people." Another university participant felt what was needed "was really careful simplicity and [greater] focus."

Reviewing the observations notes, a pervasive sense of being rushed, of urgency to get from one activity or one reading or topic to another is evident. Clearly, moving conversation to dialogue requires slow time—time to ponder, focus, reflect, explore, and test ideas and understandings. Good thinking takes time (see the conclusion). With time and engagement, language sharpens and ideas become clearer and richer, more memorable and more useful. Personal relationships deepen. The danger in being rushed, of having too much to read and too much to discuss and too little time, is that chatter may replace conversation and conversation may masquerade as dialogue. All forms of interaction are potentially pleasurable, but all are not equally powerful educationally.

Looking Ahead

The reading list was long, in part from having increased over time; as with all curriculum building, addition is easier than subtraction of content. Some readings have proved to be more timely, powerful, and deserving of careful consideration than others; but timeliness is not a function of publication date. Focus and profundity determine timeliness. As one of the teachers was quoted as saying, Goodlad's writings, for example, "felt timeless." Additionally, some issues would have been illuminated by select research studies, particularly in seeking to frame issues and to begin thinking about possibilities, but such readings must prove themselves worthy of space on a rather small bookshelf. Simply put, less is apt to be more.

The wider issue speaks to the larger civic and professional purposes of Associates, and here we return to the discussion of the themes of *awareness* and *understanding* noted earlier. Associates might be thought of as providing a broad and general introduction to a set of educational issues that are terribly important but too seldom discussed. It might also be thought of as a break, an opportunity to get away and talk—renewing, as many said—and that alone is worthwhile.

There is no doubt, greater awareness and increased understanding of the purposes and possibilities of public education represent important Associates aims. As the data indicate, participants experienced a great deal of growth in awareness and understanding, as well as development of new relationships and of feelings of being connected to the worthy moral enterprise of education. Associates was, in fact, energizing and fun. Moreover, conceptions of democracy became thicker and more closely connected to schooling in the minds of virtually every participant. A lot was accomplished, but there are limits to what can be achieved in two-day sessions occurring five times across a school year, as good as the model already is—especially when compared to other more common forms of professional development. As a seasoned veteran elementary principal wrote in the year-end evaluation, "This has been the very best professional development I have ever had."

Most of the elements that make professional development effective, as discussed in chapter 4, were present in Associates: participants sharing a work context and a common set of issues came together; the work took place over an extended period of time, with strong administrative support; and time was provided for meetings (Garet et al., 2001). Yet comments from two teachers raised an insistent set of issues. One teacher wrote in her response to the email survey sent after the new school year began, "I can't say that I consciously think about what I learned in Associates frequently." Already, memories of her experience in Associates, which she had earlier described in very positive terms, were fading. A second teacher commented that she was concerned about follow-up: "The question [is] 'What now?' You know, I could choose to put everything on my bookshelf and just leave it alone, or I could choose to do something specific.... What now?"

In support of learning, effective professional development must be sustained over time. Associates ended. What now? A middle school teacher wisely said, "Renewal is a living idea ... a way of being; we don't become renewed, it's a process." Like conversation, the challenge of professional development is to keep it going. The point was made by Goodlad as he developed and discussed the idea of renewal, the topic of the fifth and final session for this group. "Things left uncared-for tend to deteriorate.... Educational renewal is primarily designed to do two things. First, it is designed generally to prevent present conditions from deteriorating and to address problems that arise. But because schools are not yet—nor are they likely to ever be—good enough simply to maintain, renewal is, second, designed to make it possible to effect changes and to sustain those changes that prove desirable" (Goodlad et al., 2004, p. 102). The task, then, is to extend the boundaries of the commons first staked out by Associates into the schools and to keep the conversation going. District-level Associates groups and other partnership activities need to be linked to ongoing and expanded school-level Associates, an opportunity that all teachers said they would welcome.

The "thickening" of the associates' understanding of democracy presents a challenge and offers an opportunity. If Foa and Mounk were right about the deconsolidation of Western democracies, and if—as Jefferson, Tocqueville, Mann, Dewey, and Goodlad (and many others) believed—social and political democracies derive from the democratic character of their citizens, and if the "last best hope" to instill this character is our schools, then the initial and rather "thin" understanding of democratic values held by the associates casts doubt on our democratic future. How can our schools incubate democratic relationships and encourage support of and engagement in democratic institutions if our teachers' understanding is so thin? But we see an opportunity: that a comparatively small investment in time and money over one year in the Associates program has such a profoundly deepening effect on our colleagues' understanding of democracy and its essential connection to schooling is cause for optimism.

The study reported in this chapter leads to two conclusions. First, the experience of this group demonstrated that understanding and embracing the democratic purposes of schooling do not come naturally to most educators, who, quite understandably, get consumed with the business of teaching and in their busyness may neglect thinking of the expansive *whys* behind their practice. Second and consequently, schools will fulfill their democratic purposes better to the degree that educators (teacher education students, in-service teachers, administrators, teacher educators, and arts and sciences faculty who teach most of the university courses taken by preservice teachers) regularly engage with principles like those explored and celebrated in this book and with people who will share their quest for wisdom.

When left to ourselves, we humans tend to think only in terms of our personal geographies. But seldom being alone, educators are tugged in a different direction, to which both in-service and preservice teacher education must sensitively respond. We have argued for the importance of hospitality and commons enabling individuals to learn and develop as educators. Commons are places where robust dialogue is supported and expected, and they must also be places of contemplation, reflection, and, as we have suggested, communion—hence places that are renewing. Within commons, which may take many forms besides the Associates model, the human conversation finds place and beckons us to open ourselves to learning.

Conclusion

. . . .

Stewardship and
Moral Posture

> We have no need to contrive and dabble
> at "the future of the human race"; we
> have the same pressing need that we have
> always had—to love, care for, and teach
> our children.
> —Wendell Berry

In the twelfth century, architects, masons, excavators, bankers, storekeepers, farmers, blacksmiths, clerics, tailors, and many others started work on a bell tower for the cathedral church in Pisa. They were entirely dependent on each other to complete the project (which lasted for two centuries): architects required masons to cut and place stone; masons needed tools manufactured by smiths; smiths and masons purchased supplies from shopkeepers, who in turn relied on farmers and tailors (and others) to stock their shelves; bankers addressed the earthly contingencies and clerics took care of the eternal ones. Like a Jenga tower, remove a piece and introduce instability; remove many pieces and the structure collapses.

The plan called for an eight-story structure reaching a height of 183 feet. It is one of Europe's most elegant Romanesque monuments. It is famous, however, because it leans, and it leans because its foundation is too thin and the subsoil unstable (due to a fluctuating water table). The tower is unique because "it is a failure that has been occurring essentially on a continuous basis for more than

800 years. . . . What is significant however is that finally, after 8 centuries, the condition of the tower has been improved in a controlled fashion" (Education Committee of the Technical Council on Forensic Engineering, 1992, p. 3). The tower is famous for what it is not (straight) rather than for what it is (beautiful).

Our civic institutions are leaning, too, and have been leaning for some time. The argument of this book is that thin democracy and unstable democratic manners are partly responsible, and that public schools partnered with universities are uniquely situated to help correct and contain "in a controlled fashion" precarious civic leanings. In support of that argument we have convened thinkers ancient and modern, from right to left, from home and abroad, and distilled the behaviors and dispositions that students must model and must embrace in order to thicken democracy and brace public institutions.

Thick democracy and stable democratic manners rise from a foundation of attentive caring (see Weil in chapter 2), what Noddings (2010) calls *engrossment*, that often results in "motivational displacement; that is, the motive energy of the carer flows toward the needs of the cared-for. Temporarily the carer's own projects are set aside" (p. 48). The setting aside is not a renouncement but a deferral and an opening, facilitated by hospitality, conversation, and dialogue that in turn lead to pedagogical nurturing. Setting aside is the movement required for connection within the commons, and as Wendel Berry (1992) wrote, "the real name of our connection to this everywhere different and differently named earth is 'work.'"

> We are connected by work even to the places where we don't work, for all places are connected; it is clear by now that we cannot exempt one place from our ruin of another. The name of our proper connection to the earth is "good work," for good work involves much giving of honor. It honors the source of its materials; it honors the place where it is done; it honors the art by which it is done; it honors the thing that it makes and the user of the made thing. Good work is always modestly scaled, for it cannot ignore either the nature of individual places or the differences between places, and it always involves a sort of religious humility, for not everything is known. Good work can be defined only in particularity, for it must be defined a little differently for every one of the places and every one of the workers on the earth. (p. 35)

Berry's primary interest is natural ecology; ours is the civic ecology of relations that constitute what happens in and out of schools and in teacher education institutions. What Berry calls "good work" we call *stewardship*—the setting aside of immediate interests in favor of a bigger and more enduring project, and of coming to understand the self as servant. For that reason, we offer a brief discussion of stewardship as a *summa* that brings this book to a close.

Stewardship and the Tangled Bank

In the conclusion to *On the Origin of Species*, Charles Darwin (1876) drew a word landscape that portrayed his views on natural selection and evolution. It has since become a metaphor for the complex natural interrelationships studied in the field of ecology.

> It is interesting to contemplate a tangled bank, clothed with many plants of many kinds, with birds singing on the bushes, with various insects flitting about, and with worms crawling through the damp earth, and to reflect that these elaborately constructed forms, so different from each other, and dependent upon each other in so complex a manner, have all been produced by laws acting around us. . . . There is grandeur in this view of life, with its several powers, having been originally breathed by the Creator into a few forms or into one; and that, whilst this planet has gone circling on according to the fixed law of gravity, from so simple a beginning endless forms most beautiful and most wonderful have been, and are being evolved. (p. 430)

Darwin began this poetic description by alluding to "a bank"—the definite article (*a*) preceding a singular noun (*bank*) points to something unitary, one thing. Reading on, we discover that this bank, like a databank, holds an astonishing variety of assets: many varieties of birds and bushes, multiple species of insects and worms, each an individual organism, but all "dependent upon each other in so complex a manner." Unlike the orderly stacking of geologic strata, Darwin's bank is "tangled": its parts cannot be separated without changing their nature. Existence is coexistence: we are a part, not apart. Like partnering, ecology is relational not ideological.

In the organizations where we spend much of our time and effort, we often lose sight of the connections, particularly in organizing education in which the real and sometimes overwhelming demands of the classroom or scholarship leave little time for understanding and attending to the educational project as a whole (or of schooling itself in the wider democratic project). But *educational stewards* understand that all teaching is relational—ecological, to return to the Darwin text: what we do in our third grade class affects what the fourth grade teacher will do next year; an introductory college history course is part of something bigger than ourselves; students make sense of their studies not as an accumulation of disconnected academic units, but as a broadly cultural and very personal experience. The assumption of the autonomy of the classroom is a false and dangerous myth.

An example from the American jazz tradition is useful for thinking about the tangled nature of teaching: "There is an inherent tension within the jazz ensemble between the individual and the group. On the one hand, the aesthetic of music is centered on the inventiveness and uniqueness of individual solo expression; on the other, climactic moments of musical expression require the cohesiveness and participation of the entire ensemble. In an improvisational music, such as jazz, the interaction between the group and individual greatly affects the ultimate compositions and development of the music" (Monson, 1996, 66–67). Teaching is typically thought of as a solo activity: it is our class, our space, our pedagogy. One of the most difficult concepts for educators to grasp is that what I do is a part of a bigger project (derived from attentiveness); that what my students' experience in my class affects what happens in other classes; that my influence on a child or student is one of many influences. Thus, in healthy school and college ecologies we experience a social osmosis as we move from our role as a soloist to obligations as a member of an ensemble. Our friend and colleague Greg Clark (2015) has pointed out how this oscillation between the performance of a soloist and the ensemble in jazz is itself a model of democratic discourse, of the art "getting along" (p. 21).

Thinking ecologically forces the realization that systems typically have "many heads" (Andrews, 1987, p. 155) that defy the vertical, hierarchical structure of most organizations. Look at an ordinary organizational chart and note how relationships are portrayed as descending from top to bottom, while horizontal relationships are largely elided. But, in fact, "the world of work consists mostly of horizontal relationships" (Cleveland, 1985, p. 9). Vertical structures appear to control only the flow of information. Knowledge in healthy organizations is radically defused; people inevitably fill gaps in even the most carefully crafted job descriptions, else nothing works quite right (Wenger, 1998). If we were to imagine the organisms of Darwin's tangled bank as conscious, we might find that the bushes and bees, birds and worms are unaware of their interdependence, the bees so focused on their beeing that they cannot perceive the complexity of relationships that surrounds and sustains them. Or, perhaps, more often, the bees and bugs perceive the complexity primarily in terms of competition. So it is in schools and colleges where programs, grade-level, and disciplinary differences often bolstered by specialized languages and conflicting status claims produce vertical separations. Work comes to be experienced as compartmentalized, marked off by fixed borders. Such ruptures in horizontal relationships can be mended only through reminders that while we are "so different from each other," we are also "dependent on each other in so complex a manner" (in Darwin's words), and this is why we must partner. "The ability of a school to exhibit strong resilience is enhanced by the ability of school people to . . . act collaboratively from a transdisciplinary viewpoint, cutting across compartmentalized vested interests, seeking new syntheses for the meaning of knowledge from various frames of reference" (Henshaw, Wilson, & Morefield, 1987, p. 146). Once again, "we are all in this together" (Palmer, 2011, p. 44).

Stewardship and Time

Stewardship, the fourth Moral Dimension, being a form of representation, is closely related to the workings of representative democracy. The steward stands in place of another: the owner of a vineyard or a hereditary estate, the regent who stands for the monarch until she or he comes of age, the congressional representative or the board member. If educators are stewards of schools, whom do they represent? The answer of course is "the people." But who are the people? Children enrolled in the school. Their parents. Everyone in the community. But there is something more, because the interests of these groups—legitimate in demanding our best attention—are nevertheless contextually contingent.

Stewards attend to that context, but also look ahead. It is only in the long view that we can hope to represent and thus to be stewards of "We the People," understood as our neighbors, friends, and students and as an ideal: the people now and the people we imagine in the future (as we cannot conceive of future generations as anything but products of our imagination). Imagining is central to stewardship, and it is possible only when we care as deeply about imagined future generations as we do about our own. Stewardship requires long-view thinking. Stewart Brand (2000) contended that "rigorous long-view thinking makes responsibility taking inevitable because it responds to the slower, deeper feedback loops of the whole society and the natural world" (p. 18), and to illustrate, he offers the following tale from Marco Polo's travels to China:

> In the city of Tinju, they make bowls of porcelain, large and small, of incomparable beauty. They are made nowhere else except in this city, and from here are exported all over the world. . . . These dishes are made of a crumbly earth or clay which is dug as though from a mine and then stacked in huge mounds and left for thirty or forty years exposed to wind, rain, and sun. By this time the earth is so refined that dishes made of it are of an azure tint with a very brilliant sheen. You must understand that when a man makes a mound of this earth he does so for his children; the time of maturing is so long that he cannot hope to draw any profit from it himself or put it to use, but the son who succeeds him will reap the profit. (Brand, 2000, p. 53)

Today's moral stewards live in the information age, the age of tweets and screens and compressed news cycles; their students are so immersed in the pace of consumption (of information and of things) that they are often unaware that there are alternatives to this way of being. That is why educators as stewards, regardless of the courses they teach, must also be broadly educated. To be generally (or liberally) educated is to nurture an informed historical consciousness that recognizes that "the accumulated past is life's best resource for innovation" (Brand, 2000, p. 75). Historical consciousness forces us to see ourselves as the consequence of decisions made centuries ago, and to recognize ourselves as generators of what comes after.

In 1794, German philosopher Johann Gottlieb Fichte delivered a series of talks to young men who were preparing to become teachers, and he reminded them, "When I teach you I am most probably teaching unborn millions. Some among you may be well enough disposed toward me to imagine that I sense the dignity of my own special vocation, that the highest aim of my reflections and teaching will be to contribute toward advancing culture and elevating humanity in you and in all those people with whom you come into contact, and that I consider all philosophy and science which do not aim at this goal to be worthless" (1987, p. 10). Teachers who model this long view of human experience are not just stewards, but framers of future stewards who must also conceive of themselves in the "long now."

Stewardship of Mind and Memory

Long-view thinking suggests that the first claim of stewardship is to our own mind: teachers must "possess or acquire the literacy and critical-thinking abilities associated with the concept of an educated person" (Goodlad, 1994, p. 82). Transformative teachers understand the syntax of teaching: they do not teach math to students; they teach students math (students are always the direct object of our teaching and professing). Doing so requires seeing the student as more than a learner of a narrow discipline, and the discipline as more than a fixed body of knowledge. Both student and discipline are living, growing, changing. If they are to meet, the teacher must know both the student and the discipline from the inside, and in relationship to one another, which is what is meant by pedagogical content knowledge.

Seeing students as learners involves seeing them in many ways: in relation to the disciplines but most especially as educated citizens, and that broader perspective demands that teachers themselves model stewardship of the mind. A teacher we know in Massachusetts understands this: "I have learned that the best way to stay fresh in the field, to get the most, and give the most, is to continue my own process of learning and skill development. I have been fortunate enough to partake in travel, classes, seminars, workshops which have helped me change my own curriculum and contribute ideas, methods, and materials to colleagues in the field, and towards the continual growth of world languages in my community." A senior colleague in Tennessee contributed this perspective: "In ten years I will achieve the necessary age to leave the . . . classroom. I want these to be my best teaching years rather than my least effective. I do not want wobbly-arm writing on the board as a legacy. It is my time to study, to explore, and to discover." Stewards of the mind read, in and out of their disciplines, newspapers, magazines, history, biography. As students of teaching (chapter 6), their instructional empathy relies on making sure their own learning keeps pace with what they expect of their students.

Stewardship of the mind expresses itself in critical inquiry—in educators' curiosity about the nature and the effects of their practice (on the student and on the school). They understand that the schools and universities that hire them will not be the same ones that retire them (even if they spend their whole career in the same building). Schools evolve, and stewardly teachers want their school to evolve *because of* them, not *in spite of* them.

Stewardship of mind always and essentially engages *collective memory*, in at least two ways. First, partnering builds and is built on collective memory of shared activities and commitments. There is no partnership in the absence of memory, and effective partnerships are those that conscientiously curate an *archive* of the cultural artifacts they produce. That archive includes the names and writings of founders, the genealogy of core ideas and ideals, and the chronology of milestone events. "Social memory," Barbara Misztal (2003) has reminded us, is the "crucial condition of people relations, since both conflict and cooperation hinge upon it" (p. 14). Both conflict and cooperation are excavations of a shared past, and the fruitfulness of those excavations depends on the richness of the archive.

Partnerships require two types of archives. One is an authorized chronicle of partnership's activities—its official history. The other consists of the individual (usually informal) archives maintained by each participant. Chapters 1 and 2 draw on our archives. In healthy partnerships, the relationship between these two repositories is osmotic: the individual fills out her understanding of the shared past as she is exposed to its archive, and the official record is amended from time to time by the collected memories of individuals. The organization and the individuals who inhabit it must be stewards of shared experiences, each becoming a cultural genome of a shared past. Thus, collected memories and partnership histories need sharing and celebrating, for in the sharing partnerships and people are renewed.

Second, democratic institutions are as dependent on memory as are school/ university partnerships. Teachers, then, are not merely models of democratic manners; they are keepers and transmitters of democratic memory. When cultures were primarily oral, keepers of collective memory were critical for maintaining shared identity. Mnemosyne coupled with Zeus nine times, and from their union were born the nine classical muses, including Clio, the muse of history. Thus Mnemosyne (Memory) was invoked as the only way to generate and transmit the common experiences by which persons became a people. "The lack of interest *in* the past and the lack of knowledge *of* the past tend to be accompanied by authoritarian and utopian thinking and . . . 'the root of oppression is loss of memory'" (Gunn Allen, 1999, p. 589; qtd. in Misztal, 2003, pp. 14–15); we need to learn to "listen to the dead" (Grafton & Grossman,

2015, p. 37) because there is no other way to get an answer to the question of why things are as they are and to broaden the range of possible action. Bode (1937) took up this idea when he worried that thoughtful historical consciousness was being displaced by reductive bytes of information. "Our democratic institutions cannot be protected by the simple process of 'conditioning ourselves' to respond affirmatively to one set of slogans and negatively to those of . . . other movements. The idea of democracy will have to be examined and reinterpreted, in the light of rival concepts, so as to make it adequate for the conditions of present-day life" (p. 3). The sloganeering of the 1930s foreshadowed Twitter politics of our day. Not only are they bereft of history, they implicitly deny history and set us adrift. Unless educators are prepared to be the stewards of the past, our present will become unmoored.

Stewardship of Possibility

A few years ago the partnership dedicated one of its Leaders' Associates meetings to considering the commitment of "access to knowledge" in the context of the evolving demographic reality of our community—a community that had been both enriched and stretched by an unprecedented wave of mostly Hispanic immigration. Among our guests for that gathering were a mother and her primary school daughter. The mother spoke no English, and her young daughter served ably as her interpreter. The mother described her dreams for her family; the daughter, precociously poised and bright, shared her goal of becoming a doctor (an aspiration that for this family was like a moon shot). She was brimming with potential, but her family's poverty and their long-ago expired visa made these dreams all but impossible. For this family, as for many others, stingy possibility blocked ambitious potential.

Like Woodruff's (2005) urging us to "dream democracy," stewardship requires that we think about potential and possibility. Potential resides inside us, surrounded by possibility. We understand life to be just when potential and possibility exist in equal measure. For some, modest potential is awash in abundant possibility, and ample opportunity encourages every goal. For others, potential cannot or will not fill the space possibility offers it. We admire most those whose determination transcends meager possibility, and they surprise us with their accomplishments. Teachers often think about their students as "dwelling in possibility." The thought brings to mind the lines by American poet Emily Dickinson (1970), which offer a point of departure for considering just what possibilities lie ahead and what they might bring. Dickinson celebrated the infinite possibilities of poetry in contrast to the contingent limitations, the *rules*, of "Prose." However, the image of an expansive house of possibility also works as an inversion of the limited commons inhabited by many of our students and their families.

I dwell in Possibility—
A fairer House than Prose—
More numerous of Windows—
Superior—for Doors—

Of Chambers as the Cedars—
Impregnable of eye—
And for an everlasting Roof
The Gambrels of the Sky—

Of Visitors—the fairest—
For Occupation—This—
The spreading wide my narrow Hands
To gather Paradise— (pp. 483–484)

Many of our students live in commons that are unfinished houses of possibility. *Education* is a synonym for *possibility.* Democratic education is never solitary; it is an improvised dance between teacher and learner in which roles frequently and necessarily reverse. Seneca (1979) gave us the phrase *Homines dum docent discunt* (Men learn while they teach; p. 8), reminding us that we ultimately possess knowledge only in giving it away. As stewards of possibility, we learn and teach and create possibilities for others to learn and teach, in a round of expanding spheres.

The abstraction of the stewardship of possibility becomes concrete to the degree that we attend to the "gifts" of access to knowledge through pedagogical nurturing, as described in chapter 6. Access to all the subjects of the human conversation is necessary but not sufficient. For most students, mere exposure to the lessons and products of human experience is unlikely to produce the *character* required by thick democracy. Such deep learning involves what Gary Fenstermacher (1999) called "disciplined encounters" (p. 14), a phrase that captures much of the spirit of "pedagogical nurturing." Nurturing pedagogy is supportive but not soft; it is affirming, but less of the present than of the possibility (as beautifully illustrated in the story of Mr. Falker and Patricia Polacco retold in chapter 3). The moral stewardship represented by access to knowledge and pedagogical nurturing narrows the gap between potential and possibility and this, we believe, is what is meant when a student recognizes a teacher as being caring and respectful.

Stewardship and Democratic Character

The stewardship to which we aspire is expressed by the fundamental principles discussed in this book: hospitality, conversation, dialogue, a healthy commons, shared experiences, and *virtuous* listening that makes speaking meaningful. Only educators who understand these principles and consciously work to internalize them can be effective stewards because these are the principles that allow partnerships to deepen and to endure. They make possible not only *learning in organizations* but also *organizations that learn*. Peter Senge's (1990) assertion is relevant here: "In a learning organization leaders may start by pursuing their own vision, but as they learn to listen carefully to others' visions they begin to see that their own personal vision is part of something larger. This does not diminish any leader's sense of responsibility for the vision—if anything it deepens it" (p. 346).

Learning organizations are renewing organizations, and as noted earlier, renewal requires openness, humility, and vulnerability—all of which flourish only in the safety of a hospitable commons. From a nurturing commons (what Kane called the moral sphere), democratic relationships are tried out by proving contraries: safe places to test competing ideas. Mark Gerzon (1997) suggested, "An integral part of education is learning that democratic communities are strong enough to contain their deepest differences. If we avoid discussing these differences in schools, out of the misguided notion that we are protecting children from being wounded in the culture wars, we are imparting values by default. We are telling young people that we don't trust them to deal with the diversity present in their own communities. We are also telling them that we adults do not know how to deal with conflict ourselves" (p. 11).

Stewards of public education don't avoid conflict; they see conflict as an opportunity for engaged learning. That learning does not necessarily lead to concession, but it can conduce to understanding and empathy. A commons that proves contraries is not a demilitarized zone, where by common consent nothing happens. But it can become a "tangled bank," where difference is maintained but contact reminds us how fully interdependent we are. Whether that tangled bank becomes a civil or uncivil society depends on what we have called *democratic character, the manners of democracy*. To some degree cultivation of this character has been important from the beginnings of the republic. Gordon Wood (2006) wrote of George Washington, "Washington's genius, Washington's greatness, lay in his character. He was, as Chateaubriand said, a 'hero of an unprecedented kind.' . . . Washington became a great man and was acclaimed as a classical hero because of the way he conducted himself during times of temptation. It was his moral character that set him off from other men" (p. 34). Thus, like democracy, stewardship, consistent with a central theme of this book, is not a technique. It cannot be learned by training. It is not a pedagogy (though it expresses itself through pedagogy). One cannot generate a checklist of activities that constitute effective stewardship because stewardship is a *worldview* and a *way of life*. It is a particular way of understanding oneself in relation to others, as we noted earlier with Levinas's (1969) notion of "obligation," and perceiving one's time in relation to other times.

Stewardship as Moral Posture

Throughout this book we have used the word *moral* dozens of times, without introducing or interrogating it. We recognize that *moral* is a problematic word, that beyond its technical or philosophical traditions it has a history and a life of its own. For one, *moral* is salvific; for another it is oppressive. For many *moral* suggests dogma and codes and is anything but hospitable. Michael Oakeshott, whose voice is prominent in this book, worried about moralizing, but still found room for the moral. Elizabeth Corey (2013) suggested one way to get at his moral stance: for Oakeshott, "the disposition that comes with liberal education is a moral disposition that consists of the willingness to be refuted and to admit what one does not know" (p. 94). Further, "one view, which Oakeshott rejected, sees human beings primarily as workers, an organism concerned above all to satisfy desires, to get ahead in the world, to be better than others, to make more and more money. According to this view, education is what helps us do these things well. . . . [It] . . . becomes an instrument for a kind of life that Oakeshott saw as slavish and flat. Identity consists in our being successful exploiters of the earth" (p. 94). An alternative view is one we have sought to describe, that sees education as the bridge between potential and possibility. "Human possibility [is] virtually unlimited—or limited only by one's own imagination. In the moral life of self-enactment and self-disclosure there are multiple opportunities for pursuing radial and surprising paths. . . . The gifts of such an education is thus perspective, liberation, and courage. One is no longer slave to the purposes and values of the world into which one happens to be born and one is freed from imperatives of conformity to present ideas of value" (Corey, 2013, p. 95). Our sense of *moral* flows from these ideas. It is grounded in the recognition that education is inherently relational, that it involves doing things to and for other individuals (some in an unequal relation of power) and that it is moral to the degree that it is grounded in noncontingent fundamental principles that foster self-enactment: that it nurtures the processes that make it possible for the human to become humane (see the introduction).

Soviet writer Vldimir Alekseevich Soloukhin's (1973) story "Rasporyazhenie" (The directive) is an engaging illustration of moral responsiveness. The story's first-person narrator is the father of a two-year-old girl who is gravely ill from double tonsillitis and pneumonia. The father and mother rush their daughter to the overcrowded hospital, where they wait to be attended. "Mother helped by sitting next to our little girl," the story goes. "Whenever she opened her eyes and her consciousness cleared up, and the world around her was a dark . . . spot, then her mother was always in that spot. It could be no other way. If for some reason that spot was empty, maybe the girl wouldn't open her eyes ever again." The hospital staff finally arrived to admit the toddler, but informed the stunned parents that policy did not permit the mother to join her in the ward. Their "pitiful babbling about humanity, about the child's unique needs, and about 'mama therapy' that we had read about in *Health* magazine, made not an impression on the impassive people in the white coats." Knowing that the child could not possibly survive without her mother, the father left instructions that the girl should not be admitted until he returned. He dashed to the clinic's department head, who sadly informed him that the policy was a directive of the ministry, "a directive no one had the right to break." Off he went to the head doctor. "You're out of luck. . . . There's a directive from the minister that no one has the right to break. It's a recently issued directive, so it's untouchable," he was told.

Finally, a friend got the father access to the minister himself, who, after hearing the story responded wearily, "Yes, there is a directive. There are good reasons for it. You simply don't know the full picture. Yes, it was my directive. But since it's mine, I'm not going to be the first one to break it." Surrendering to the inevitable, the father returned to the hospital but on arriving in the waiting room found no sign of his little family. Finally, a nurse's aide—not a nurse, not a doctor, not the department head—a nurse's aide, entered, carrying the child's clothes. "Are these yours?" she asked the father.

> "Yes, yes, but where are they?"
> "They're in the good section. By themselves. No one will bother them. . . ."
> "But how could you? Even the Ministry couldn't, the direct connections."
> "I don't know about any direct connections."
> "But did someone tell you to?"
> "No need of that. It was obvious we needed to admit the girl."
> "But they allowed her mother, too."
> "It was obvious that the girl would be better off with her mother. Your daughter will be fine. Go home. Bring some juice tomorrow or something to eat. Maybe some raspberry jam."

The story is about the unhealthy ecology of the Soviet health care system, and we can perhaps chuckle too smugly at its lapses. But are we or our schools invulnerable to the lacunae in *rational* communication that characterize many large bureaucracies, even those embedded in democracies? Are we too comfortable in our vertical hierarchies? So comfortable we feel no need to listen? What sort of stewards are we? How often do policies disserve the individuals they were designed to serve? How easy is it for us to isolate ourselves in our office (the ministry), classroom (the ward), or role (professor, doctor, nurse, minister, nurse's aide), and to forget that what we do is a part (surely an important part) of something bigger—a tangled bank. When hurried, how often do we ask, "What are you going through?"

In E. B. DeVito's poem "Graduates" (chapter 3), we read that "learning slips in and comes to stay / while you are faced the other way." Facing the other way—attentive, hospitable, empathetic—is what we mean by moral posture.

Stewardship and the Quest for Wisdom

Paul Woodruff (2005) has reminded us that it is impossible to know the future, and that therefore "any government is government by ignorance" (p. 153). Even experts with "good" data never know the outcome of any particular decision or the impact of policy (see Gardner, 2011). Our predictive capacities are limited by many things beyond the fact that our predictions themselves often change the future. Regardless, the future is always imaginary. But, Woodruff argued, this does not mean that we cannot choose well: "the ability to make good decisions without knowledge was called *euboulia* by the ancient Greeks—good judgment" (p. 153). And later, "In democracy, every adult citizen is called upon to assist in managing public affairs. Therefore, the democracy should see that every citizen has the ability to do so. Citizen wisdom is common human wisdom, improved by education" (p. 156). Woodruff cautioned that this broad ideal was unfortunately narrow in application: in Athens, as still today, generally those who would receive the education necessary for citizen wisdom were sufficiently wealthy to be members of the privileged classes.

Tragically, access to this kind of knowledge (what we now call a broadening general education as opposed to narrow vocational training) was limited from the days of Athenian democracy through the founding of our republic. Only a few had access to "rigorous encounters with all the subject matters that comprise the human conversation." What distinguished the founders from the common soldiers was their access to a broad, "classical" education (Wood, 2006, p. 15). Not until the nineteenth century did we begin to recognize the ideal of universal education to promote citizen wisdom.

Horace Mann was perhaps the greatest champion of public (or "common") education in nineteenth-century America. He was the most influential voice in making a claim for *common schooling* as the right and obligation of all citizens, in contrast to the traditional notion of education as an aristocratic privilege as widely accepted in his day. In September 1837, soon after his appointment as secretary of the Board of Education for Massachusetts, Mann, an attorney, politician, and committed reformer, made his first county circuit to build support for the idea of a state system of public schooling. Mann had taken on the secretary's job before fully knowing what he was getting into. To find out, he would wear thin a pair of breeches riding his mare around the state, speaking, meeting with influential citizens, and visiting schools.

As Jonathan Messerli (1972), Mann's biographer, described him, Mann was an intense and nervous person driven by an insistent sense of duty, whose spirits rose or fell with the reception he received at each and every one of his many stops. While he was frequently welcomed by large and enthusiastic audiences, not every meeting proved cordial. Arriving in Northampton, as reported by Messerli, Mann found a room in the Mansion House and called on Franklin Dexter, a bumptious yet important figure within the state.

> No sooner had Mann broached the subject of enlightening and elevating the common people than Dexter cut him off and gave his opinion on the undertaking in clear and unambiguous terms. To him it was plain for anyone to see who would not let himself be misled by all the nonsense about democracy and the wisdom of the majority. Society had been, was, and always would be sharply divided into two classes, commoners who were destined by nature to work and support themselves by the sweat of their brow and an aristocracy of birth and position who were obligated to guide and govern the less fortunate. . . . [I]t was the duty of the American wealthy and well-born to prevent ingress into their ranks by those below. Only in such a way could a society maintain standards of morality, justice, and good taste. (p. 271)

Shaken by Dexter's assault, Mann returned to his room reportedly feeling "helpless." "Once one granted Dexter's division of society, then the entire scheme of a comprehensive public system of education, which furnished avenues of upward mobility for all children regardless of race, creed, or financial position, emerged as a foolish and even dangerous experiment" (p. 271).

Messerli speculated that perhaps Mann pondered what Dexter had said, acknowledging the position Dexter represented: "[Perhaps] even the lowliest needed a modicum of literacy if they were to know their place, remain law-abiding and docile, and show proper deference to those above them, but schooling which was the vehicle for a mobility that crossed class lines and challenge[d] the established order was an American form of Jacobinism" (pp. 271–272). Thus Mann's ideal would be resisted vigorously. The idea of mass public education required defending, and different arguments would be necessary with different audiences. Citizenship demands have grown exponentially since Mann's time, even as we are in danger of ignoring the differences between "mass public education" as conceived in the nineteenth century and broad general education as we understand it now. After his meeting with Dexter, Mann rode on, and so must we, in defense of the publicness of public education, to promote citizen wisdom as not being limited to an aristocracy of wealth, position, or privilege.

In 1949 the faculty at the University of Chicago reprised education's prominent role in nurturing *euboulia* in its now familiar declaration: "If the United States is to be a democracy, its citizens must be free. If citizens are to be free, they must be their own judges. If they are to judge well, they must be wise. Therefore, the business of [general] education in a democracy is to make free men wise" (Staff, Social Sciences 1, College of the University of Chicago, 1949, p. v). This statement expresses the aspiration central to the Agenda for Education in a Democracy. It will always remain aspirational, incomplete. Although a learning outcome addressing democratic character is unlikely to ever be fully satisfied, this doesn't mean it should be discarded. That imperfectability might be expressed in the popular wisdom of Wasserman and Leigh's "impossible dream" to "reach the unreachable star" or through Fichte's (1987) more scholarly musing: "It is part of the concept of man that his ultimate goal be unobtainable and that his path thereto be infinitely long. Thus, it is not man's vocation to reach this goal. But he can and he should draw nearer to it, and his true vocation *qua man* ... lies in endless approximation to this goal" (p. 9).

During the Renaissance, artists regularly signed their name after the Latin word *fecit*, which is "made by" in the preterit tense. In the seventeenth century the practice changed subtly but significantly. In place of *fecit* they wrote *faciebat* (imperfect tense, meaning "was being made"), a "work in progress," which "indicated that they did not view their work to be finished, but rather that they considered it in the process of execution, because art, as a liberal activity, never reaches a state of perfection" (Portús, 2016, p.188; translation ours). If our partnership were to be signed as paintings were, the signature would read *faciebat anno 1983*, because the sustained partnership of democratic education is a liberal activity and because, like learning itself, the quest for wisdom is never finished.

Faciebat anno 2017, Provo, Utah

Appendix

. . . .

Moral Dimensions,
Commitments, and Postulates

The Moral Dimensions of Teaching

Democracy: "Enculturating the young into a social and political democracy" (Goodlad et al., 2004, p. 29).

Access to Knowledge: "Providing access to knowledge for all children and youths" (Goodlad et al., 2004, p. 29).

Nurturing Pedagogy: "Practicing pedagogical nurturing with respect to the art and science of teaching" (Goodlad et al., 2004, p. 30).

Stewardship: "Ensuring responsible stewardship of the schools" (Goodlad et al., 2004, p. 32). ,

The BYU–Public School Partnership Commitments

We believe

1. Public education is the cornerstone of a civil and prosperous democratic community.
2. Education is a public imperative, a moral endeavor, and a shared responsibility for all members of society.
3. Public schools exist to provide access to education for all, which includes both academic mastery and personal development for the purpose of maximizing students' potential to participate fully and productively in society.

4. The university supports schools by preparing educators who master their disciplines and who understand and implement curriculum and instruction that support their students' learning and development through ongoing research and inquiry leading to dialogue and action that directly benefit schools.

We **commit** to

1. *Civic Preparation and Engagement*: The Partnership prepares educators who model and teach the knowledge, skills, and dispositions required for civic virtue and engagement in our society.
2. *Engaged Learning Through Nurturing Pedagogy*: The Partnership develops educators who are competent and caring, who promote engaged learning through appropriate instructional strategies and positive classroom environments and relationships.
3. *Equitable Access to Academic Knowledge and Achievement*: The Partnership develops educators who are committed to and actively provide equitable access to academic knowledge and achievement through rigorous mastery of curriculum content and instructional skills.
4. *Stewardship in School and Community*: The Partnership assists educators in becoming responsible stewards in their schools and communities by dedicating themselves to shared purpose, simultaneous renewal, and high standards of educator competence and learner performance.
5. *Commitment to Renewal*: The Partnership fosters in educators a commitment to renewal through consistent inquiry, reflection, and action within their professional practice, resulting in continuous improvement. (http://education.byu.edu/cites/new_statement.html)

Postulates

Over the years, Goodlad and his associates at the Institute for Educational Inquiry have published an evolving list of "postulates," setting forth conditions necessary for organizing and maintaining transformational educator training programs. A postulate is a stipulation, but also an agreement, and the term refers to what is *necessary* and to the *collaborative* nature of that necessity. Commitment to postulates such as these is the point of departure for enduring partnerships. University faculty and faculty leaders—in schools of education and their arts and sciences collaborators— share stewardship for ensuring that these conditions are in place at their institutions.

Postulate 1: Programs for the education of the nation's educators must be viewed by institutions offering them as a major responsibility to society and be adequately supported and promoted and vigorously advanced by the institution's top leadership.

Postulate 2: Programs for the education of educators must enjoy parity with other professional education programs, full legitimacy and institutional commitment, and rewards for faculty geared to the nature of the field.

Postulate 3: Programs for the education of educators must be autonomous and secure in their borders, with clear organizational identity, constancy of budget and personnel, and decision-making authority similar to that enjoyed by the major professional schools.

Postulate 4: There must exist a clearly identifiable group of academic and clinical faculty members for whom teacher education is the top priority; the group must be responsible and accountable for selecting diverse groups of students and monitoring their progress, planning and maintaining the full scope and sequence of the curriculum, continuously evaluating and improving programs, and facilitating the entry of graduates into teaching careers.

Postulate 5: The responsible group of academic and clinical faculty members described above must have a comprehensive understanding of the aims of education and the role of schools in our society and be fully committed to selecting and preparing teachers to assume the full range of educational responsibilities required.

Postulate 6: The responsible group of academic and clinical faculty members must seek out and select for a predetermined number of student places in the program those candidates who reveal an initial commitment to the moral, ethical, and enculturating responsibilities to be assumed, and make clear to them that preparing for these responsibilities is central to this program.

Postulate 7: Programs for the education of educators, whether elementary or secondary, must carry the responsibility to ensure that all candidates progressing through them possess or acquire the literacy and critical-thinking abilities associated with the concept of an educated person.

Postulate 8: Programs for the education of educators must provide extensive opportunities for future teachers to move beyond being students of organized knowledge to become teachers who inquire into both knowledge and its teaching.

Postulate 9: Programs for the education of educators must be characterized by a socialization process through which candidates transcend their self-oriented student preoccupations to become more other-oriented in identifying with a culture of teaching.

Postulate 10: Programs for the education of educators must be characterized in all respects by the conditions for learning that future teachers are to establish in their own schools and classrooms.

Postulate 11: Programs for the education of educators must be conducted in such a way that teachers inquire into the nature of teaching and schooling and assume that they will do so as a natural aspect of their careers.

Postulate 12: Programs for the education of educators must involve future teachers in the issues and dilemmas that emerge out of the never-ending tension between the rights and interests of individual parents and interest groups and the role of schools in transcending parochialism and advancing community in a democratic society.

Postulate 13: Programs for the education of educators must be infused with understanding of and commitment to the moral obligation of teachers to ensure equitable access to and engagement in the best possible K–12 education for all children and youths.

Postulate 14: Programs for the education of educators must involve future teachers not only in understanding schools as they are but in alternatives, the assumptions underlying alternatives, and how to effect needed changes in school organization, pupil grouping, curriculum, and more.

Postulate 15: Programs for the education of educators must assure for each candidate the availability of a wide array of laboratory settings for simulation, observation, hands-on experiences, and exemplary schools for internships and residencies; they must admit no more students to their programs than can be assured these quality experiences.

Postulate 16: Programs for the education of educators must engage future teachers in the problems and dilemmas arising out of the inevitable conflicts and incongruities between what is perceived to work in practice and the research and theory supporting other options.

Postulate 17: Programs for the education of educators must establish linkages with graduates for purposes of both evaluating and revising these programs and easing the critical early years of transition into teaching.

Postulate 18: Programs for the education of educators require a regulatory context with respect to licensing, certifying, and accrediting that ensures at all times the presence of the necessary conditions embraced by the seventeen preceding postulates.

Postulate 19: Programs for the education of educators must compete in an arena that rewards efforts to continuously improve on the conditions embedded in all of the postulates and tolerates no shortcuts intended to ensure a supply of teachers.

Postulate 20: Those institutions and organizations that prepare the nation's teachers, authorize their right to teach, and employ them must fine-tune their individual and collaborative roles to support and sustain lifelong teaching careers characterized by professional growth, service, and satisfaction.

Source: Goodlad, J. I. (1994). *Educational renewal: Better teachers, better schools.* San Francisco, CA: Jossey-Bass, pp. 72–93. See also http://www.ieiseattle.org/Publications/postulates.htm.

Acknowledgments

We express our appreciation to our colleagues in the Brigham Young University Public School Partnership, with whom we have conversed for more than two decades, and whose collective wisdom and genuine goodness inform this book. We also are grateful for the encouragement of our friends in CITES (The Center for the Improvement of Teacher Education and Schooling), who have given us helpful feedback along the way. We must also mention Bernard Badiali, Steven Baugh, Greg Clark, Cori Mantle-Bromley, and John Patten, who nudged our thinking along at critical times. Sharon Black was remarkably generous in sharing her editorial skills. And lastly, we are grateful to Al Merkley, who played a key role in the data gathering for chapter 7.

Wherever we looked we found teachers. Where we found teachers we learned. In places of learning we encountered the thickness of democracy.

References

Agenda. In *Oxford English Dictionary*. http://www.oed.com.

Alberty, H. B., & Alberty, E. J. (1962). *Reorganizing the high-school curriculum* (3rd ed.). New York, NY: Macmillan.

Alter, C., & Scherer, M. (2016). The truth is out there in 2016. Way out. *Time, 188*(15), 28–32.

Andrews, R. (1987). The school–community interface: Strategies of community involvement. In J. Goodlad (Ed.), *The ecology of school renewal* (pp. 152–169). Chicago, IL: National Society for the Study of Education.

Apple, M. (1979). *Ideology and curriculum*. London, England: Routledge and Kegan Paul.

Aristotle. (1943). *One man in the universe: Metaphysics, parts of animals, ethics, politics, poetics* (Lousie Ropes Loomis, Ed.). Roslyn, NY: Walter J. Black.

Aristotle. (1999). *Politics* (Benjamin Jowett, Trans.). Kitchener, Ontario: Batoche Books.

Ayres, L. P. (1909). *Laggards in our schools: A study of retardation and elimination in city school systems*. New York, NY: Russell Sage Foundation.

Bakhtin, M. (1984). *The problems of Dostoevsky's poetics* (Caryl Emerson, Ed. and Trans.). Vol. 8 of Theory and History of Literature. Minneapolis: University of Minnesota Press.

Barber, B. R. (1997). Public schooling: Education for a democracy. In J. I. Goodlad & T. J. McMannon (Eds.), *The public purpose of education and schooling* (pp. 21–32). San Francisco, CA: Jossey-Bass.

Barber, B. R. (1998). *A passion for democracy: American essays*. Princeton, NJ: Princeton University Press.

Barnett, C. (2005). Ways of relating: Hospitality and the acknowledgement of otherness. *Progress in Human Geography, 29*(1), 1–19.

Bartholomew, S. S., & Sandholtz, J. H. (2009). Competing views of teaching in a school–university partnership. *Teaching and Teacher Education, 25*(2), 155–165.

Bauman, Z. (2008). *Does ethics have a chance in a world of consumers?* Cambridge, MA: Harvard University Press.

Bauman, Z. (2011). *Collateral damage: Social inequalities in a global age*. Malden, MA: Polity Press.

Bauman, Z. (2012). *This is not a diary*. Malden, MA: Polity Press.

Bauman, Z., & Donskis, L. (2013). *Moral blindness: The loss of sensitivity in liquid modernity*. Malden, MA: Polity Press.

Bauman, Z., & Raud, R. (2015). *Practices of selfhood*. Malden, MA: Polity Press.

Bell, T. H. (1988). *The thirteenth man: A Reagan cabinet memoir*. New York, NY: Free Press.

Berliner, D. C. (2009). MCLB (Much Curriculum Left Behind): A U.S. calamity in the making. *Educational Forum, 73*, 284–296.

Berliner, D. C. (2011). Rational responses to high stakes testing: The case of curriculum narrowing and the harm that follows. *Cambridge Journal of Education, 41*(3), 287–302.

Berliner, D. C., & Biddle, B. J. (1995). *The manufactured crisis: Myths, fraud, and the attack on America's public schools*. Reading, MA: Addison-Wesley.

Berliner, D. C., & Glass, G. V. (2014). *50 myths & lies: America's public schools and the real crisis in education*. New York, NY: Teachers College Press.

Berry, W. (1992). *Sex, economy, freedom and community: Eight essays*. New York, NY: Pantheon.

Bevins, S., & Price, G. (2014). Collaboration between academics and teachers: A complex relationship. *Educational Action Research, 22*(2), 270–284.

Bjorklund, D. F., & Pellegrini, A. D. (2010). Evolutionary perspectives on social development. In P. K. Smith & C. H. Hart (Eds.), *The Wiley-Blackwell handbook of childhood social development* (2nd ed., pp. 64–81). Oxford, England: Wiley-Blackwell.

Bode, B. H. (1937). *Democracy as a way of life*. New York, NY: Macmillan.

Bode, B. H. (1940). *How we learn*. Boston, MA: D. C. Heath.

Book, C. L. (1996). Professional development schools. In J. Sikula (Ed.), *Handbook of research on teacher education* (2nd ed., pp. 194–210). New York, NY: Macmillan.

Brand, S. (2000). *The clock of the long now: Time and responsibility*. New York, NY: Basic Books.

Breault, R., & Breault, D. A. (2012). *Professional development schools: Researching lessons from the field*. Lanham, MD: Rowman & Littlefield.

Broudy, H. S. (1988). *The uses of schooling*. New York, NY: Routledge.

Broudy, H. S., Smith, B. O., & Burnett, J. R. (1964). *Democracy and excellence in American secondary education: A study in curriculum theory*. Chicago, IL: Rand McNally.

Buchmann, M. (1986, April). Reporting and using educational research: Conviction or persuasion (Occasional Paper no. 96). Institute for Research on Teaching, Michigan State University.

Bullough, R. V., Jr. (1988). *The forgotten dream of American public education*. Ames: Iowa State University Press.

Bullough, R. V., Jr. (1999). Past solutions to current problems in curriculum integration: The contributions of Harold Alberty. *Journal of Curriculum and Supervision, 14*(2), 156–270.

Bullough, R. V., Jr. (2001). *Uncertain lives: Children of promise, teachers of hope*. New York, NY: Teachers College Press.

Bullough, R. V., Jr. (2005). Teacher vulnerability and teachability: A case study of a mentor and two interns. *Teacher Education Quarterly, 32*(2), 23–39.

Bullough, R. V., Jr. (2007). Ali: Becoming a student—A life history. In D. Thiessen & A. Cook-Sather (Eds.), *International handbook of student experience in elementary and secondary school* (pp. 493–516). New York, NY: Springer.

Bullough, R. V., Jr. (2012). Against best practice: Outliers, local studies and education research. *Journal of Education for Teaching, 38*(3), 343–357.

Bullough, R. V., Jr. (2014). The way of openness: Moral sphere theory, education, ethics, and classroom management. *Teachers and Teaching: Theory and Practice, 20*(3), 251–263.

Bullough, R. V., Jr. (2014/2015). Higher education and the neoliberal threat: Place, fast time, and identity. *Journal of Thought, 48*(3/4), 13–32.

Bullough, R. V., Jr. (2016). Status and quality of teacher education in the US: Neoliberal and professional tensions. In J. C.-K. Lee & C. Day (Eds.), *Quality and change in teacher education: Western and Chinese perspectives* (pp. 59–75). New York, NY: Springer.

Bullough, R. V., Jr., & Baugh, S. C. (2009). Developing professional learning communities in a university–public school partnership. In C. Mullen (Ed.), *The handbook of leadership and building professional learning communities* (pp. 39–49). New York, NY: Palgrave Macmillan.

Bullough, R. V., Jr., & Hall-Kenyon, K. M. (2011). The call to teach and teacher hopefulness. *Teacher Development, 15*(2), 127–140.

Bullough, R. V., Jr., Patterson, R. S., & Mayes, C. (2002). Teaching as prophecy. *Curriculum Inquiry, 32*(3), 311–330.

Bullough, R. V., Jr., & Smith, L. K. (2016). Being a student of teaching: Practitioner research and educator study groups. In M. L. Hamilton & J. Loughran (Eds.), *International handbook of teacher education* (Vol.2, pp. 305–352). New York, NY: Springer.

Bullough, R. V., Jr., Young, J., & Draper, R. J. (2004). One year teaching internships and the dimensions of beginning teacher development. *Teachers and Teaching: Theory and Practice, 10*(4), 365–394.

Burbank, M. D., Kauchak, D., & Bates, A. J. (2010). Book clubs as professional development opportunities for preservice teacher candidates and practicing teachers: An exploratory study. *New Educator, 6*, 56–73.

Burwell, R., & Huyser, M. (2013). Practicing hospitality in the classroom. *Journal of Education and Christian Belief, 17*(1), 9–24.

Camus, A. (1957). *The fall.* New York, NY: Knopf.

Carey, K. (2017). Dismal voucher results surprise researchers as DeVos era begins. *New York Times*, February 23, p. A20.

Carnegie Forum on Education and the Economy. (1986). *A nation prepared: Teachers for the 21st century.* New York, NY: Author.

Castle, S., Fox, R. K., & Souder, K.O.H. (2006). Do professional development schools make a difference? A comparative study of PDS and non-PDS teacher candidates. *Journal of Teacher Education, 57*(1), 65–80.

Castle, S., & Reilly, K. A. (2011). Impact of professional development school preparation on teacher candidates. *National Society for the Study of Education, 110*(2), 337–371.

Chechov, A. (1920/1972). *"The Cook's Wedding" and other stories* (Constance Garnet, Trans.). Vol. 12 of *The Tales of Chekhov.* New York, NY: Macmillan.

Choo, S. S. (2014). Cultivating a hospitable imagination: Re-envisioning the world literature curriculum through a cosmopolitan lens. *Curriculum Inquiry, 44*(1), 68–89.

Churchill, W. S. (1898/1989). *The story of the Malakand Field Force.* New York, NY: Norton.

Clark, G. (2015). *Civic jazz: American music and Kenneth Burke on the art of getting along.* Chicago, IL: University of Chicago Press.

Cleveland, H. (1985). *The knowledge executive.* New York, NY: E. P. Dutton.

Cochran-Smith, M., Feiman-Nemser, S., McIntyre, D. J., & Demers, K. E. (2008). *Handbook of research on teacher education* (3rd ed.). New York, NY: Routledge.

Corey, E. (2013). The aesthetic and moral character of Oakeshott's educational writings. *Journal of Philosophy of Education 47*(1), 86–98.

Council for the Accreditation of Educator Preparation. (2013). Standard 2: Clinical partnerships and practice. http://CAEPnet.org/standards/standard-2.

Croft, S. J., Roberts, M. A., & Stenhouse, V. L. (2016). The perfect storm of educational reform: High states testing and teacher evaluation. *Social Justice 42*(1), 70–92, 147.

Curtius, E. R. (1953). *European literature and the Latin Middle Ages* (W. Trask, Trans.). New York, NY: Pantheon.

Darwin, C. (1876). *On the origin of species by means of natural selection*. London, England: Clowes and Sons.

DePencier, I. B. (1967). *The history of the laboratory schools: The University of Chicago, 1895–1965*. Chicago, IL: Quadrangle Books.

Derrida, J. (2000). *Of hospitality: Anne Dufourmantelle invites Jacques Derrida to respond* (R. Bowlby, Trans.). Stanford, CA: Stanford University Press.

Derrida, J. (2002). Hospitality. In *Acts of religion* (M. Dooley & M. Hughes, Trans.) (pp. 356–420). New York, NY: Routledge.

DeVito, E. B. (1989). Graduates. *American Scholar, 58*(2), 282.

Dewalt, K. M., Dewalt, B. R., with Wayland, C. B. (1998). Participant observation. In H. R. Barnard (Ed.), *Handbook of methods in cultural anthropology* (pp. 259–299). Walnut Creek, CA: AltaMira Press.

Dewey, J. (1900). *The school and society*. Chicago, IL: University of Chicago Press.

Dewey, J. (1904). The relation of theory to practice in education. In *The third yearbook of the National Society for the Scientific Study of Education* (pp. 9–30). Chicago, IL: University of Chicago Press.

Dewey, J. (1910). *The influence of Darwin on philosophy: And other essays in contemporary thought*. New York, NY: Henry Holt.

Dewey, J. (1916). *Democracy and education*. New York, NY: Macmillan.

Dewey, J. (1927). *The public and its problems*. New York, NY: Henry Holt.

Dewey, J. (1933). *How we think*. Lexington, MA: D. C. Heath.

Dewey, J. (1938). *Experience and education*. New York, NY: Macmillan.

Dewey, J. (1939a). *Freedom and culture*. New York, NY: Putnam.

Dewey, J. (1939b/1988). *Creative democracy—The task before*. Carbondale: Southern Illinois University Press.

Dickinson, E. (1970). *The complete poems of Emily Dickinson* (Vol. 1) (R. W. Franklin, Ed.). London, England: Faber.

Dobson, A. (2014). *Listening for democracy: Recognition, representation, reconciliation*. New York, NY: Oxford University Press.

Donskis, L. (2013). Introduction. In Z. Bauman & L. Donskis, *Moral blindness: The loss of sensitivity in liquid modernity* (pp. 1–16). Malden, MA: Polity Press.

Draper, S. M. (2010). *Out of my mind*. New York, NY: Atheneum Books.

Education Committee of the Technical Council on Forensic Engineering of the American Society of Civil Engineers. (1992). *Failures in civil engineering: Structural, foundation and geoenvironmental case studies*. New York, NY: American Society of Civil Engineers.

Ellis, J. J. (2016). *The quartet: Orchestrating the second American revolution, 1788–1989*. New York, NY: Knopf.

Everson, K. E. (2017). Value-added modeling and educational accountability: Are we answering the real questions? *Review of Educational Research, 87*(1): 35–70.

Fallows, J. (2017). Despair and hope in the age of Trump. *Atlantic Monthly*, January/February, 13–15.

Fenstermacher, G. (1999). Agenda for education in a democracy. In Wilma Smith & Gary Fenstermacher (Eds.), *Leadership for educational renewal* (pp. 3–28). San Francisco, CA: Jossey-Bass.

Fichte, J. G. (1987). Some lectures concerning the scholar's vocation (Daniel Breazeale, Trans.). In Ernst Behler (Ed.), *Philosophy of German idealism* (pp. 1–38). New York, NY: Continuum.

Fish, S. (2011). My life report: Things done well, things done less well. *New York Times*, October 31. https://opinionator.blogs.nytimes.com/2011/10/31/my-life-report/?_r=0.

Fisler, J. L., & Firestone, W. A. (2006). Teacher learning in a school–university partnership: Exploring the role of social trust and teaching efficacy beliefs. *Teachers College Record, 108*(6), 1155–1185.

Foa, R. S., & Mounk, Y. (2016). The danger of deconsolidation: The democratic disconnect. *Journal of Democracy, 27*(3), 5–17.

Freire, P. (1970). *Pedagogy of the oppressed*. New York, NY: Herder and Herder.

Freire, P. (1998). *Teachers as cultural workers: Letters to those who dare to teach*. Boulder, CO: Westview.

Fuller, T. (1991). Foreword. In M. Oakeshott, *Rationalism in politics and other essays* (pp. xiii–xxi). Indianapolis, IN: Liberty Fund.

Furlong, J., Whitty, G., Whiting, C., Miles, S., Barton, L., & Barrett, E. (1996). Redefining partnership: Revolution or reform in initial teacher education? *Journal of Education for Teaching, 22*(1), 39–55.

Gadamer, H.-G. (2011). *Truth and method*. New York, NY: Continuum.

Gardner, D. (2011). *Future babble: Why expert predictions are next to worthless and you can do better*. New York, NY: Dutton.

Gardner, J. W. (1984). *Excellence: Can we be equal and excellent too?* New York, NY: Norton.

Garet, M. S., Porter, A. C., Desimone, L., Birman, B. F., & Yoon, K. S. (2001). What makes professional development effective? Results from a national sample of teachers. *American Educational Research Journal, 38*(4), 915–945.

Gerzon, M. (1997). Teaching democracy by doing it! *Educational Leadership, 54*(5), 6–11.

Giles, H. H., McCutchen, S. P., & Zechiel, A. N. (1942). *Exploring the curriculum*. New York, NY: Harper & Brothers.

Gittins, A. J. (1994). Beyond hospitality? The missionary status and role revisited. *International Review of Mission, 83*, 397–416.

Goodlad, J. I. (1984). *A place called school: Prospects for the future*. New York, NY: McGraw-Hill.

Goodlad, J. I. (1987). Structure, process and an agenda. In J. I. Goodlad (Ed.), *The ecology of school renewal* (pp. 1–19). Chicago, IL: National Society for the Study of Education.

Goodlad, J. I. (1990). *Teachers for our nation's schools*. San Francisco, CA: Jossey-Bass.

Goodlad, J. I. (1993). School–university partnerships and partner schools. *Educational Policy, 7*(1), 24–39.

Goodlad, J. I. (1994). *Educational renewal: Better teachers, better schools*. San Francisco, CA: Jossey-Bass.

Goodlad, J. I., Mantel-Bromley, C., & Goodlad, S. J. (2004). *Education for everyone: Agenda for education in a democracy*. San Francisco, CA: Jossey-Bass.

Goodlad, J. I., & McMannon, T. J. (Eds.). (1997). *The public purposes of education and schooling*. San Francisco, CA: Jossey-Bass.

Grafton, A., & Grossman, J. (2015). Habits of mind. *American Scholar, 84*(1), 31–37.

Green, T. F. (1999). *Voices: The educational formation of conscience*. Notre Dame, IN: University of Notre Dame Press.

Greenblatt, S. (2011). *The swerve: How the world became modern*. New York, NY: Norton.

Gunn Allen, P. (1999). Who is your mother? Red roots of white feminism. In C. Lemert (Ed.), *Social theory: The multicultural and classic readings* (pp. 585–594). Boulder, CO: Westview.

Gurian, M., & Stevens, K. (2005). *The minds of boys*. San Francisco, CA: Jossey-Bass.

Gutmann, A. (1999). *Democratic education*. Princeton, NJ: Princeton University Press.

Habermas, J. (1984). *The theory of communicative action I: Reason and the rationalization of society*. Cambridge, England: Polity Press.

Hall, D. L., & Ames, R. T. (1999). *The democracy of the dead: Dewey, Confucius, and the hope for democracy in China*. Chicago, IL: Open Court.

Hall, S. S. (2010). *Wisdom: From philosophy to neuroscience*. New York, NY: Knopf.

Hallie, P. P. (1994). *Lest innocent blood be shed: The story of the village of Le Chambon and how goodness happened there*. New York, NY: HarperPerennial.

Hamilton, M. L., & Pinnegar, S. (2015). Dialogue as a tool for knowing. In M. L. Hamilton & S. Pinnegar (Eds.), *Knowing, becoming, doing as teacher educators: Identity, intimate scholarship, inquiry* (pp. 143–157). Bingley, England: Emerald.

Hansen, M. T. (2009). *Collaboration: An interview with Morten T Hansen*. Conducted by Alistair Craven. Bingley, England: Emerald. Emeraldgrouppublishing.com/learning /management_thinking/interviews/pdf/Hansen.pdf.

Harari, Y. N. (2017). *Homo deus: A brief history of tomorrow*. New York, NY: Harpers.

Hargreaves, A., & Fullan, M. G. (1992). *Understanding teacher development*. London, England: Cassell.

Hargreaves, E. (2013). Assessment for learning and teacher learning communities: UK teachers' experiences. *Teaching Education, 24*(3), 327–344.

Harre, R., & van Langenhove, L. (1999). *Positioning theory*. Oxford, England: Blackwell.

Henshaw, J., Wilson, C., & Morefield, J. (1987). Seeing clearly: The school as unit of change. In J. Goodlad (Ed.), *The ecology of school renewal* (pp. 134–151). New York, NY: National Society for the Study of Education.

Hoffert, R. W. (2001). Education in a political democracy. In R. Soder, J. I. Goodlad, & T. J. McMannon (Eds.), *Developing democratic character in the young* (pp. 26–44). San Francisco, CA: Jossey-Bass.

Holder, J. B., & Flessas, T. (2008). Emerging commons. *Social & Legal Studies, 17*(3), 299–310.

Holmes, R. (2005). *In the footsteps of church: A study in character*. New York, NY: Basic Books.

Holmes Group. (1986). *Tomorrow's teachers*. East Lansing, MI: Author.

Holmes Group. (1995). *Tomorrow's schools of education*. East Lansing, MI: Author.

Horn, I. S., & Little, J. W. (2010). Attending to problems of practice: Routines and resources for professional learning in teachers' workplace interactions. *American Educational Research Journal, 47*(1), 181–217.

Houston, W. R. (1990). *Handbook of research on teacher education*. New York, NY: Macmillan.

Hughes-Warrington, M. (2012). The ethics of internationalisation in higher education: Hospitality, self-presence and "being late." *Educational Philosophy and Theory, 44*(3), 312–321.

Hullfish, H. G., & Smith, P. G. (1967). *Reflective thinking: The method of education*. New York, NY: Dodd, Mead.

Jeffrey, A., McFarlane, C., & Vasudevan, A. (2012). Rethinking enclosure: Space, subjectivity and the commons. *Antipode, 44*(4), 1247–1267.

Johnson, M. (1993). *Moral imagination: Implications of cognitive science for ethics*. Chicago, IL: University of Chicago Press.

Kagan, R. (1981). *The evolving self*. Cambridge, MA: Harvard University Press.

Kamola, I., & Meyerhoff, E. (2009). Creating commons: Divided governance, participatory management, and struggles against enclosure in the university. *Polygraph, 21*, 5–27.

Kane, R. (2010). *Ethics and the quest for wisdom*. New York, NY: Cambridge University Press.

Kelchtermans, G. (1996). Teacher vulnerability: Understanding its moral and political roots. *Cambridge Journal of Education, 26*(3), 307–323.

Kridel, C. A., & Bullough, R. V., Jr. (2007). *Stories of the eight-year study*. Albany: State University of New York Press.

Lamont, C. (1959). *Dialogue on Dewey*. New York, NY: Horizon Press.

Latham, N. I., & Vogt, W. P. (2007). Do professional development schools reduce teacher attrition? Evidence from a longitudinal study of 1,000 graduates. *Journal of Teacher Education, 58*(2), 153–167.

Lemert, C. G., & Gillan, G. (1982). *Michel Foucault: Social theory as transgression*. New York, NY: Columbia University Press.

Lencioni, P. (2004). *Death by meeting: A leadership fable*. New York, NY: Harcourt.

Levinas, E. (1969). *Totality and infinity*. Pittsburgh, PA: Duquesne University Press.

Levinas, E. (1985). *Ethics and infinity*. Pittsburgh, PA: Duquesne University Press.

Levine, M. (Ed.). (1992). *Professional practice schools: Linking teacher education and school reform*. New York, NY: Teachers College Press.

Levine, T. H. (2011). Experienced teachers and school reform: Exploring how two different professional communities facilitated and complicated change. *Improving Schools, 14*(1), 30–47.

Lindert, P. H. (2003). Voice and growth: Was Churchill right? *Journal of Economic History, 63*(2), 315–350.

Lippmann, W. (1939). The indispensable opposition. *Atlantic Monthly, 164*, 186–190.

Lubienski, C. A., & Lubienski, S. T. (2014). *The public school advantage: Why public schools outperform private ones*. Chicago, IL: University of Chicago Press.

Lukianoff, G., & Haidt, J. (2015). The coddling of the American mind. *Atlantic, 316*(2), 42–52.

Macris, V. (2012). Towards a pedagogy of philoxenia (hospitality): Negotiating policy priorities for immigrant students in Greek public schools. *Journal of Critical Education Policy Studies, 10*(1), 298–314.

Madison, J., Hamilton, A., & Jay, J. (1787/1987). *The Federalist Papers*. New York, NY: Viking Penguin.

Madrick, J. (2017). America: The forgotten poor. *New York Review of Books, 64*(11), 49–50.

Maieutic. In *Oxford English Dictionary*. http://www.oed.com.

Mann, H. (1867/1848). *Annual report on education*. Boston, MA: Horace B. Fuller.

Martin, J. (2010). *The Jesuit guide to almost everything*. New York, NY: HarperOne.

Mayhew, K. C., & Edwards, A. (1936). *The Dewey school*. New York, NY: D. Appleton–Century.

McLaughlin, C., & Black-Hawkins, K. (2004). A schools–university research partnership: Understandings, models and complexities. *Journal of In-Service Education, 30*(2), 265–284.

Messerli, J. (1972). *Horace Mann: A biography*. New York, NY: Knopf.

Misztal, B. (2003). *Theories of social remembering*. Maidenhead, England: Open University Press.

Monson, I. (1996). *Saying something: Jazz improvisation and interaction*. Chicago, IL: University of Chicago Press.

Moss, T. (2014). Spatiality of the commons. *International Journal of the Commons, 8*(2), 457–471.

Mullen, C. A., Samier, E. A., Brindley, S., English, F. W., & Carr, N. K. (2013). An epistemic frame analysis of neoliberal culture and politics in the US, UK, and the UAE. *Interchange, 43*(3), 187–228.

Naas, M. (2003). *Taking on the traditions: Derrida and the legacies of deconstruction.* Stanford, CA: Stanford University Press.

National Association for Professional Development Schools (NAPDS). (2008). 9 Essentials. www.napds.org/nine-essentials.

National Commission on Excellence in Education. (1983). *A nation at risk: The imperative for education reform.* Washington, DC: US Government Printing Office.

National Council for Accreditation of Teacher Education (NCATE). (2001). *Standards for professional development schools.* Washington, DC: Author.

N'gom, M., & Nistal, G. (Eds.). (2012). *Nueva antología de la literatura de Guinea Ecuatorial.* Madrid, Spain: Sial.

Noddings, N. (2003). *Happiness and education.* New York, NY: Cambridge University Press.

Noddings, N. (2010). *The maternal factor: Two paths to morality.* Berkeley: University of California Press.

Nolan, J., Grove, D., Leftwich, H., Kelly, M., & Peters, B. (2011). Impact of professional development. *Teachers College Record, 113*(14), 372–402.

Oakeshott, M. (1959). *The voice of poetry in the conversation of mankind: An essay.* Cambridge, England: Bowes & Bowes.

Oakeshott, M. (1991). *Rationalism in politics and other essays.* Indianapolis, IN: Liberty Fund.

Obermayer, B., & Obermaier, F. (2016). *The Panama papers: Breaking the story of how the rich and powerful hide their money.* London, England: Oneworld.

Palmer, P. (1998). *The courage to teach.* San Francisco, CA: Jossey-Bass.

Palmer, P. (2011). *Healing the heart of democracy: The courage to create a politics worthy of the human spirit.* San Francisco, CA: Jossey-Bass.

Papay, J. P. (2011). Different tests, different answers: The stability of teacher value-added estimates across outcome measures. *American Educational Research Journal, 48*(1), 163–193.

Patterson, R. S., & Hughes, K. H. (1999). The Utah Associates program for leaders. In W. F. Smith & G. D. Fenderstermacher (Eds.), *Leadership for educational renewal* (pp. 271–288). San Francisco, CA: Jossey-Bass.

Patterson, R. S., Michelli, N. M., & Pacheco, A. (1999). *Centers of pedagogy: New structures for educational renewal.* San Francisco, CA: Jossey-Bass.

Penuel, W. R., Fishman, B. J., Yamaguchi, R., & Gallagher, L. P. (2007). What makes professional development effective? Strategies that foster curriculum implementation. *American Educational Research Journal, 44*(4), 921–958.

Petrie, H. G. (Ed.). (1995). *Professionalism, partnership and power: Building professional development schools.* Albany: State University of New York Press.

Pivovarova, M., Amrein-Beardsley, A., & Broatch, J. (2016). Value-added models (VAMS): Caveat emptor. *Statistics and Public Policy, 3*(1), 1–9.

Plato. (1953). *Collected works of Plato* (Benjamin Jowett, Trans.) (4th ed.). Oxford, England: Oxford University Press.

Pliny the Elder. (1855). *Natural history of Pliny, Book 35.36* (J. Bostock & H. T. Riley, Trans.). http://www.perseus.tufts.edu/hopper web.

Pohl, C. (1999). *Making room: Recovering hospitality as a Christian tradition.* Grand Rapids, MI: Eerdmans.

Polacco, P. (1998). *Thank you, Mr. Falker.* New York, NY: Philomel Books.

Polly, D. (2016). Considering professional development school partnerships in light of CAEP standard two. *School–University Partnerships, 9*(3), 96–109.

Portús, Javier Metapintura. (2016). *Un viaje a la idea del arte en España*. Madrid, Spain: Museo Nacional del Prado.

Putnam, R. D. (1995). Bowling alone: America's declining social capital. *Journal of Democracy, 6*(1), 65–78.

Radhakrishnan, S. (Ed. & Trans.). (1953). *The principal Upanishads*. New York, NY: Harper and Brothers.

Ravitch, D. (2013). *Reign of error: The hoax of the privatization movement and the danger to America's public schools*. New York, NY: Knopf.

Riley, K. (2015). Reading for change: Social justice unionism book groups as an organizing tool. *Perspectives on Urban Education, 12*(1), n.p.

Robison, J. E. (2007). *Look me in the eye: My life with Asperger's*. New York, NY: Crown.

Rooney, E. (2015). "I'm just going through the motions": High-stakes accountability and teachers' access to intrinsic rewards. *American Journal of Education, 121*(4), 475–500.

Rorty, R. (1979). *Philosophy and the mirror of nature*. Princeton, NJ: Princeton University Press.

Rose, M. (2015). School reform fails the test. *American Scholar, 84*(1), 18–30.

Rose, R., & Mishler, W. (1996). Testing the Churchill hypothesis: Popular support for democracy and its alternatives. *Journal of Public Policy, 16*(1), 29–58.

Ruitenberg, C.W. (2009). Educating political adversaries: Chanteal Mouffe and radical democratic citizenship education. *Studies in Philosophy and Education, 28*(3), 269–281.

Sartre, J.-P. (1966). *Being and nothingness* (Hazel Barnes, Trans.). New York, NY: Washington Square Press.

Sax, D. (2016). *The revenge of analog: Real things and why they matter*. New York, NY: PublicAffairs.

Schneider, M. K. (2016). *School choice: The end of public education?* New York, NY: Teachers College Press.

Schön, D. A. (1983). *The reflective practitioner*. New York, NY: Basic Books.

Schön, D. A. (1987). *Educating the reflective practitioner*. San Francisco, CA: Jossey-Bass.

Schultz, D. (2013). Democracy is the worst form of government. In D. Schultz (Ed.), *American politics in the age of ignorance: Why lawmakers choose beliefs over research* (pp. 85–106). New York, NY: Palgrave Macmillan.

Seligman, A. B. (1997). *The problem of trust*. Princeton, NJ: Princeton University Press.

Seneca the Younger. (1979). *Epistulae morales* (Vol. 1) (R. M. Gummere Seneca, Trans.). Cambridge, MA: Harvard University Press.

Senge, P. M. (1990). *The fifth discipline: The art and practice of the learning organization*. New York, NY: Doubleday.

Simanowski, R. (2016). *Data love: The seduction and betrayal of digital technologies*. New York, NY: Columbia University Press.

Simmons, R. (2003). *Odd girl out: The hidden culture of aggression in girls*. Boston, MA: Mariner Books.

Sizer, T. R., & Sizer, N. F. (1999). *The students are watching: Schools and the moral contract*. Boston, MA: Beacon.

Smith, A. (1759/1937). *An inquiry into the nature and causes of the wealth of nations*. New York, NY: Modern Library.

Smith, R. W., & Imig, S. (2016). Taken by the numbers: How value-added measures distort our view of teachers' work. In T. Pett, A. Good, & S. M. Putman (Eds.), *Handbook of research on professional development for quality teaching and learning* (pp. 634–651). Hershey, PA: IGI Global.

Snow-Gerono, J. L. (2005). Professional development in a culture of inquiry: PDS teachers identify the benefits of professional learning communities. *Teaching and Teacher Education, 21,* 241–256.

Soder, R. (2001). Education for democracy: The foundation for democratic character. In R. Soder, J. I. Goodlad, & T. J. McMannon (Eds.), *Developing democratic character in the young* (pp. 182–205). San Francisco, CA: Jossey-Bass.

Soloukhin, V. (1973). Rasporyazhenie. In *Olepinskie prudy* (pp. 153–159). Moscow, Russia: Sovremmenik. Unpublished English translation by David Hart.

Sörensen, M. P., & Christiansen, A. (2013). *Ulrich Beck: An introduction to the theory of second modernity and the risk society.* London, England: Routledge.

Staff, Social Sciences 1, College of the University of Chicago (Eds.). (1949). *The people shall judge: Readings in the formation of American policy.* Vol. 1, part 1. Chicago, IL: University of Chicago Press.

Stallings, J. A., & Kowalski, T. (1990). Research on professional development schools. In W. R. Houston (Ed.), *Handbook of research on teacher education* (pp. 251–263). New York, NY: Macmillan.

Standing, G. (2011). *The precariat: The new dangerous class.* New York, NY: Bloomsbury Academic.

Stanley, J. H. (1992). *Children of the Dust Bowl: The true story of the school at Weedpatch Camp.* New York, NY: Random House.

Stoll, L., Bolam, R., McMahon, A., Wallace, M., & Thomas, S. (2006). Professional learning communities: A review of the literature. *Journal of Educational Change, 7,* 221–258.

Streeck, W. (2016). *How will capitalism end? Essays on a failing system.* London, England: Verso.

Tarcov, N. (1996). The meanings of democracy. In R. Soder (Ed.), *Democracy, education and the schools* (pp. 1–36). San Francisco, CA: Jossey-Bass.

Terence. (n.d.). *Heautontimorumenos: The self tormentor.* http://www.gutenberg.org/files/22188/22188-h/files/terence3_4.html.

Tocqueville, A. de. (1835/1840/1947). *Democracy in America.* New York, NY: Oxford University Press.

Toulmin, S. (2001). *Return to reason.* Cambridge, MA: Harvard University Press.

Trilling, L. (1950). *The liberal imagination: Essays on literature and society.* New York, NY: Charles Scribner's Sons.

US Department of Education. (2013). States granted waivers from No Child Left Behind allowed to reapply for renewal for 2014 and 2015 school years. August 29. https://www.ed.gov/news/press-releases/states-granted-waivers-no-child-left-behind-allowed-reapply-renewal-2014-and-2015-school-years.

Van Laere, K., Peeters, J., & Vandenbroeck, M. (2012). The education and care divide: The role of the early childhood workforces in 15 European countries. *European Journal of Education, 47,* 527–541.

van Laerhoven, F., & Ostrom, E. (2007). Traditions and trends in the study of the commons. *International Journal of the Commons, 1*(1), 3–28.

van Manen, M. (1991). *The tact of teaching: The meaning of pedagogical thoughtfulness.* London, Ontario: Althouse Press.

van Manen, M. (1994). Pedagogy, virtue, and narrative identity in teaching. *Curriculum Inquiry, 24*(2), 135–170.

van Manen, M. (2012). The call of pedagogy as the call of contact. *Phenomenology & Practice, 6*, 8–34.

Webb, R., Vulliamy, G., Sarja, A., Hamalainen, S., & Poikonen, P.-L. (2009). Professional learning communities and teacher well-being? A comparative analysis of primary schools in England and Finland. *Oxford Review of Education, 35*(2), 405–422.

Weil, S. (1951). Reflections on the right use of school studies with a view to the love of God. In *Waiting for God* (pp. 57–66). New York, NY: Putnam.

Weinstein, D., & Weinstein, M. (1984). On the visual constitution of society: The contributions of Georg Simmel and Jean Paul Sartre to a sociology of the senses. *History of European Ideas, 5*, 349–362.

Wenger, E. (1998). *Communities of practice: Learning, meaning, and identity.* New York, NY: Cambridge University Press.

Willingham, D. T. (2009). *Why don't students like school?* San Francisco, CA: Jossey-Bass.

Winitzky, N., Stoddart, T., & O'Keefe, P. (1992). Great expectations: Emergent professional development schools. *Journal of Teacher Education, 43*(1), 3–18.

Wisdom. In *Oxford English Dictionary.* http://www.oed.com.

Wood, D. R. (2007). Professional learning communities: Teachers, knowledge, and knowing. *Theory into Practice, 46*(4), 281–290.

Wood, G. (2006). *Revolutionary characters: What made the founders different.* New York, NY: Penguin.

Woodruff, P. (2005). *First democracy: The challenge of an ancient idea.* New York, NY: Oxford University Press.

Woodruff, P. (2011). *The Ajax dilemma: Justice, fairness and rewards.* New York, NY: Oxford University Press.

Wordsworth, W. (1836). *The excursion.* London, England: Moxon.

Wu, M. (2014). Hundun's hospitality: Daoist, Derridean and Levinasian readings of Zhuangzi's parable. *Educational Philosophy and Theory, 46*(13), 1435–1449.

Yin, R. (1989). *Case study research.* Newbury Park, CA: Sage.

Young, R. E. (1990). *Critical theory of education: Habermas and our children's future.* New York, NY: Teachers College Press.

Zeichner, K., & Conklin, H. G. (2017). Beyond knowledge ventriloquism and echo chambers: Raising the quality of the debate in teacher education. *Teachers College Record, 119*(4), 115–150.

Zinkin, M. (1998). Habermas on intelligibility. *Southern Journal of Philosophy, 36*(3), 453–472.

Zyngier, D. (2012a). Re-discovering democracy: Putting action (back) into active citizenship and praxis (back) into practice. In P. R. Carr, D. Zyngier, & M. Pruyn (Eds.), *Can educators make a difference?* (pp. 57–90). Charlotte, NC: Information Age.

Zyngier, D. (2012b). Rethinking the thinking about democracy in education: What are educators thinking (and doing) about democracy? *Education, 2*, 1–21. doi:10.3390/educ 2010001.

Zyngier, D. (2013). Democracy will not fall from the sky. The Global Doing Democracy Research Project: Seeking to understand the perspectives, experiences and perceptions of teachers in relation to democracy in education. *World Studies in Education, 14*(2), 5–23.

Zyngier, D., Traverso, M. D., & Murriello, A. (2015). "Democracy will not fall from the sky": A comparative study of teacher education students' perceptions of democracy in two neo-liberal societies: Argentina and Australia. *Research in Comparative & International Education, 10*(2), 275–299. doi:10.1177/1745499915571709.

Index

About the Authors

ROBERT V. BULLOUGH JR. is a professor of Teacher Education at Brigham Young University and Emeritus Professor of Educational Studies at the University of Utah. Currently he serves as associate director of the Center for the Improvement of Teacher Education and Schooling (CITES). His most recent books include *Preschool Teachers' Lives and Work: Stories and Studies from the Field*, with Kendra Hall-Kenyon (2018); *Adam's Fall: Traumatic Brain Injury* (2011); *Counternarratives: Studies of Teacher Education and Becoming and Being a Teacher* (2008); and *Stories of the Eight-Year Study: Reexamining Secondary Education in America*, with Craig Kridel (2007).

JOHN R. ROSENBERG is the Washington Irving Professor of Spanish and American Relations at Brigham Young University and former dean of the College of Humanities. He is the author of *The Black Butterfly: Concepts of Spanish Romanticism* (1994) and *The Circular Pilgrimage: An Anatomy of the Confessional Autobiography in Spain* (1998).